Hauntingly
Familiar

Virginia Renaud

This story is based on real events, however the names of some of the characters were changed to preserve anonymity. Places and some incidents are either the product of the author's imagination, or were used fictitiously. The author acknowledges the trademarked status and trademark owners of various products referenced in this book which have been used without permission. The publication/use of these trademarks is not authorized, associated with or sponsored by the trademark owners.

Dedication

For my husband Dan, who continually shows me how much he loves me. Your patience, unconditional love and support mean more than you will ever realize.

And for my family, who have not had it easy with me in their midst. Thank you for putting up with me when all you really wanted to do was scream in frustration and throw your hands into the air. Thanks for not doing that. It made the job of writing, editing and publishing this work so much easier. I am sure the next one will be a smoother process.

Acknowledgments

Sue and Diane Renaud, I still can't believe how you managed to re-create my memories on film! Pure magic.

Martin Renaud, thank you for publishing first and braving the learning curve so I could ask you so many questions! A million thanks for your wisdom and patience– if my calculations are correct, that should be about one thank-you per question …

And Pam Mason, a very unique thank you to you for helping me remember. And for teaching me that sometimes, it's okay to forget. Hauntingly Familiar would still only exist in the pages of that battered orange duo-tang if not for your wisdom and support.

Contents

Forward

A Fly on the Wall

The story you are about to read is a tale of my childhood. It really happened. I grew up in a haunted house that probably looked like every other house in those days. It wasn't your typical rambling Victorian, neglected by its owners and sadly in need of renovation. It was a modern, well built, North American Rancher. Quite beautiful for its day, it didn't look like anything strange could happen there. In fact, my mother often joked, in the early days of our move, that she felt rich just being able to move into a place like that.

I still think fondly about that old house, but someone asked me recently if I had the chance to move back into it ... would I?

Not on your life.

The reasons? Well, I believe they'll become apparent.

As it happens, I am not, nor have I ever been a fly on the wall. Oh, it wasn't for lack of trying, of course. The skill of eavesdropping was a developing part of my repertoire back in 1979, but there are limitations. Therefore, the following conversation is a work of fiction, pieced together from half-sentences spoken aloud by my parents in unguarded moments over the years, and things my sister probably wishes she'd kept to herself. Of these unguarded moments, there've been few, but each one noteworthy. Today my parents' answer, is still that this is a flight of fancy and my wild imagination at its best.

I will leave it to you to judge for yourself.

The events that inspired this story awakened in me an unquenchable thirst for the paranormal. As I look back today, a conversation I had with my brother-in-law several months ago still echoes resoundingly in my head.

"I still don't understand what happened. It's weird, after all these years, even after writing this book," I told him.

"Maybe you aren't meant to understand," he said, as he broke eye contact with me and stared out the window. "Maybe you were supposed to learn something about yourself."

His comment was more accurate than he could have known.

It is my sincere hope that you enjoy reading Hauntingly Familiar as much as I have enjoyed writing it. Bear with me while I tell you how my paranormal adventure began.

House for Sale

1

"David, it's been three months."

"And four days," the young man said to his friend.

"Hey, don't shoot, I'm the good guy remember? But look, can we talk sense here? Three months is too long to put your life on hold. Grief will take its own time, I got that, but bills won't wait. Have you been back to work yet?"

"No," he admitted. "The business can go for awhile without me, but … look, I can't sleep, and as long as that's an issue, I can't do my job. I can't even form a coherent thought, much less give out good advice. Besides, the last thing I want to look at is a pool. I just see …" David's expression grew tight and he blinked fiercely.

"Look, I'm not trying to pry, but how are you paying the bills?" The taller man's tanned features showed his concern. "Do you need money?"

"No. We're fine." The clipped comments left no room for discussion. "Look, I know you're just trying to help, but selling? I mean, man you don't understand what you're saying. Our business is here, and …."

"The business is downtown," Tony interrupted. "You don't have to leave the area, but it might be a good idea to let go of the house."

"You don't know what this house means to us." David kicked savagely at the gravel under his feet and looked over his shoulder at the modest farmhouse. "At least it used to."

The tall man inhaled and exhaled slowly. He wasn't here to fight. "You're right. I'm not in your shoes and I can't judge. But it's just a house, David, really. Maybe it's time to consider Plan B. Look here, this is 1979. House prices are climbing in a way I've never seen before. The cash would

5

come in handy and you know it. Besides, changing your address isn't giving up."

"Tony, just drop it, okay?" the young man replied, his face tired. "I wouldn't know where to start, what to say … I can't even concentrate, much less negotiate. This whole thing is tearing us apart. It's harder still on Becca. Nothing's been right since the accident."

"Yeah," Tony shuffled his feet and ran a manicured hand through his dark hair. His gold rings caught the sunlight for a moment and David winced, remembering their high school promises to each other about 'striking it rich'. Looked like Tony had a handle on that one.

"But you know," David continued. "You're right about one thing."

"Yeah?"

"It's not fair. You got that part right." A fierce light seemed to kindle in the man's eyes for a moment. "I'll think about what you said, and talk it over with her." Tony's mouth opened in shock.

"That's all I can promise," David said, raising a hand to forestall his friend.

"It's enough. Look, I want to help you. Geez, I'm watching you fall apart, and it's killing me!"

David's head jerked up and he stared at his friend. It was many years since high school, but that deep connection was still as strong as ever. Could he really care that much? Was he trustworthy? He wished he knew Tony better. Maybe if he hadn't been so wrapped up in the business. No, he couldn't start thinking like that. He'd travelled too many times already down that road. Things were hard, but they were likely to get harder, and with every nut coming out of the woodwork claiming to help he had to be wary, didn't he? Absently his gaze came to rest on the shiny patent leather shoes his friend now wore and he laughed in spite of himself.

"Nice farm shoes."

Tony had the grace to look uncomfortable. "Yeah, well, yours is the only farm I'm visiting today. No barn tours." The men smiled at each other, remembering their days of fast cars and crazy schemes.

David was the first to break eye contact. Those days were long since passed. In fact, it felt like a lifetime ago. His world had been ripped apart, and all that was left behind was a house he didn't want to live in and a wife who was becoming someone he didn't know.

What did he have to lose?

"Well Tony" he said, running one hand through his short hair. "I guess there's nowhere to go but up, right?"

Tony squinted at his friend suspiciously. "What are you saying?"

"I guess it's time to move on."

~~~~~~~

Two months later …

The first time I saw the house I was in a bad mood and didn't really care what was going on. My parents usually did things that I wasn't interested in. I trailed behind them, bored and oblivious.

The realtor unlocked the solid oak front door. It swung inward with a drawn-out squeak.

That got my attention and my head snapped up in response to the sound.

"Touring haunted houses now?" I muttered. Mom dropped back beside me and poked me in the ribs.

"Be nice," she said through gritted teeth.

"Come on in," the realtor said, moving to one side and waving us into the living room. "You'll notice this house is a great set-up for parties. Over here you have a wood-burning fireplace, and just in front of it, this is called a *conversation pit*. It's very popular just now in all the modern homes. See how it adds to the spacious living room? That recessed area can be used for cozy nights by the fire or adding a little colour to your parties! Nice touch, huh? And there you have a built-in bar to serve your guests. If you'll just come on over this way, to your right, you'll see that the large country kitchen has ample cupboard space. Note this convenient pass-through to the adjoining entertainment room." The tall dark-haired realtor tossed these words over his shoulder as he walked ahead and waved his arms for emphasis.

I had no inkling, no indication, that anything was different about this place. The first few house tours had been mildly entertaining, but by the eighth walk through I was eye-rolling at everything and just wanted to be done. How long had we been at this? One week? Two? Geez, it felt like forever. Too bad I wasn't old enough to stay at home by myself yet.

"All the appliances are in good shape and as you can see, there are two bathrooms and …" he walked further down the hall, throwing open doors as he went. "… three bedrooms in the house. Note the vaulted ceilings and extensive use of sky lights." He gestured again as he walked, my parents and I trailing behind.

"This is an executive home," he said. "The wood-burning fireplace will come in handy this winter." His voice droned on and on. I was only interested in retracing my steps through the front door and getting back to my own room and my new Nancy Drew novel.

Mom walked briskly to the kitchen and began busily pulling open cupboard doors.

Oh great. We were gonna be there for hours, I thought darkly.

Pulling out a kitchen chair, I plunked myself down in it to wait, crossing my arms in a long-suffering pose, and propping my feet on an adjoining chair. I'd have never done that at home, but mom seemed too wrapped up to notice.

Suddenly, I sat bolt upright at the intrusion of a strange noise. Running footsteps echoed down the empty hallway to my right. I jumped up automatically and peered down the long, very empty hallway.

"What the heck is going on around here?" I wondered aloud.

Turning back around, I could see my father and the realtor talking in the recreation room and my mom still in the kitchen, admiring all the cupboard space...I thought the owners were away? Was someone still home after all?

Mom crossed the room and beckoned me to follow her.

"Mom, is someone here?" I asked.

"Don't be silly, of course not," she said, taking my elbow and leading me to catch up with dad and the realtor as they walked to the back of the house. She grinned at me. "You're gonna want to see this part."

"But of course summer is coming and the piece de resistance," Tony's cultured voice built to a crescendo, as we joined them in the next room. "... your very own in-ground pool!"

"What?" My confusion disappeared in an instant. This place had a pool? Well, now I was interested. How come I was always the last to know about these things?

I raced to my parent's side just as the realtor slid open the glass door to wave at the back yard pool with another game-show gesture.

Probably Italian.

My parents came to stand next to him, expressions of both concern and excitement mingling on their faces.

My boredom instantly forgotten, I ran to it, ponytail flying.

"I love it!"

"Virginia!" mom called, coolly intercepting me. "Back from the edge! It needs a good cleaning and lots of care before anyone goes near it." She

8

was looking at the dark green water with distaste. "They've really let it go. You can't even see the bottom." She turned back to me. "Please baby, stay back from the edge."

"They've had a tough couple of months, I'm afraid," The realtor said, pausing to grab a hankie from his pocket. "Excuse me," he apologized. He sniffed and wiped his eyes and nose before continuing. "Darn allergies."

"Uh, it's pretty bad Tony," dad said, looking at the pool.

"Oh, a little chlorine and it'll be perfect!"

Mom continued to look doubtful, her green eyes still fixed on me, but I was invested now. Time to turn on the charm.

"Mom, just think how great it'll be, having our very own pool! It'll feel like we're rich!"

"I know, I know, but there are plenty of other things to see," she said, looking meaningfully at the realtor. "Tony?"

We moved off down a gravel path that paralleled the pool fence. There were massive trees, huge, green lawns, paddocks for the horses and even a cute little chicken house with fake shutters. It was so different from the other properties I'd seen. It was greener than anything we had on our whole street and almost eerily quiet.

Eventually we reached the fourteen-stall barn.

The building didn't just sit there, it loomed. Moss clung to the roof in spots and the wood had weathered to a dark grey. Once the sliding door was opened, the pungent smell of livestock manure wafted out.

Well, no place was perfect.

"Pee-yu!" I backed away, holding my nose. "How many animals are in there?"

The central corridor of the barn looked empty, and the stall doors stood open, awaiting occupants. Small shuffling noises spoke of mice and I stepped closer to my mom. Just to be sure.

"There's been no livestock in here for quite some time," Tony said. "But I'm sure it wouldn't take too much to …."

His sentence was cut short by a jarring, mechanical sound. I wasn't the only one wincing and covering my ears. The long mechanical clacking went on and on, but Tony only smiled, raising his hands apologetically and shaking his head.

"Trucks. They get a few big ones along here," he said, indicating the road out front. "It's a gravel truck route, but there's a court order now to shut down the gravel pit, so that noise is only temporary. Can't happen fast enough if you ask me."

Was it my imagination, or did our enigmatic realtor's eyes darken as he spoke? His casual demeanor seemed to disappear in an instant.

Mom sensed it too. "Oh Tony," she said, laying a hand on his. "What is it?"

"Nothing," he muttered, shaking his head as though to clear away unwanted thoughts. "Shall we?" We all walked inside the barn. As I turned to look behind me out the barn door, I did a double take. A little kid was playing on the road! Wait. Was he on the road or beside it?

"Mom! There's a kid on the road out there!" I shouted. All eyes were on me as I gestured at the boy I'd seen.

"What kid?" Mom's face showed her alarm and she rushed toward the door. "A child? Where?" Turning back to me, she looked confused.

"There," I said, pointing at him again. He was walking now, ambling easily up the driveway towards us. "Who is that? Does he live here?"

"Ginny, I don't know who you're talking about," mom said. "There's no one there." She patted my arm in a gesture meant to soothe and returned her attention to dad and their examination of the barn.

"Hmmm, could be dry rot in here, Tony," my dad said, his attention riveted on the wooden cross members of the aging barn. "Have to replace these doors too, and that loft isn't much to speak of."

Dad poked at wooden beams, peered at ceiling rafters and rolled the barn doors back and forth on their long metal tracks widening the doorway and my view of the young boy.

"Daddy, that kid's coming over here," I warned. Dad flicked a gaze at me that said very clearly *Not now*!

Mom stood to one side, shuffling her feet and looking uncomfortable, her eyes on the interchange between her husband and the realtor.

"Mommy," I said, pointing at the driveway and the approaching figure. "He's coming. What do I say?"

"In a minute honey," she told me. She was nervously watching her husband as he slowly shook his head.

Tony the realtor continued to talk to my parents, leaving me frustrated and just a little apprehensive about this visitor that somehow escaped detection.

My thoughts were angry. Talk about obsessed, my parents were house crazy!

"I want you to realize that my clients are very motivated to sell," Tony was saying. Suddenly the tone of his voice shifted and despite the visitor, I found myself staring at him with suspicious eyes. "I wasn't going to tell you this, but this couple is really interested in moving on quickly. You see, they've suffered a great tragedy. Lost their only child a couple of months ago."

"How?" mom said. "Not drowned?" With one hand she reached up to clutch the crucifix hanging around her neck and with the other, she grabbed my hand protectively.

"No, nothing like that. It wasn't even on the property. The point is, they want to move on. I'm sure you can understand." Tony shifted his weight uneasily. "I know you've seen a lot of houses, but believe me this one is special. It's well built and in your price-range. Honestly folks, it's been a very difficult time for them, and they need a quick sale. I promised to help them get back on their feet. You know, this house is so suitable; I couldn't pass up the opportunity to show it to you. It's a rancher, like you asked for, so there are no stairs. It's got a barn for your horses. It's got a pool for your little daughter there," he looked at me and grinned. "And it's a five-acre parcel. It was built six years ago. Frankly, I think it will suit your needs. I know these people and they are ready to deal."

Dad turned from his inspection of the loft opening and rolled his shoulders. "It's a lot to consider, Tony, and I do feel for the family but I can't pay full price, the barn's not a total write-off, but it still needs work. There's no way this was built six years ago."

Tony smiled, "No, the barn was pre-existing, the house was built afterwards. You have to admit the price is amazing. It sits at $25,000 less than any other comparable property in the area. You won't find a better deal. Why don't we talk about it back in my office?"

Mom stepped forward. "William, I like it better than the others we've seen so far."

"It has a pool!" I said, not forgetting my selfish focus. "Did you see the pool?"

The adults laughed and smiled at each other, breaking the tension. I smiled too, and in that instant I remembered the boy in the driveway. But even as I scanned the open area to the right and left, I could catch no sight of him. Where had he gone so fast?

"Your other daughter's into horses, is she not?" Tony said, speaking a little faster. "I almost forgot to show you, there's a lighted riding ring just over there." He walked through the open doorway at the side of the barn and stepped gingerly into the barnyard, mud oozing dangerously up the sides of his leather dress shoes. A metal box was mounted on a pole just outside the sturdy split-rail fence and he reached for it. "You're gonna love this," he said as he threw the stiff switch and eight large lights came on, illuminating the field like a baseball diamond, transforming the twilight into high noon.

"Whoah," dad said. His light brown hair turned suddenly golden as he stepped into the glow of the powerful lamps. The effect was surreal.

I clapped my hands together in sheer delight. "Wow!"

"I can't deny it, Tony, this place is amazing. Diana's gonna love that, for sure," mom replied, glancing at her husband, still bathed in the bright lights. "I think we've seen enough."

Obviously pleased with himself, our smiling realtor led us back to the house, chatting merrily about the great neighbourhood and the excellence of the local school.

I skipped ahead, churning up the loose gravel underfoot.

School! Ugh! Resist! Don't think about it. I was going to be the new kid … again!

I was already picturing myself swimming and diving in our very own pool, floating free, my long hair fanned out behind me in the crystal blue waters. I could almost feel the warmth of the sun on my skin.

"Oh!" A woman's voice cut through my daydream as I rounded the corner of the house and nearly collided with two people coming the other way.

"Hi," Tony said, catching up quickly. "We were just leaving." He darted a look at his watch as mom moved up to take my hand. "Um, I thought you wouldn't be back until eight."

"Sorry, my fault. Just needed a couple of things, and I totally forgot you were going to be here." His clothes were neat and clean, and his brown hair was cut short, but his eyes were haunted. I think that's what struck me the most about him. He looked lost.

The woman who clung to his hand was petite, and very thin. Her eyes looked past us, and her straight black hair emphasized the pallor of her skin. Despite the shock of our near collision, she kept her dark eyes averted. In her fist, she held a rumpled up tissue.

An awkward silence followed, and mom's quick nudge indicated that I was making it worse by staring so I put on what I hoped was my best smile and beamed it at her.

Who were these people anyhow? Why were they acting so creepy?

"It's alright, we're about done anyhow," Tony assured them. "We were just on our way to the cars." He tried to manage a laugh but it came out like a weak cough.

"Sorry Tony, I forgot you were showing the house," the man said. "I can't remember much of anything these days."

Tony scratched at his chin; a five o'clock shadow was already beginning to form. "That's okay Dave, it's no problem. I'd like you to meet Elizabeth and William." Mom and dad stepped forward and shook hands with the couple awkwardly, casting glances back at me. Tony smiled and held one hand out to me. "This is their daughter, Virginia."

"I'm Rebecca," the small woman said. She stepped back and a huge sigh escaped her lips as she looked at the house. She took in my grin and managed a weak smile in return, nervously plucking at the seams on the leg of her faded blue jeans.

"Is this your house?" I asked abruptly and felt mom stiffen at my side. The previously distant woman focused tired eyes on my face as she answered.

"Yes," she said, her expression growing tender. "You're awfully grown up. How old are you?"

"People tell me that lots," I answered. "I'm nine."

"It's nice to meet you. Do you like the house?"

"It's great," I told her. "Did you guys build it? I really like the pool."

David stepped up and took his wife's hand in his. "Actually, young lady, we did." He managed to look embarrassed. "My company built the pool and I'm afraid it needs a good cleaning. We've been a bit distracted lately."

"I think the house is lovely," intervened my mother. "The country motif is charming."

The tiny woman smiled, but the action didn't touch her eyes. Her expression said she wasn't listening anymore.

"We're looking forward to a fresh start." The young homeowner looked at his wife and squeezed her hand. "Rebecca and I have so many memories; it feels like we're tripping over them. It's almost like our son is still here with us."

The woman dropped his hand and turned away. Suddenly, her shoulders shook and I could hear sobs erupting from her thin frame. She sat down abruptly on the corner of the concrete walkway and stared straight ahead, her eyes seeing nothing as tears poured down her cheeks.

"He is," she whispered through her sobs.

"Oh no, honey, I'm sorry." David said, moving to his wife and putting a protective arm around her, holding her to him as she continued to cry.

With his free hand, he extended it to my dad and our realtor. He shook hands briskly with the two men, obviously making an effort to resurrect the situation. "I'm sorry about this; we aren't trying to make this more awkward than it is. We're just exhausted."

"That's understandable," mom said. "You've been through a lot. Tony mentioned …."

Tony stepped forward and cleared his throat. "Well, we're done here so I'm gonna take these folks back to the office to look at some papers." Tony turned to my parents. "That okay with you?"

They smiled encouragingly at him and nodded.

The man named David seemed not to hear us as he fumbled in his pocket briefly, handing Tony a small paper. "You can reach us at this number; we aren't staying here anymore."

"Did you want me to lock up?" Tony asked, holding up the key.

David took the key and waved him off. "It's alright; I'll take care of it."

As we got into the car, I turned sharply, expecting to see them staring after us, but they'd already gone.

"Dad?"

"Yeah?"

"What's wrong this those people?"

My parents looks at each other but didn't answer my question. I looked longingly at the house, feeling strangely attached to it now, imagining the day when I would live there.

Which bedroom would be mine?

Suddenly, an image danced at the edge of my vision.

A face at the window?

I rubbed my eyes with gusto but when I looked again there was no one.

Wait. Had those curtains been closed before?

I laughed at my own paranoia. What was I thinking?

Chaos

2

It had been days, but I couldn't stop thinking about the strange, sad people at the farmhouse and the curious face in the window that I did or didn't see. So wrapped up in my own thoughts, I was fully in the room before I realized the implications of the scene around me. Our usually pristine dining room table was strewn from one end to the other with overlapping pieces of paper and my parents sat, huddling over each one anxiously. Tony was seated across from them, equally intent, his strong aftershave wafting over to me as he gestured and smiled.

That man seemed to enjoy paper far too much.

They weren't paying any attention to me, so I made myself busy with whatever came to hand, trying to tell myself that there were lots of other houses. Trying very hard not to think about the house that could be ours and the pool that occupied my imagination.

I knew the papers could mean only one thing. This was the part dad called "negotiating." Apparently, the house sat on five acres of land. I knew that was a lot, but I couldn't grasp how big that was. I was used to living within easy sight of our neighbours, our back yards touching.

Fields surrounded this new house. Lots and lots of fields. After living so close to our neighbours, it was a strange and exciting prospect to have all that space.

"Diana, did you see the pool?" I asked, unable to keep it from my mind.

"Yeah, how could I miss it? It's green."

"I know, but dad already said he'd fix it. Did you know that the guy who's selling the house actually owns the pool shop in town? He knows

15

about all the stuff to put in there so it'll be beautiful. It's going to be so fun!"

"That's *if* we get it," she reminded me. "It's not final yet." She and I slouched on the sofa in the living room, the television playing a Three's Company episode.

"When you went out there yesterday, what did you think? Didn't it feel like home?" I asked her. Diana shrugged. "Did Tony show you the outside lights?" I couldn't stem the constant flow of questions.

"What? Oh the riding ring? Yeah, I loved the lights!" She was warming to the subject now. "Yeah, they're definitely nice. Looks like a professional set-up. I know Koko would love it." Diana laughed. "She's going to think she's a show horse when ... sorry, *if* she gets inside that riding ring. Can't you just imagine her prancing around like she's royalty?" We both laughed at the mental image of the somewhat paunchy brown and white Pinto attempting to prance.

As our laughter died down, I sighed happily. "I can't believe it! Our own pool!"

"Hang on a sec, kiddo," Diana cautioned. "There's a whole house attached, you know. Besides," she jerked a thumb at the kitchen, "they're still negotiating." A small frown touched her face. "It did feel familiar, though, almost homey, like I'd been there before. It was weird. I honestly felt like I would turn around and see my own things in the bedroom." She shook her head. "Strange how that." She stopped suddenly and looked at me, her expression a bit startled. "Hey sis, did you get the feeling ...."

"Of what?" I interrupted.

Straightening the waist of her sweater, she averted her eyes. "Never mind," she said, shaking her head for emphasis. "It's nothing. Just ... nothing."

"Diana," I asked slowly, "did you meet the owners?"

"No," she replied. "Did you?"

"Yeah, I think so. They came right when we were leaving. The lady was really sad and she actually started crying, right in front of us. I felt really bad for her."

"Oh wow. Really? How come?"

"Well, mom and dad said they lost their kid, and that's why they're selling the house. I guess he must have died. How sad for them." I wasn't sure how to say what had been whirling around in my head for two days, so I just blurted it out. "Diana, did you see any kids there when you went with mom and dad?"

"Where? You still talking about the farm house?"

"Yeah. Was there a little boy there?"

"Don't be stupid. Nobody's living there right now. He must have been a neighbour."

"*Inside* the house? Look who's being stupid!"

"What are you talking about inside? There was nobody inside..Geez!"

"Look, I saw someone inside the house; I'm not making this up. I think it was the same person I saw in the driveway, before. Remember I told you?"

"Oh yeah, that little kid you saw near the barn? That's crazy. He was just a neighbour. And what would anyone be doing inside an empty house? Did you tell Tony, or mom and dad ?"

"No."

"And why not?"

"Well, because I felt bad for the people, I guess. The woman was really crying ...."

"Yeah? So what does that have to do with anything?"

"So if the kid died," I said. "Maybe, what I saw ...."

My sister let out a low whistle, followed by a mocking chuckle.

"So that's why you didn't ask? Because their kid died, and you *might* have seen a little boy in their house, only there shouldn't *be* anyone in the house? Where do you come up with this stuff?"

"I didn't come up with it, I saw it."

"And where did you *perhaps* see this supposed person?"

"At the bedroom window when we were leaving. I saw his face."

Diana was shaking her head. "You just thought you saw something. Other stuff can look like faces, sometimes. Maybe the window was dirty."

I sighed. "It was there one minute and gone the next, Diana. The curtains were open, I saw his face there, clearly. A little boy. I'm *not* wrong, Diana."

"Oh, puh-lease," she said. "Maybe their niece or nephew is staying with them."

"Nope. They aren't even staying there. They told us so."

"Okay, so what does that prove? Who's the kid?"

"I dunno."

"Hmm," she said. "I know where this is going, my dramatic sister. Ever hear of the power of suggestion? I suppose you think you saw a ghost? Stuff like that doesn't really happen."

17

I slumped and looked off to my left with a deep sigh. "Fine. Don't believe me."

"Don't worry, I won't," she said, flipping her curly hair over one shoulder and fixing me with a superior look. "So what then? You think the place is haunted? Oooh-creepy!" She waggled her fingers at me and rolled her eyes, making me laugh. "You're so gullible! You watch too much T.V."

"Okay, don't rub it in. Maybe I did imagine it." I sank down further into the sofa cushions and tried to put it out of my mind. "Speakin' of T.V., you watchin' this?" I asked her, a couple of minutes later.

"Yeah, don't turn it off," she said, eyeing me.

"And you say I watch too much T.V.," I said as I went down the hall to read and settled down with my newest mystery. After a few pages, though, all I could think of was the house. Who was that mysterious boy I saw in the bedroom window? Could it have been a real person? And what about that little boy I noticed standing in the driveway? He was definitely real. Did the people have a second son? If so, why were they keeping him a secret? Something didn't add up.

As evening approached, mom and dad's excitement intensified.

Diana stirred the contents of a large cook pot, her light red hair falling to her shoulders in waves. I turned my head to one side and squinted at her. She looked like someone in a grocery store ad. I stifled a laugh and turned to walk away.

"Not so fast shorty," she said, still stirring. "I still need you to set the table. Mom! Dad! Can we clear the table for dinner?"

"What?" mom answered.

"The table," Diana said, pointing. "Can we clear it?"

"Oh, sure," she said, hurrying to the table to scrutinize the piles of paper. "Just put all these papers … um, on the coffee table in the living room, I think. We'll move them back after supper." She looked behind her at the doorway to the next room. "Daddy's mixing me a drink, I'll be right back."

"Okay, we'll set the table then." Diana turned to me as mom moved into the other room. "Of course, when I say *we* I really mean *you*."

"Thanks," I replied sticking my tongue out at her.

Although we never took telephone calls during dinner, Tony's calls were the exception. He called several times, interrupting supper so often that my sister and I were finished long before our parents had taken their first bites.

Later, the friendly realtor was back in our home, and Diana and I cleared the dinner dishes. Mom and dad grinned excitedly at each other, as the previous stacks of papers were replaced.

I hung back in the doorway, trying to be quiet so no one would tell me to run along.

"It's a done deal. We just need signatures." Tony's strong voice rang with triumph.

"I can't believe it!" Mom's voice fairly squeaked.

"Well, that's it kids!" dad called out to my sister and I.

"We're moving, you guys!" mom added, rushing forward to grab both of us in a big group hug. "We've got the house!"

"Yup. Now we just gotta sell this one and then we're off to the farm!"

Dad seemed excited at the prospect of gentleman farming.

I could hardly believe my ears. Tony's "done deal" phrase had me giggling out loud. Even Diana was smiling. I had a tough time falling asleep that night.

"Dad," I said, the next morning at breakfast. "Um, I've been thinking. These people with the house, you said they don't have kids?" The problem of the little boy was still stuck firmly in my head.

Mom and dad exchanged a startled look and mom turned to me. "No honey, not anymore. They lost their only child. Remember?"

"Yeah … about that. What do you mean lost? He ran away?"

The adults exchanged long looks. "No," mom said. "He passed away."

"Oh." I chewed my lip and thought about my earlier conversation with Diana. "That means he died, right?"

"Yes."

"Oh. Do they have other kids?"

"I'm quite sure they don't," he said gravely. "Why?"

"Well, remember we were looking at the barn, and I said I saw a little kid in the driveway? Remember dad?"

My father nodded, still frowning slightly. "Yes, so your mother said. And?"

"Well, the way he walked up the driveway, it just seemed to say, *I live here*. Then, after, when we were going home, I turned around to look at the house again and I swear, I saw him, in the bedroom window."

"Inside the house?" dad asked his eyebrows rose in surprise. "Quite impossible." He shook his head emphatically. "The house was empty. There was no way anyone could get inside. You couldn't have seen that."

"I know what I saw, dad."

My statement hung in the silence as the seconds ticked by. Mom and dad frowned at me and then at each other, obviously wondering if I was making this up and why.

"The mind plays funny tricks sometimes," Diana said, breaking the awkward silence. "Patterns and all that. People have done studies on it."

"You were tired," mom agreed. "It was a long emotional day for all of us."

"Yeah, your baby blues are still bloodshot, kiddo," dad said. Even Diana chuckled at that.

"Let's not have any more talk about seeing things, we all need to get started on our day. We have a lot to do. Tony wants an Open House by Saturday."

"But Mom," I protested. That 'seeing things' comment made me mad.

"I know what you think you saw, Virginia, but it's just not possible. Think about it logically."

I frowned hard and headed down the hall. The low rumble of adult voices was still audible, even through my closed door. I could guess what they were saying. My "wild imagination" was their favourite topic.

~~~~

Over the next three weeks, I rarely saw my parents without a dust rag, a paintbrush or a screwdriver in their hands. What couldn't be spruced up was carefully packed or hauled off to the dump. The spring sunshine called to my mother and she spent long hours outdoors, planting pansies. Two huge plum trees in full flower dominated our front yard. Our house had never looked this good.

Although the mystery of the strange boy was still uppermost in my mind, I knew better than to talk about it to my family.

Our first Open House attracted a lot of attention. Fifteen business cards were left piled on the counter when we got back from our trip to the ice cream parlour. To a nine year old, a spontaneous trip to the ice cream parlour was the best and most memorable part of the process, but my parents had a different perspective. I remember feeling that their reactions were very strange.

"I'm a wreck," mom said as we sat down on the red vinyl seats, ice cream cones in hand. "Right now, people are going through my house, pointing out its flaws. I hate it."

Dad turned to his wife. "Try not to think about that, dear. All it takes is one, right?" Dad nodded at her and winked at me, taking a bite of his ice cream. "We have time, don't worry."

"I know," she said, holding his hand in hers and smiling. "It'll work out, won't it?"

Dad squeezed her hand, "Sure it will."

~~~~~

"The end of the month is nearly here," mom said to my sister, as they sat together in our living room one evening, several weeks later. "It's making me nervous. I don't know why the house isn't sold yet."

I turned back to the open pantry cupboard and continued rummaging. "Don't worry Mom, the right people are coming tomorrow." It didn't seem like a problem to me.

Diana turned around to make a face at me and I heard my mother's gentle answering chuckle. "If you say so, honey." She always treated my affirmative statements this way. I was used to being humoured. It didn't bother me much.

The next day brought a few more people to our house, including a couple who'd been once before. I beamed at them as we crossed paths at the front door. "Hello again," I said, remembering them immediately.

"Hello to you," the man and his wife answered politely.

"We're going for ice cream," I told them, matter-of-factly, as we filed out the front door. "Enjoy your new house."

They seemed to think that was funny and giggled behind their hands.

"Enjoy your ice cream," they called, disappearing further inside my home.

When we got back, I was sent to change my ice-creamed shirt, but I clearly heard Mom's exclamation all the way down the hall.

"Oh! They loved it!" She said.

I smiled and hummed to myself. The right people had come after all.

~~~~~

A couple of days later, a spring storm unleashed its fury all over Mom's delicate flowers; the rain that hit the windows did so with a

21

staccato beat. It poured all day, casting darkness over the house even at midday. I watched as blossoms drifted to the ground. Mom was in a black sort of mood so I kept the information about the destroyed pansies to myself.

Dad laughingly attributed this bad mood to "legal mumbo-jumbo."

I wasn't sure what it meant, but I guessed that it had something to do with Tony and his piles of paper. Tony had been showing up with regularity, always with more paper, and they would sit around the table for hours, talking. Since this was labeled "adult talk" I wasn't invited.

As though I'd been able to conjure him up just by thinking, the sudden shrill ring of the doorbell jarred the air, and Tony the realtor appeared on our doorstep. He was grinning, his teeth very white against his tanned skin and the backdrop of the storm outside. I grinned back at him, secretly wondering if his hair ever moved. His black hair lay slicked back against his head, perfectly combed and unmoving even in that terrible gale.

"The nice couple that toured through the other day has offered to buy our house," mom told us, as she and dad moved to the kitchen table with Tony.

"Told ya," I said. "Nothing to worry about."

"Yes honey, so you did." mom grinned at me for a moment and shook her head. "Another of your lucky guesses, huh? Well," she straightened up and pushed at her pinned-up hair. "We have some papers to sign, and some phone calls to make. T.V. off, if you please."

Diana switched off the T.V. in the living room and retreated to her room. I took a quick look at the kitchen, but the sight of all the papers on the table made my eyes glaze over. Paperwork! Again! Yuck, they could have it. I didn't understand the significance of all the seriousness and paperwork and it felt like they were wasting time with all this foolishness when I was already gearing up for a move.

~~~~~

"KIDS!"

Dad's shout, a short time later, brought me back from the world of amateur sleuthing and I reluctantly put down my book. "Get in here, we have big news!"

Dad was on his feet, his face wreathed in smiles. Mom stood at his side, her smile even bigger.

"What's going on?" Diana said, coming up behind me.

"What do you guys think of this?" Tony answered, entering the room. In his hands, he held a red-lettered sign about the size of a large envelope that read: SOLD. "I'm gonna go paste this on your sign outside. You can all get started packing!"

Our family was moving.

That summer was the first time I ever truly knew the meaning of "overwhelmed." Moving day approached and I started living out of cardboard boxes, as my things rapidly disappeared. Dad, as anxious as I was, seemed to make excuses to drive past the new house almost every day. Of course, I went with him.

"Drive slow dad," I said, as I stared hard at every window and examined the long expanse of gravel in both driveways.

"What are you looking for?" he asked, a grin covering his face.

"Just looking." I couldn't tell him the real reason. He'd only laugh and say I was acting crazy. As each day passed and still I saw nothing, I was starting to think maybe dad was right.

It was moving day at last, and we were first to arrive at the new house, our long, black station wagon crammed to the ceiling with boxes, plants and clothing.

"It's almost like I've lived here before." I said, spinning in a circle, my arms wide.

Mom laughed. "I've never seen you so happy!"

Even Diana found nothing to complain about. She and I wandered through the empty rooms, noting the dents in the carpets where furniture had once stood.

"Well, it's quiet now, but just wait 'til the moving van gets here," my sister said. "Then you'll know the real meaning of chaos."

"Everybody go and move your cars," dad quickly announced to the growing number of friends and relatives. "The movers are finally here and I want them to have direct access to the house. Just pull up to the barn. Use the second driveway, it leads straight there."

"What? You own that too?" Uncle Ted seemed amazed.

"Such as it is," he chuckled. "Came with the house. Every property has its eye sore."

"What about that ratty-lookin' house next to it?" Aunt Phyllis wanted to know.

"No, that's not ours. That property is owned by our neighbour to the south. They've got all this land in crops, so they've got no time to fool around with an abandoned house."

"But don't you think it's creepy?" Aunt Phyllis said.

"Not particularly Phyllis. Umm … were you moving your car or did you want me to take care of that for you?"

"Alright, alright I'm going."

The living room had a weird square depression at one end, just in front of the fireplace that my sister called "the pit." It was carpeted the same as the surrounding floor and looked like you could break an ankle if you weren't looking. With a name like "the pit" it didn't even sound appealing. But Diana thought it was great, and currently, it was the only space not piled high with boxes so I jumped down to investigate.

With my body laid flat out on the carpeted surface, I closed my eyes, thinking how life would be different here. Of course, I'd have to go to a different school and that would be awful, but I'd been the new kid before. I knew what to hide and how to act. Dad *did* say I could have my own horse, so that was something, anyhow, but ….

My thoughts abruptly detoured as a sharp sound intruded. It was out of place in a home where I was the youngest child. Did I imagine it? Sitting up slowly, I'd almost convinced myself I was just overtired when I heard it again, distinctly. The happy giggle of a toddler made me stand up and spin around. My youngest cousin was eight and that didn't sound like him. Who else was here?

Checking around the house, I realized I was alone. All the adults, it seemed, had taken a break and they were out on the large back lawn, sipping from beer bottles and plastic cups. I felt my body relax. Obviously sound carried in the country. Laughter can float in from anywhere, my logical mind told me. It was probably just a neighbour.

"Hey Ginny, come on out here and join us!"

Dad's voice rose above the din.

I started for the open back door, but before I could go through, a flash of colour passed by the opposite window. I only caught a glimpse but knew it had to be my young cousin, Bradley.

"Ginny, you coming out?" dad called. "We're all taking a break. Mom made punch."

"In a minute dad," I replied through the open doorway. I was already moving towards the front of the house, intent on catching my younger cousin unawares when dad's next statement made me pause.

"You better get your fill of the punch before Peter and Brad show up. Your Aunt Denise is bringing them over soon. You know what those boys are like!"

What??

So if my cousins weren't even there yet, who just went past the window? In a state of frustration, I flung open the front door, revealing a line-up of cars and trucks. Not a soul lingered.

———

The rest of the day was filled with stilted sentences, frustration, and a growing sense of unease. The latter was all mine.

Mom said to "be helpful", but since my Aunt Phyllis' idea of helpful was to give me weird jobs, I ended up drifting towards the back door, intent on escape.

Think. I just had to think.

"Has anyone seen the box labeled pots and pans?" mom asked, her head partially inside a kitchen cupboard. "It was right here a minute ago and now it's gone! How can I cook the hot dogs for our lunch if I can't find a pot?"

"William, the back door keeps re-locking, is there some mechanism that I'm just not seeing?" Auntie Julia, my mom's sister, was trying to get back into the house with an armload of linens and she was locked out … again. Dad rolled his eyes and jogged over to help.

"Liz, where's the keys to the station wagon? The van's here with the second load and it's in the way again." Aunt Phyllis asked as she wafted through the room, dragging the scent of her ever-present cigarette with her, as she gazed around searching for Mom.

"Oh, for Heaven's sake!" mom said harshly, appearing from around the corner. "Phyllis, put that thing out, would you please?" Phyllis merely shrugged and went back outside.

"Somebody better think about lunch, I'm getting hungry!" Uncle Jack announced loudly.

"If I could find those pots, you'd already have it!" mom snapped, pressing the palm of her hand to her perspiring forehead.

"Watch your back, coming through!" Yelled a man in blue coveralls on one end of Mom's elaborate sofa. Mom jumped up to direct him, dropping the dish she'd been carefully unwrapping, letting it fall back into the box with an ominous sound of breaking glass.

"No, no, the living room's this way!" She pointed, dodging ahead of the men.

"Where do you want this?" Another mover asked, awkwardly holding a black leather armchair in his grip. "In here?" He started down the hallway as mom came running once again.

"In the master bedroom," she called to the disappearing coveralls as she ran down the hall after him.

"Which one is the master bedroom?" he yelled back.

"Where does this go?" said another coverall behind me. "It's got no label."

In the midst of the chaos, Uncle Ted hefted a box to his shoulder and grunted with the effort. "Whew! You got a lotta junk, Will!"

Dad wiped his hands on the front of his jeans and smiled. "That happens when you have a family, Ted. Your turn's coming. I'm gonna laugh when you and Phyllis move. Then we'll really see some junk! I remember what your room looked like."

"Sure, sure, keep laughing," Uncle Ted replied, grinning.

"Ginny," dad called, noticing me by the back door. "Don't just stand there, pitch in." Turning back to my uncle, he grinned. "Well? One more truckload?"

"One?" The big man scoffed. "Mom must've dropped you on your head when we were kids! Look around you; this is just the first wave."

Dad groaned and followed his brother through the open door as I ducked out the back. My boy cousins had finally arrived, only to disappear just that fast, with a soccer ball in hand. I found a flowering tree behind the house with a perfect "v" shape about six feet up the trunk. I figured I could hide out there and peek through the branches at the house.

It looked funny to see all the people rushing past the windows, trying to cram all our stuff into a house that now looked too small to hold it. I was pleased with my concealed perch. No one would notice me there. And maybe I could put all those strange wonderings to rest if I just thought about them awhile.

As I prepared to climb, something unusual caught my eye. A large cardboard box sat on the grass all alone. A hastily scribbled label read: POTS AND PANS. Since the moving van and all the people were coming and going from the other side of the house, I realized no one was going to find it there.

"Mom," I called, hauling open the sliding glass door at the back of the house. "I found your box."

"What honey? What box?"

"The pots and pans box you were looking for."

"Finally!" She interrupted. "Where?"

"Outside on the grass," I pointed to my right, indicating the patch of lawn to the north of the house.

"What? Out that side? Well, of all the ridiculous... thank you sweetie," she said, running up to me and giving me a huge hug. "Lunch is saved! Now you don't try and lift it. That sucker's heavy."

As I turned away, I heard her holler for Uncle Jack, directing him to the errant box.

My new tree was located on the edge of the north lawn, adjacent to the fenced pool deck. After awhile, sitting there didn't seem like such a good idea. My legs cramped from the awkward position, and I felt like any moment someone would holler at me for not helping. Maybe my cousins had come back and were looking for me. Or maybe pigs had learned to fly.

I wiggled my way around to jump down.

And that's when I saw him.

He was small and pale, maybe six years old. He stood about 20 feet away, and watched me intently.

I looked back at him for a moment, trying to decide if this was the same kid I'd seen before.

"Hi," I called out waving awkwardly with one arm while I hung on to the tree with the other.

The boy just stood there, and if he said anything, I didn't hear it. What was he staring at? I turned instinctively to check behind me, but there was nothing.

When I turned back again, he was gone.

I shook my head in wonder. What was going on?

A moment later, my attention was diverted by another coverall carrying something white in through the door at the far side of the house.

"My bed!"

Discussions

3

About three days after the big move, I awoke to the sound of my parents having a discussion. My usual method of discovery leaned towards eavesdropping. An amateur sleuth in the making, I'd read every mystery book I could get my hands on, so I had a few tricks up my sleeve. One of them was to grab a blanket or scarf and muffle the sound of my breathing so I could get closer and hear every word.

"Added to that, I found all the lights on again!"

Dad was discussing quite loudly this morning.

"Shush," muttered my mother. "The kids are still sleeping."

"Well I find it bloody frustrating when I work hard to bring in money and all night long, it's being wasted. The house was ablaze with light again last night! What are these kids thinking? Do they have any concept of how expensive electricity is nowadays?"

"I don't understand it myself, Will. I double-checked the house before I went to bed and there weren't any lights on at all in the rest of the house. The kids must've gotten up later."

"They know the rules. Just because it's a new house, that doesn't change anything. Heaven only knows how much more this house will cost us; we don't need wasteful habits making it worse! Someone's going to answer me about this, I can assure you!"

Of course, by someone, I knew he meant Diana and me.

Later, after the discussion died down and a suitable period of silence followed, I made a sleepy-eyed entrance into the kitchen. Dad was seated at the kitchen table with his newspaper.

"Good morning sleepyhead," mom greeted me affectionately with a warm hug. "Sleep well?"

I smiled happily, playing up a luxurious stretch as dad watched suspiciously.

I could win an award.

"Sort of," I replied, wiping my eyes. "It's a little cold in there."

"Oh," she said, looking nervously at dad.

"Well, by all means let's turn up the furnace too," he replied, his tone heavy with sarcasm. "What's a few more dollars poured down the drain?" With that, he slammed down his paper and left the room.

Even though I knew why dad was ticked off this morning, I chewed my lip and wished I could take my comment back. His actions were surprising. This wasn't the dad I was used to. Mom caught my eye and smiled comfortingly. "Don't worry. Daddy didn't sleep well last night. Look, I've made pancakes! Eat up!"

When Diana finally put in an appearance later that morning, my father re-appeared from the living room where he'd obviously been stewing over the problem.

"Now see here you two," he said as we sat at the kitchen table, backs and faces straight. "You both know there's no parading around the house after bed time. I don't appreciate it when you leave lights on all night."

"What?" Diana said. "Why are you looking at me? I was in bed."

"Well I didn't do anything," I said. "I was too busy freezing."

Dad's dark look told me to drop it.

"Look, the lamps in this house are perfectly good and they do not suddenly turn themselves on in the middle of the night." His deep blue eyes were angry-looking behind the wire-rimmed glasses he always wore. "Are you trying to tell me you have no idea how all the lights in the living room, dining room, kitchen and family room were left blazing last night after mom and I turned them all off and went to bed?"

Diana and I looked at each other in surprise. Lights going on by themselves? Neither of us knew what to say. We were as confused as anyone.

"Dad, I was in my room all night. I was exhausted. You've been working us like dogs!"

Dad narrowed his eyes as Diana went on. "When I went to bed the house was dark. I never touched any of the lights out here," she said. "Why would I?"

My parents turned the full effect of their "tell-me-or-else" look on me. But I was no more help than she'd been. My only crime was eavesdropping, not turning on lights in the dead of night.

"I was in my room, dad," I said. "My lights were off. I was trying to sleep. Honest!" I wondered if mom and dad believed me, the looks they directed at each other were skeptical. "Daddy, I wasn't out of bed."

"Well, whatever the case, both of you need to understand that this light business had better not happen again."

"Yes dad," we answered.

"Will, this heat issue in Ginny's room sounds serious," mom said. "We can't have her roaming the halls all night, trying to get warm."

"Who's roaming?" I complained.

"Never mind Virginia," mom said.

"I'll look into it," dad promised. "Good thing summer's around the corner. We'll be looking for ways to cool down. You'll love it then. Which reminds me, I've got to talk to those folks at the pool place!"

That night, dad presented me with a new portable heater for my room, and two peaceful, warm nights passed. Coincidentally, there were no additional lighting issues either. Dad seemed to feel vindicated, but continued to grumble about "electrical anomalies".

"The house isn't exactly old," he commented. "I'd expect this sort of stuff in an older home."

There were three bedrooms in the house, and being the smallest person, I got the smallest room. It was set in the exact center of the house and as such, it had no windows.

Mom said it looked like it was built as an afterthought.

It was not the ideal bedroom for a little girl, but I hung colourful posters on the walls and once my furniture was all in place, it looked kind of cute. With the help of stuffed animals, it looked bright-er and *more* cheerful, but no amount of decorating made up for the lack of daylight. I couldn't help feeling cut-off from the rest of the family every time my door was closed. Being at the center of the house, dad said it should have been 'like an oven' but it wasn't. Sometimes, long after everyone had gone to bed, the air in my room would grow gradually cooler, until it felt like I lived inside a refrigerator. The plummeting temperature was enough to wake me up, and I would fight with the covers, wrapping myself up tight to try and stay warm. The small porcelain heater dad gave me glowed red with purpose and the promise of delicious heat, as I cranked it up to maximum, but, inexplicably my breath still steamed into the air, the tip of my nose stinging with the sudden cold. Still other times, I had no need of a heater, throwing off my bed covers in the middle of the night and awakening with a halo of sweaty hair.

As if by coincidence, several of our lamps seemed to develop a life of their own, going on and off at random, usually resolving to stay on sometime after midnight. Mom and dad slept with their door open so they could figure it out, but despite sleeping lightly and prowling the house after midnight, dad never caught anyone. He was fit to be tied.

One night, around one a.m., I'd been trying to get to sleep for hours, but my body trembled with a paralyzing fear I didn't understand. Why did I feel so scared?

I wrestled between being brave and seeking help. Eventually, I padded barefoot across the hallway to tap on my parent's open door.

"Hmm, what is it?" dad answered.

"Daddy? Mom?" I whispered. "It's me."

"Come in sweetheart," mom said, instantly awake. I crept into the room, shadows looming large in the corners. The moon gave off a faint glow through the curtains and I used this to navigate to the side of the bed where my mother lay.

"What does she want?" dad's voice rumbled in the darkness.

"It's alright, Will," mom whispered as I approached her in silence. "It's just Ginny. Go back to sleep." Her hand strayed to my head and she stroked my hair lovingly, beckoning me to join her on the edge of the massive bed. "You had a nightmare?"

I shook my head and bit my lower lip. "I just can't sleep."

"Aw honey, it's a new house. There are plenty of new noises but we're safe. You'll be alright. Can you go back to bed?"

My eyes widened at the thought.

Mom smiled comfortingly as she registered my fear. "Alright, well, you're a little old for this, but I'm too tired to argue; you can curl up here. Let's get some rest."

Without another word, she moved over next to dad and I crawled under the covers. The warmth of my mother's body had transferred to the sheets beneath me and I soon felt my muscles begin to relax.

"Gin," mom asked quietly. "Did you leave a light on?"

"No," I mumbled sleepily.

Dad was up and out of bed in an instant. "Damn," he muttered.

"What?" I dragged myself back from the edge of sleep to understand what was going on.

"Never mind sweetie," mom said, stroking my hair in a gesture I remembered from earliest childhood. "Go to sleep." Unable to fight it, I soon fell into a dreamless sleep.

~~~~

"She has her own bed," dad said at breakfast the next morning. "She needs to learn how to stay there."

I started to answer, but a quick look from mom hushed me and I returned to my Cheerios.

"Will, I know you're irritable this morning. That light thing is perplexing, but please don't take it out on her. Just try to relax. It's a new place, full of new noises and she's reacting, that's all. This will pass. Besides, we have more important things to worry about," she told him, moving off towards the sink. "Like this faucet for instance. It was on again this morning, and water was pouring down the drain when I got up to make coffee. Handle all the way up to the top. And before you start, I was the first one up. The kids didn't go near it. Defective or something."

Dad sighed, "I'll go get my toolbox."

"Will that really help?" mom asked, a weary look on her face.

"It's all I can think of," he mumbled, leaving the room in search of his tools.

During the daytime hours, I spent my time divided between unpacking boxes and exploring the vast backyard of my new home. We had five acres of land and I was determined to explore it all. I felt comfortable there, as though I'd known this place before, but when I tried to tell my mom about it, I wasn't sure she understood.

"It's weird, but I just keep thinking I've been here before," I told her.

"You have," mom said. "We took a tour of it together. I remember how fascinated you were with the place."

"But it's different than that, mom. It's like I've already lived this."

"Oh, that's called déjà vu honey; when I walked through, I felt it too. People have that all the time. It feels … different, doesn't it?" She smiled and touched my cheek. "I don't know why, but I keep thinking about your sixth birthday party. Can't seem to get it out of my head." She squinted at the sunshine, streaming through the windows. "Maybe I'm just remembering what the realtor called it when he showed it to us: a party house."

As comfortable as the daytime hours were, night brought new levels of tension.

Everyone in my family seemed to be feeling the strange unease. Worse still, was the fact that I ended up at my parent's bedside in the small hours of the night, more than I ever had in our previous house.

"It's Friday, let's relax tonight," said dad "Lord knows we could all use it. There's a T.V. special on. That channel comes in great with our new antenna." He opened cupboards and peered into the fridge. "What do you guys want to have for supper?"

"Yay! Movie night!" I cried. "Can we have pizza?"

"Well … yeah. Why not?" dad agreed.

Later, with aluminum T.V. trays before us, we chomped on pepperoni pizza and watched the screen as police cars careened violently after the bad guys, who always seemed just out of reach.

I munched my pizza appreciatively. "This is great, dad!" I said. "Who's that guy in the red car again?"

Dad laughed and rolled his eyes. "You're as bad as your mother; can't you keep the story line straight?"

Mom went back and forth to the kitchen several times during the course of our movie, coming back with napkins, forks, knives and drinks.

"Elizabeth, you're missing it!" dad called as she disappeared from the room yet again. "If you don't see this part, then the whole movie won't make sense. You'll be asking more questions than Ginny."

His only answer was the sound of glassware clinking together and a sharp clicking, as of plates being stacked. Out of the corner of my eye, I watched him grow irritated as he waited for Mom's response. The kitchen in this home shared a wall with the family room. It had a pass-through over the sink, like a window without glass that looked directly into the adjoining family room. It conveyed sound easily between the two rooms, so you could always tell when someone was around. Dad frowned. We could all clearly hear the sound of someone washing dishes in the kitchen, yet mom didn't say a word.

Dad turned around to peer through the opening. "Honey, leave those dishes, you're gonna miss the whole thing. The girls will clean …." He was standing now, his pizza forgotten. "Liz! Where did you go? Don't you hear me?"

"Coming," her voice carried from the hallway beyond the kitchen. "What's the problem? Can't a girl go to the washroom now?"

"What?" dad stared at her in wonder as she came into the room, patting her hair into place. Absently scratching at his chin, he turned around and sat back down. "Oh, I wondered where you'd gone, that's all."

Diana and I frowned at each other. We were just as puzzled by dad's behaviour as we were about the sound of dishwashing. Clearly there was no one in the kitchen.

"Dad, uh …" Diana ventured.

"Sound carries," he mumbled, turning back to the TV. "Whoah, did you see that? There they go again!" He pointed at the screen excitedly in an obvious attempt to change the subject.

But someone had been in the kitchen a moment ago and if it wasn't Mom, then who was it? It was a mystery and it made no sense that dad was ignoring that.

Later, mom brought out a deep-dish apple pie, still warm from the oven.

"Mmm!" I said. "I love your apple pie! It's the best!"

"What a wonderful idea this was," mom said, laughing. "I feel almost normal!" She began serving the pie, as my sister and I eagerly held out our plates, but out of the corner of my eye, I noticed that dad wasn't laughing.

"Liz," he said, "Do you remember earlier when I was calling you?"

"Yes," she answered, calmly re-inserting errant apple slices back inside the pieces she'd cut.

"Were you in the washroom the whole time I was calling you?"

"Of course, dear, where else would I be?"

"Not in the kitchen mucking about with the plates and glasses, for instance?" He raised his eyebrows at her as though he'd caught her in a fib.

"What?" she asked. "What's that supposed to mean? I thought the girls were doing the dishes tonight? That's what we talked about." She turned to look at Diana, then me, our heads bent over our plates. "Girls?"

"Yeah, we're gonna do 'em after we're done eating, Mom." Diana told her.

"There," she said, turning back to her husband. "Problem solved. Now, was there anything else, or can I relax with my pie?"

Later that evening, with the movie over, dad shook his head and muttered to himself as he followed his wife into the living room, grabbing the newspaper as he went.

The next day, mom was back in the kitchen, diligently unpacking even more boxes into the ample cupboard space. "Look at all this room," she said dreamily. "I've wanted to do this since the first day, but there are always so many things to be done around here!" She wasted no time ripping the packing tape off of about ten cardboard boxes.

"Now you'll know where everything goes, Ginny," she said, handing me a stack of dessert plates. "You and Diana still have to do dishes and I don't want to hear you telling me there's no room to put stuff away. Just look at this kitchen! It's huge!"

I sighed and started plotting a dishwashing mutiny.

In answer to the unpredictable lights, mom changed out every light bulb, calling it a precaution while dad went from plug to plug with some kind of hand held device he called a "meter." He said he was checking for "electrical anomalies" but I was just glad they didn't blame me anymore for leaving on the lights.

The "blame game" in which my parents tried to find the lighting culprit, had gotten them nowhere. It seemed there was a lamp in the living room that now had the reputation of being "tricky" and the switch in the family room was labeled as being "sticky". Anything else was simply ignored and switched off when necessary. No one really wanted to talk about it.

~~~~~~

"Diana how're those stalls coming? Did you mount those locks on the stall doors, like I asked? Those horses of yours are costing me a fortune the longer they stay at that boarding place. Let's see if we can't get them into the barn by the weekend, hmm?"

"Okay. Do you think the barn is secure enough, dad?"

My sister and father were talking together in low tones as I ambled past.

"It'll have to be for now. Too many other things to do around here. That leaky faucet is making me crazy. It just won't stay fixed. I can't figure out how it can slip all the way to the top like that. Must be a build-up of pressure or something. Darn thing only seems to happen at night"

"Okay dad," she said, with a resigned tone. "I'll get onto those stalls tomorrow, but how are we getting them here without a horse trailer anyhow?"

"We're borrowing one from a neighbour down the road," dad replied. "He's a friend of your Uncle Ted's. His trailer's big enough to take both horses in one trip."

"Well, I hope Koko behaves herself," Diana commented, running her hand through her wavy hair. The natural curls bounced up and over the top of her head, effectively giving her a 'mane' of her own.

My sister was the designated horse person in our family. She knew a lot about horses and their myriad of accessories. A few years prior to our move, she'd acquired a full-sized horse. Her name was Koko and she was a curious mixed-breed of quarter horse, Morgan and Pinto, making her strong, belligerent and easily the most cantankerous animal I'd ever known, but her stamina and pride were unmatched. The first time our eyes met, the large barrel-chested beast had taken an instant dislike to me. So intent was she on this hatred that she had learned to kick sideways, no doubt so she had a better shot at nailing me in the leg as I walked past. For horse shows, Diana patiently braided red ribbons into her mane and tail, telling all who ventured near that she was a kicker. I viewed this as an understatement and told her she needed to paint the whole horse with that colour! Most people were surprised to discover that this horse was not only a kicker, but a stomper, a leaner and just a bad attitude on horse legs!

My pony Charlie had been my sister's first horse. He was a squat, brown and white Shetland with a heart of gold. He had enormous dark eyes lined with white eyelashes and his white mane stuck out at wild angles, no matter how many times I tried to brush it into some sense of style. He was slow and patient, often giving a little wheeze when I had to tighten the girth strap on my saddle. Both horses were being lodged in a field at a friend's house until we could bring them home.

"Look kiddo," Diana said to me, as I followed her out to the barn the next day. "I'm finished school, except for a few exams, but you've got a couple more weeks left. You'd better get back inside and get ready. Is mom driving you?"

"But I don't want to go to school, it's so boring!" I complained. I still wore my pajamas, but I'd pulled on my cowboy boots over my bare feet.

"You can help me later; the horses aren't even here yet. Dad and I go to get them next Saturday. There'll be lots of stuff to do once they arrive, I promise."

Sighing to myself that life wasn't fair, I returned to the house and got ready for school. "What's the fun of living in a new house if you have to go to school every day?" I asked mom as we sat in the car on the way to school. "Technically, half of the chores are mine, you know."

Mom chuckled to herself and shook her head, both hands on the steering wheel and her eyes on the road. "Anxious, aren't we? You always want everything yesterday!"

"School's already done for the year. There's nothing to do, we're just marking time. Wouldn't you be bored?"

"You'll have plenty of time after school is over," she said. "Besides, you're going to a new school in the Fall, this is your last chance to spend time with your classmates and build some lasting memories. Wasn't your teacher talking about a year-end party?"

"Sure," I said, my tone sarcastic. "Probably something like a petting zoo. She seems to think we're children!"

"I swear, Ginny, you're nine going-on sixteen!"

No matter how many times I heard that, Mom's favourite phrase always made me smile.

———

"Come on Mom, I just want to go look around," I whined a few days later after breakfast. I was the last one up, the rest of my family already busy with their own Saturday agendas, the summer sun glowing through the filmy white curtains, warming the room.

"What if you step in a gopher hole or something?" mom replied. "You could twist your ankle. How would you get help? I don't feel good about that." Mom, a city girl and a self-proclaimed mud-hater got her country living information from the books she found at the library.

"A gopher hole, Mom? Are you kidding? Do we even have gophers around here?" I asked sarcastically. "What about if I stay in the yard where you can see me?"

"Oh, alright ... fine." She returned her attention to the huge tangle of clothes hangers protruding from a laundry basket on the floor. "I've got to get this sorted out. I swear your father must've packed this." I gave her a quick sideways look to see if she would say anything else.

"Go on," she said, waving her hands at me in a sweeping motion. "Stay in the yard ... and watch for reckless gophers." This last part was delivered with a short chuckle, and I smiled back, grabbed some sneakers and bolted for the back door.

I ran down the gravel path to the cross-fenced paddock and the green fields beyond. The warm air was tinged with the smell of fresh-cut hay, dandelions and manure. Technically, I counted this as the yard, but mom probably wouldn't, so I moved fast.

Soon, I emerged into the large oval-shaped riding ring, surrounded by the tall light posts at each corner. It smelled better there, and the cedar shavings crunched underfoot. I looked back briefly at the house, but there was no sign of Mom.

"Free for the moment," I thought.

Just as I ducked through the last fence into the back field, I saw a familiar flash of colour. Quickening my pace, I approached warily.

"Hey," I called out. Was there someone there by those bushes? It was hard to tell. As I drew nearer, I saw a familiar sight. It was a small boy. He had wind-blown, dark hair and was dressed in blue jeans and a brown short-sleeved shirt. He stood uncertainly near the fence that separated our property from the neighbours, watching me approach. His body language said he was ready to run.

"Well, hello again," I said, giving him a friendly wave. Wasn't he a bit young to be out there by himself? Again! By now, I was sure he was the same kid I'd seen that day in the driveway. Maybe I'd finally get those answers I was looking for.

He walked toward me, but suddenly stopped short. His whole manner was hesitant.

"It's okay," I told him. "Come on, I could use a friend."

He pointed at his chest questioningly.

"Yeah, you," I laughed. "You see anyone else out here?" He walked toward me and his lips parted in a smile, revealing pearly white baby teeth. I guessed his age at probably about five or maybe six.

"What's your name?" I asked.

"Bobby," he said, his voice near to a whisper.

"Call me Ginny," I told him. "Haven't I seen you before? You live around here?"

"Um ... I think so." He was frowning at me in a confused sort of way.

Trying to put him at ease, I continued. "I just moved in. This place is great!"

"Yes," he agreed, smiling at last and looking around.

"You looking for someone?"

He nodded, then seemed to change his mind and shook his head 'no'.

"Okay," I laughed. "Have you been here before?"

"Yes!" he answered eagerly.

"So what are you doing out here then?" I asked.

The frown returned quickly and I hastily added, "Not that it matters."

I stuck my hands in the back pockets of my shorts and squinted into the sun. "It's great out here, isn't it? Hey, I'm gonna look around, I heard there's some horse trails. You want to come?"

The boy nodded slowly.

The new property held treasures, like a tiny creek and winding horse trails. The creek waters were so clear I could clearly see the tiny, round pebbles, in shades of green, brown, grey and blue, lining the creek bed. It meandered through the property at an angle, crossing the back field, shielded by small, leafy saplings and blackberry bushes with slowly ripening fruit on them. At first I walked cautiously, not wanting to leave him behind, but soon, it became obvious he had been there before, and he was just as comfortable with the place as I was. We crawled under the low-hanging tree boughs together, and slid on our heels down the angled, muddy embankments of the winding creek.

"It's not fair," I said to him, giggling as I tried to brush the caked mud off my knees. "I'm filthy and you haven't got so much as one spot!"

The boy was openly grinning now.

I sat, throwing small rocks into the gurgling creek waters. The satisfying splash brought a smile to both our lips. I watched him out of the corner of my eye. Each time I picked up another stone, he'd peer at it carefully, stretching his neck for a better look before it launched into the water.

"You like rocks?" I asked.

He nodded. "A lot."

I darted a quick glance at him out of the corner of my eye.

He was so small to be here alone.

"So do your mom and dad know you're here?"

"No," he replied sadly.

"Oh," I said, trying to sound understanding. "Had a fight? Are you running away?" Again, he seemed too young for that, but what did I know?

"No!" His answer was quick and sharp and it brought a frown to my face.

"Well okay then, relax," I told him. "I won't tell. Honest."

He seemed to settle down after that, and we spent the time in companionable silence, with just the sound of the rushing water filling our ears. Awhile later, we wandered back toward my house. The direction didn't seem important. We were comfortable in each other's company. It occurred to me more than once that this boy had to be older than I first thought. While his body was that of a six year old at best, his manner was considerably older. He seemed to say a lot without uttering a single word.

"Let me show you my tree," I said as we ducked through the last fence. "The branches are just perfect for sitting in."

"Oh yeah," he whispered. "I know this one."

I tilted my head in wonder, but said nothing. He'd been here before. Probably a friend of the boy who died, I thought sadly.

We walked past the chicken coop and his head turned sharply to the left. "What's that?" He asked, looking at me intently.

I nodded at the chicken barn. "We've got babies, you wanna see?" Carefully, I pulled open the spring-loaded door and we peered in. A heat lamp cast its red glow over the bodies of the young chicks as they wandered around their enclosure, peeping at each other.

"Dad wants to be a real farmer so we're raising chickens. He got them yesterday. They're so tiny, aren't they?" A sudden loud clucking drew my attention on the other side of the partition. "Those three hens were here when we bought the place. They lay eggs every day." I paused to shudder and make a face. "Laying eggs … yuck!"

Bobby laughed and the musical sound got my full attention. I'd heard that sound before, but where?

We stayed awhile, poking long stalks of grass through the wire mesh of the fence. Bobby giggled with delight as the hens plucked each one from my grasp, carrying it across the yard, their bodies swaying ponderously as they ran.

His laugh was so familiar.

Suddenly, the screen door banged. "Uh-oh, there's Mom, let's go before she remembers some chore I forgot to do!" I said, pointing at my mom as she emerged from the back door. We ran back to the nearest paddock and ducked through.

"You're really familiar with this place, aren't you?" I asked him.

He turned sharply to me and his eyes, blue as they were, seemed to look right through me. I shuddered involuntarily and his smile turned to a frown again.

"You're cold?" he asked. The concern in his voice was strange. Most six year-olds couldn't care less how I felt, unless it was somehow preventing them from having fun.

"I-I don't know. Just all of sudden ... weird right? It's summer and I'm cold." I laughed, but Bobby didn't. He simply stared.

"What are you looking at?"

"You," he said, his expression still serious.

What a charmer, I thought. Laughing, I reached out to tousle his hair in an imitation of my big sister, but he drew back.

"No!" he said sharply.

"Oh, I'm sorry. Did I scare you?"

He didn't answer. Hmm, I thought. Let's try this again.

"Where do you live?"

For an answer, he just narrowed his eyes and frowned at me.

Well? What was his problem?

He looked down at his sneakers, the toes of them peeking out from under his dark denim jeans, the knees almost worn through from use. When he looked up again, his expression was sad.

"What did I say?" I asked.

The small boy shook his head. He stood there a moment, kicking at the rocks we stood on, as though there were words he couldn't bring himself to say. His little foot didn't even seem to make an impression.

What a strange little boy he was. Expressive one minute and silent the next.

"Hey, do you like swimming? My dad's gonna fix up that pool pretty soon, and we can go swimming together sometime. Would you like that? Do you know how to swim?"

Again, the musical giggle I found so familiar was my only answer. He looked at me with a wondering gaze.

"What?" I asked, suddenly embarrassed. I was confused by his reaction. It was this new community, I thought. Kids wandering around alone. Everybody had horses; maybe going swimming wasn't as popular as I thought.

We walked in silence, not caring where our feet took us. Eventually I was startled to find that we had arrived at the neighbour's cornfield, the stalks already grown waist high. It marked the edge of my property, and I was still a city-dweller at heart so I stopped and watched him continue to walk into the field.

"Hang on a sec," I called to him. "Is that the way to your house?"

He just seemed to ignore me, plunging into the field, not looking back.

"Um … hey?" I rose up on my tiptoes, but after a minute more, all I could see was the occasional corn stalk bending as he passed, moving deeper into the field. He was shorter than me, and it wasn't long before I couldn't see him at all. "Huh, weird little kid," I muttered to myself. I stood out there hugging my arms around my middle. Why was I so cold on such a warm day? Where did this kid live if a cornfield was a short-cut? The sun cut at the corners of my eyes and I realized that the afternoon was fading. It would be dinner soon and I knew I'd be in trouble if I didn't get back in time to set the table. I skipped down the path, spewing little rocks out left and right as I ran, smiling. I had a pretty good story to tell at dinner tonight!

Hayloft

4

"Look, I know it's a busy time of year, but it's also hot as blazes and besides, my daughter's birthday is coming soon. I need help getting this pool ready."

A couple of days later, dad was talking on the phone as I walked into the room. He waved at me and smiled as he waited for the person on the other end to respond.

"Uh-huh …yeah, that's right. Mm-hmm … yes … well, the problem is, the whole thing is green … yup, dark green … oh … yeah … yeah? Okay … well that makes sense. I'll try that, but how much am I gonna need? … yeah … the shape? Oval. The measurement is 36 by 18 … oh really? Wow! That much? … Okay, I see … and after that? … Mm-hmm and how much of that do I need? … And where are you? Yup, okay I got it." Dad said, writing something down on the scrap of paper in his hand. "Okay, I'll see you in a few minutes. Bye."

Dad hung up the phone and turned to face me. "Trying to get a pool guy *here* is harder and more expensive than I thought," he told me. "But I found a compromise. The folks at the store are teaching me how to fix the problem myself. I just gotta bring down a sample of pool water and they'll set me up. Tell your mother I went to town so she doesn't worry. To hear that guy talk, it sounds like I'm going to become a chemist before all of this is finished," he laughed.

"We are still planning to have a pool party, aren't we dad?" I asked.

"Sure sweetheart, just as soon as I figure out how to make the pool waters clear instead of green." With that, he chuckled, picked up his keys and went out the laundry room door.

"I'll be back in about an hour," he called back over his shoulder. "Hold off inviting your friends until after I try this magic potion."

"Okay."

As dad pulled closed the outer door, I rested my hand against the second interior door that separated the laundry room from the rest of the house. I was deep in thought. It was already practically the middle of summer and no pool! What if he couldn't make it nice again? Would we have to drain out all the water and start again? How long would that take? What if I couldn't have my pool party after all? I shook my head and mentally changed gears, frowning. What if I did have the pool party and all of my guests got terrified by ghosts?

Which scenario was worse?

~~~~

Later that morning, Mom's voice carried to me through the pass-through from the kitchen. "Ginny, your sister's got the flu; I need you to do the horses."

Mom stood at the kitchen counter filling the kettle with fresh water as I reluctantly returned to the kitchen. "Better make sure they have enough hay in the outside feeders, and then you can let them out into the side paddock."

I blew at my bangs in exasperation. I had plans today. This was gonna take forever. "Well, before there's any more drama, you better get going," mom said. "When you're done I'll have some lunch ready for you."

With nothing left to do but agree, I set off for the barn.

The feeders consisted of a metal-framed trough, fastened to the fence. Diana usually put a scoop of sweet feed inside to make sure Koko cooperated with the daily routine. The hay was always just thrown down on the dry ground directly beneath.

"No problem," I said. It was to be the first and last time I would ever do the job alone.

"Okay, I stand corrected. Problem. Big Problem," I said to myself, a few minutes later, looking at the place in the feed stall where the hay should have been. Only a few whisps of dried glass lay on the bare

44

concrete. Not even a mouthful for a hungry horse. That meant I had to go to the loft. Alone.

My rubber boots made clunking sounds as they hit each rung of the old wooden ladder.

"If there's anybody up here," I called, "you'd better get lost 'cause I got work to do." Talking made me feel a little braver as I headed upstairs into the eerie darkness.

There was a rough-cut hay chute in the center of the loft floor. As I opened it, its rusty hinges squeaked loudly. Light flooded through the opening from the barn below and helped to give me enough light to work by. A flashlight would have been a good idea, but I wasn't noted for thinking ahead.

The bale was heavy, but I was nothing if not determined. Tugging and pushing, the oblong hay bale finally reached the edge of the chute.

I'd seen Diana do this before, and I thought I knew what I was doing. I pushed at the bale from first one side and then the other; finally, I heard a great tearing sound as the large bale fell ponderously down through the chute. I was pleased with my show of strength, but not with the effect. The bale had landed so hard that its twine snapped with the force of impact, scattering hay everywhere … but that wasn't the worst of it. The wooden trap door of the chute dangled in the opening below, twisting back and forth on one rusty hinge.

Great. I'd broken the chute. Now I was gonna get it.

A small piece of twine was still attached to the trapdoor, but it twisted tantalizingly out of reach. If I could just get that and haul the whole thing back up, I could tie it in place and maybe I could even fix it before dad found out. I was handy with a screwdriver.

"Okay," I lay down on my tummy and inched toward the opening. Stretching as far as I could, I still couldn't touch the twine. I needed another two inches … damn! My waist was level with the edge of the opening and I felt gravity's tug. I sat up in a hurry, breathing hard. Nix to that.

The narrow column of light coming through the open chute didn't do much to dispel the gloom in the old loft. The wood was weathered a dark grey and shadows lurked everywhere. A rush of cool air hit me in the face as I straightened up and brushed at it instinctively.

"I'm gonna go down now," I called out. I didn't really know why I said that, but saying it made me feel better. "You'd better leave me alone."

Poor choice of words.

Backing up to the loft ladder to descend, my pant leg caught on something. I kicked to shake it loose. A nail? A bit of old wood? With a small tearing sound, my leg came free.

Great. I was going to catch it for that now, too.

I peered into the gloom at the head of the ladder trying to see what had grabbed me but all I saw were bits of loose hay and the short railing that bordered the stairway.

"Imagination?" I muttered, trying to chuckle. Diana went down this thing all the time.

Another blast of icy air blew my hair back as I stood on the top rung of the ladder, getting my balance. It was summer! Where was this icy wind coming from?

Now I have *never* liked heights. I have had to deal with my fair share of ladders, perhaps trying to dispel my instinctive fear, but it's always the same routine. My heart pounds, my palms get sweaty and I can feel my grip loosening. It's a race to get to the ground, but my shaking legs don't want to cooperate.

I've worked hard to overcome it, taking on impossible tasks in the hope that I won't be held prisoner by this fear, but it's always the same.

My life-long fear of heights did nothing to help me that day.

Even with my natural flair for the dramatic, I couldn't have predicted what happened next.

What light there was illuminated the bottom half of the ladder and I focused on that. Awkwardly groping for the second rung, I heard a bang on the floor right behind me. "What the!" My foot slipped off the top rung and with the other still groping in mid air, I was left clinging to the short support railing by my hands, while both legs struggled to find those elusive ladder rungs.

"Oh, finally!" I said angrily as my feet touched solid wood. I took a slow breath to quiet my racing heart. "Something fell over, that's all."

A moment later, my bravado disappeared.

Soft, scuffing noises on the hay-strewn floor made me jump.

Suddenly, I recognized them for what they did: footsteps. Approaching footsteps.

Squeaking in terror, I groped for the next step, desperate to get down.

I got one foot on the next rung down before I was jerked up by the cuff of one sleeve.

Was I caught on something?

My ears strained for any kind of clue, whether I wanted to believe it or not.

Whatever had me, it held me fast! My legs flailed against the ladder in panic, bumping painfully against the rungs where my lower torso hung down in the space below. I was now suspended by my arms, one hand grasping the ladder while the other seemed to hang in space.

With amazing force, my arm and slowly my whole body began to rise.

Panic gripped my insides. I was being lifted toward whatever held me! What was going on?

"Stop it!" I screamed. With an energy born of fear and desperation, I twisted my body frantically, fighting to get away.

Suddenly, inexplicably, I fell backwards, released as though whoever had me had decided I wasn't worth the effort. My upper torso, arm and hand smacked painfully against the hard wooden edge of the ladder and I scrambled for a foothold, nearly tumbling backwards down the ladder. My booted feet found purchase on the rungs at the last second and I wasted no time feeling my way, still without much light, my panic making me awkward, trembling all over.

What was going on?

Something banged loudly against the head of the ladder, only a few feet from my face and I screamed anew.

That's when the barn lights went out.

I wasn't aware of falling, but the concrete floor rushed up to greet me with alarming speed.

I remember that I couldn't breathe for a moment. I was conscious of a searing pain hammering through my body. I tried to move, but couldn't. Everything was dark. How bad was I hurt? Did that really just happen?

I lay there, frozen in fear, listening for the sounds of pursuit that didn't come. Eventually, fear won out over injury, and I got shakily to my feet. A low rumble intruded on my clouded mind.

Pain wracked my body. "Wh-who's there?" I called. I really didn't want an answer.

The low rumble sounded again. What was that? A truck going past? No ... this was closer.

A sharp wave of vertigo assailed my senses and I nearly fell again. My head ached like I'd been hit with a baseball bat, but all I could think of was getting out of there.

Somehow I found the barn door and limped through.

Impossible as it seemed, no one would be coming to my rescue. I was supposed to be "old enough" to manage these simple chores. Simple. Ha! The absurdity of it made me want to laugh.

I needed my Mom, I needed my bed…maybe I even needed a doctor. Or a shrink.

Much later, I lay on my bed feeling sore and confused.

I heard voices again, but this time, they were just outside my bedroom door.

"It was a damn good thing she didn't fall any further, or she'd be much worse off."

The voice belonged to my father.

"Well obviously she's just too little. I blame myself," mom replied.

"Now, you couldn't know she would tackle a full bale of hay, Liz," dad replied, the tone of his voice was soothing. "Normally I leave an open bale in the feed stall and I just forgot today, with everything going on … the fact that she got up and walked back to the house is a very good sign. No permanent damage, just a few scrapes and bruises. It's a farm. Stuff like this happens and she's a tough kid."

"Ye-es," mom didn't sound convinced. "But what about those claims? What do you make of that?"

"Dark in there," dad said, as though that were explanation enough. "She just tripped that's all. As for those ramblings of footsteps and being pushed, the simple answer is, she's a natural-born storyteller; we've always known that. And remember, she did hit her head, so she's no doubt a little confused."

"Thanks doc," I mumbled sarcastically, my lips feeling thick and clumsy. I leaned back deeper into my pillows and closed my eyes. All I could think about was staying still, but I was angry at his choice of words. Storyteller? Ramblings? Nice. That's what I get for telling the truth.

The next day, I was a mass of bruises, but being a "tough kid", I was up and around, doing my chores and not loving it. I was still angry about my parents' reaction, but there wasn't one thing I could do about it.

"Now then, whatever possessed you to drag a full bale of hay through that old chute?"

Mom put her hands on her hips and stared hard at me.

"There wasn't any in the feed stall and the horses needed it."

"And you are incapable of asking for help?"

"Um, no."

"And have we ever asked you to get hay from the loft by yourself?"

"No."

"And all these facts didn't register with you at all, hmm?"

"Well, I ...." Mom's level gaze froze the rest of my sentence. I realized there was nothing I could really say to that.

"Well, there's only one thing left to do, I suppose. Come here," mom said, her tone conciliatory.

Suspicious, I followed her into the laundry room, where she opened a closet door and exposed a puddle of multi-coloured fur, nestled into a cardboard box filled with mittens and toques.

"Ooh!" I squealed, hurting my own head with the sound. "Kittens." My excitement sent up a wailing discord of kitten mewling and I covered my ears, giggling with newfound happiness.

"Tiger must have had her babies while I was busy with you," mom said. "I found her in here this morning."

"How many?" I asked.

"Five," mom said, grinning. "Which one do you want?"

"What? Oh Mom, really? Daddy said we had to get homes for all of them!"

"Your dad softened once they were born," she said, grinning. "He and I agreed you could pick one for your very own. You've had a rough time. Maybe this little thing will cheer you up."

I crouched next to the box and looked them over. The mother cat gingerly stepped into the box and arranged herself in a crescent shape around them. Their eyes were still closed and they groped blindly toward their mother. Tiger's green eyes blinked at me lazily.

"You're a good little mother, Tig," I said. "Can I help with one?" Tiger stretched forth one of her white-tipped paws and meowed. "I'll take that as a yes," I said. "Mom, look at that orange tabby, isn't it a doll?"

"Sure is," mom said. "It's a boy doll, though."

"Boy or girl, it doesn't matter, he's adorable!"

"Then you'd better decide what to call him," she said. "Adorable isn't really a name." She laughed softly. "Now remember, you can't pick them up right now. They're too small. They need their mummy." With that, she ushered me out of the room, closing the wooden Dutch door that separated the rooms.

I was left peering through the squares of glass in the upper half of the door, a grin permanently etched on my face.

I stayed glued to those kittens for the rest of the day, but mom announced early the next morning that despite my adventures on Saturday, it was time to earn my keep, as she put it.

"Your chores are backing up young lady, so it's time to get a move-on. Your dad and sister need your help. The kittens will still be here."

~~~~

"Well, you didn't know how to work it," dad said, as we sat down to dinner. He rested both elbows on the table and clasped his hands. "You busted the lip off of the underside of that chute when you pushed the bale through. Now I'm gonna have to fix that, too. You shouldn't have tried doing that alone."

"Yes dad," I replied, wondering how I was ever going to set foot in that barn again without being scared to death.

"And as for that ladder," he continued. "Well, I know it's always too dark in that barn, even in the daytime. I'm wiring up some lights so you can see where you're going. Can't have you tripping and falling all over everything."

I stared at him, open-mouthed. He was putting it all down to clumsiness?

"Diana needs help cleaning the tack tomorrow," mom interceded. She looked meaningfully at dad before continuing. "It'll be good for you to get back in there right away."

I was going to have to swallow my fear. I just hoped it wouldn't come back on me.

Bobby

5

"I never knew we had this much tack!" Diana commented, as we labored to wipe down each leather strap with our damp rags. The bar of saddle soap glistened in the sunshine that poured in through the open barn door. The freshly cleaned leather smelled good.

I struggled to keep up with my sister, my smaller biceps straining under the weight of a saddle as I lifted it off its rack. "Yeah, and it weighs a ton!"

"Quit complaining," she said. "At least you got a new cat out of the deal. Bruises heal."

"Oh, aren't you understanding?" I commented drily. "I have the scare of my life and all you can say is, 'bruises heal'?"

"Sorry," she winced. "I guess that was a bit callous."

"A bit," I said.

"Had to be scary, huh?" She asked. "I mean, that ladder is bad enough without the lights going off. You must've been freaked, being in there all by yourself."

"Yeah," I said. "All by myself …."

Diana stopped and looked at me with a startled expression. Just then, dad came in, conversing with Grandpa. Mom followed a step behind, a notepad in her hand. I loved my Grandpa and wanted to rush in for a hug, but I sensed the tension and kept my distance.

"Humph," he said, as the two of them toured the old structure. "This old place won't last much longer. Did you see this? It's spreading into the

51

joists. No. A re-build is what you really need; otherwise, it's like throwing good money after bad."

I winced as I watched their retreating backs.

"Dad," mom said, addressing Grandpa, "We can't afford it right now. Are you sure we can't shore it up somehow?"

Grandpa turned and smiled at Diana and me.

"Never said it couldn't be done," he said. "But it's not going to be easy."

"This is gonna cost," I heard dad say, looking around at the aging timbers. "I knew it was too good to be true."

~~~~

"Dad, what's the matter with the pool?" I asked for what had to be the twentieth time.

"I'm working on it," came the static reply, as he moved out of earshot.

"Okay," I sighed. This had become a familiar litany.

"Alright lazy bones," mom said, intercepting me as she came in from outside. "Time to be useful pajama-girl." She smiled and pointed to a list I hadn't noticed before.

Reluctantly, I traded my pajamas for jean shorts and a halter-top. I saw no way out of this long list of chores, but at least I'd be comfortable doing them.

The fresh scent of wood filled my nostrils and I breathed it in gratefully, crossing the old barn's threshold. There were two sawhorses and various pieces of new two-by-fours left in the corridor, but my excitement soon faded. It still looked the same, the dreary silvered wood staring back at me so bleak and uninviting … and cold. Why was it always so cold? The large, sliding doors at either end of the building were wide open, admitting the summer sunshine in all its splendor. It should have been warmer just from that. It was mid July and a glorious summer day outside of that barn. I looked up and saw one improvement that made me smile, though. Large white fluorescent lights ran in a dotted line down the center corridor. The barn now, at least, had light.

"Hey kiddo." dad asked, coming up behind me. "So how about getting these stalls done properly? I just got a new load of shavings. They're in there." Dad indicated the last stall on the right and handed me a list. "Rest of the chores are on there."

"Uh, okay," I said uncertainly, glancing at the list in my hand. Apparently, that was the source of the new wood smell. Shavings always smelled divine to me. "Uh, dad ..." I paused, unsure how to voice the concern I felt.

"I know, I know, when's the barn gonna be done, right?"

"Well yeah, but ... can you stay and help me? I mean, the barn's um, big." "Kinda creepy", is what I wanted to say, but couldn't. Dad frowned at me in silence as though he could hear my thoughts.

"What's the matter with you? You don't have to live in it, you know. Just get busy. Grandpa and I put some lights in there so it'll be a lot safer. If we're ever gonna get this thing finished, I got work to do. As long as we know you'll be staying out of the loft ...." He let the sentence dangle with meaning.

"Yeah, yeah. Okay. I get it," I said. "Ground floor only. I promise."

"Good girl." Dad walked away quickly, his trusty black-handled hammer in one strong hand.

Hmm. Safer? I wonder.

Hesitantly, feeling small and vulnerable, I breathed in the scent of the fresh pine shavings, trying to gain confidence from the familiar odour. A footstep sounded behind me.

I turned sharply. "Dad, I ...."

A chill jolted through me at the sight of the empty corridor.

"Dad?"

Whirling around, an all-too-familiar frisson rippled down my backbone.

Damn! Despite dad's best efforts, I felt anything but safe here.

I felt like crying, but I knew that would do me no good. My parents never budged on what they considered "responsibility", and tears were just gonna make me feel worse.

Resolutely, I approached the stall that held the pile of shavings. It faced me like a mountain. I could see the summer sunshine flooding tantalizingly through the doorways, small dust motes illuminated in its golden light. Inside where I stood with my worried frightened self, it was cold. A tingling sensation crept inch by inch across my shoulder blades. I shivered and hugged myself, determined to be okay.

"Cold?" A voice said from behind me.

I jumped and whirled around, a scream escaping my lips.

"Dad!" Feeling like a fool, I rushed forward and hugged him. "You scared me."

"Obviously," he chuckled. "Are you gonna stand there all day or get some work done?" He shook his head. "Maybe this is too big a job for you after all. Can't have you getting hurt again."

I was never as relieved in my life as I was at that moment.

"So let's get started then."

Dad was as good as his word. Soon, the old shavings were removed from the stalls and bright new wood chips took their place, lending the barn a clean, woodsy smell. Dad's strong arms wielded the shovel and wheelbarrow with ease and I hurried to keep pace.

"Met any of the local kids yet?" dad asked, as he helped me fill the wheelbarrow.

"Yeah, I met one, but he's only six."

"Oh, I see. And where did you find a six year old?" dad asked, as he wheeled the full load into the last stall.

"Actually he found me. He must be a neighbour. He's just a little guy. Kinda quiet, always wears brown! Every time I see him, he's wearing another brown shirt." I laughed at my dad's quizzical expression.

"Brown, huh?" he said. "Very fashionable."

I tried to appear casual as I snuck a peak behind me, the nervous feeling still there.

"Six, that's mighty young to be wandering around by himself. Does he ride?"

"I don't know, maybe. But you know he doesn't seem to care if he's by himself. I think he'd be comfortable anywhere."

"Strange," dad said. I agreed with him, but I was more concerned with the prickling sensation inching over my scalp and upper back. This was ridiculous. My dad was right there, but it felt exactly like someone unseen was watching me. And it didn't feel friendly. My heart raced. Where were they hiding? I twisted in a circle, looking everywhere.

"Would you cut that out?" dad said, laughing. "You're driving me crazy, watching you spin around like that. Honestly, you kids! Can't stop dancing for five minutes! Let's get a move-on!"

"Sorry," I mumbled.

"Hey," he said, his expression softened and he put down his shovel and dug into the pocket of his baggy work jeans. "I just remembered, Grandpa and I found something you might like." He pulled out a battered cardboard box and handed it to me. It fit in the palm of my hand. The cardboard was dusty and misshapen, but the lid was still securely in place.

"What is it?" I asked in wonder. "Where did you find it?"

"In the wall, of all places," dad replied. "We were pulling off some of the rotted plywood from the workshop walls. It was sitting on one of the cross beams. Weird huh?"

"Nothing surprises me about this place anymore," I muttered darkly.

"What?"

Dad's frown said he didn't appreciate my remark.

"Um, I just said what a nice surprise," I fibbed, smiling sweetly. The faded blue cardboard had seen better days, but when I finally worked the top off the box, I found a crystal pendant, resting in a tarnished puddle of metal, torn strips of paper acting like a nest. The metal chain was hopelessly tangled, but the pendant caught and held my attention; it looked brand new somehow, and seemed to refract light in a myriad of ways, all at once.

"It's beautiful," I whispered.

"Yeah, pretty thing isn't it?" He agreed. "I know you like crystals. I thought of you right away when we found it."

The work continued better after that. For some reason, I felt better with this new treasure tucked securely in my own pocket.

~~~~

Later that night after dinner, my treasure still tucked in the pocket of my barn jacket, I tried to confide my worries to Diana.

"Don't you find it creepy in there?" I asked her. "I always feel like someone's watching me."

"Like who? The horses? The mice? It's a barn," Diana said. "They're all drafty and a bit cool. It's good for the horses. I've never been in a barn that was as warm as a house. You want it to be creepy, so it is. That's all. Stop inventing things where there aren't any. It won't kill you to do your chores."

"It might," I said, only half joking. "And I'm not inventing … can't you go with me?"

"Humph," Diana said, eyeing me. "Every time? I've got things to do without you."

"You could try to help your little sister," I said, playing the sincerity card.

She pursed her lips and struck a pose of disbelief. "Not likely."

"But Diana, it's big and scary."

"Look, as long as you agree NOT to go in the loft AT ALL, we don't have a problem. You can go by yourself to do your chores."

"Nuh-uh," I said, shaking my head.

"Look, you can either haul your butt outa bed when I go out there or you can go alone. Those are the two options. I don't have the patience to coddle you."

"Oh, you two," mom said. She looked at us and grinned affectionately. "Ginny, what you need is motivation. How about having some friends over after you do your chores? Have you met any of the neighbour children yet?"

"Just one," I said. "But he's just a little kid. He couldn't help me much. There isn't anyone my age here."

"Oh really?" mom said. "How little is little?"

"I don't know, maybe six."

"That's strange. He didn't have anyone with him?"

"Nope, just him."

"Hmm, well that doesn't seem right, does it?"

"Yeah, but I think people are like that around here. They just sort of show up ... don't you remember? You saw him."

"No, I don't think so dear," she said, removing the dinner plates to the countertop. "I'd have remembered that, I think."

I frowned. Why did mom say that? Perhaps she just didn't notice.

~~~~

My Shetland pony Charlie eyed the bedraggled looking carrot I'd snuck from the fridge. He tossed his head and whinnied his approval as I fed it to him, his shaggy mane bouncing up and down as he chewed his way through the rubbery skin.

"Good old horse," I said, scratching between his ears. Charlie closed both golden eyes and sighed. The summer sun warmed both of us. I stroked his brown and white flanks, thinking of riding. I could saddle him by myself and ride in the back field, as long as I told mom where I was, but that would mean going into the barn alone again.

Shaking my head in defeat, I spied a great big oak tree. It shadowed not only the driveway, but also part of the house. I waved to Charlie and ran to it, scrambling up easily amongst the vibrant green leaves, farther up again, the bark scraped and crunched under my sneakers. I felt a rush of adrenaline. Nothing could touch me here. As I settled into the uppermost branches, the sunshine dappled across the green grass and I smiled.

I still remember that moment. I can still feel the rough bark against my back and the smell of nature filling my nostrils. I can still remember the thrill I felt, looking down at my new home from that vantage point and wondering why it couldn't look this grand all the time.

And down there, looking small and sad, was the small boy I had come to call 'friend'. Bobby, that little neighbour boy, had obviously come to play again. With the sun full on him, his brown hair shone like something other-worldly.

He was seated cross-legged on the gravel driveway, but there was something odd about his actions. Although he was facing me, I could tell he hadn't noticed me way up in the tree. As I watched him, his head moved rhythmically, like he was either listening to music or talking to someone. Only there was no music and no one else around. I continued to watch, truly puzzled now as he tried to stand up, only to fall back down to the gravel with a little puff of dust, repeating the action with absurd determination.

His expression was unreadable from that distance, but something about his body language told me he was angry.

What was he doing? Was he alright?

"Hey Bobby!" I called. "You better cut that out or people will think you're crazy!"

I was obviously too far away for him to hear me. He continued to sit on the ground, his body slumped forward. He seemed to be drawing in the dust with his fingertips and I couldn't be sure but it looked like he was talking.

To whom?

I swung down from the branches of the tree, intent on going to him, but as I did so, a bit of colour caught my eye and my heart dropped.

What was my sweater doing in the barn? I remembered wearing it back into the house last time. My necklace was still probably in the pocket, too.

"Hey Bobby!" I called out, as my feet hit the ground. "BOBBY!!!"

His head came up with a start and he stared at me. His grin was slow to start, but by the time I approached, it was dazzling. What a cute kid.

I was going to be in big trouble if I didn't get to that sweater before Koko's teeth left their mark, and now I was worried about my treasure too.

"Hey, I just gotta grab my sweater and put it back in the house." I laughed. "Maybe it'll stay there this time. I wonder who brought it out here?"

As I turned to go in the barn door, Bobby appeared in front of me, blocking my way.

"No," he said.

"Yes," I argued. "I don't want to go in there either, but it'll just take a second."

His gaze slid from my face.

"I'll be fast, believe me. Stop being so weird," I replied, mock-punching his arm.

He dodged out of the way but did not smile.

"Look, my dad found the coolest necklace in the wall of the workshop. Lemme show you."

"Where?" he asked.

"In the workshop," I said. "It was tucked into the wall or something."

Bobby looked shocked, which only made me laugh harder. I was taking any opportunity to laugh and be silly, putting off going back into the dead air of that place, but knowing I had to.

"Come on, I'm dead if Koko rips that sweater and she will. She's mean and she hates me —"

"Don't." His voice was high pitched and scared. "That's a bad word."

"What is?"

Bobby looked around cautiously. "Dead," he whispered. "You shouldn't say that."

"O-okay. I won't. I'm sorry. Come on, come with me," I wheedled. "I ... I just don't want to go in there alone. It'll just take a second."

"Okay," he replied at last. "Just to the door."

"Fine."

We walked together to the barn and I went inside, distracted by Bobby's obviously heightened fear as he halted just inside the door. The cool air enveloped us like a shroud. The red and blue sweater was draped over an open stall door at the far end. I still didn't remember leaving it there.

"Bobby?"

When he didn't answer, I whirled around. He was several feet back, stopped just inside the doorway, those intense blue eyes staring, but not at me.

"What are you looking at?" I asked worriedly.

58

He didn't answer, but his eyes were round with fright.

"Bobby, you're scaring me," I cried frozen with indecision, my eyes darting everywhere, trying to see what he saw. Finally, when I could stand it no longer, I ran the last few feet and snatched the sweater, beating a hasty retreat back through the barn and into the sunshine.

"Got it." I announced triumphantly, looking around. I frowned in sudden disappointment. Bobby was gone.

~~~~

My little friend didn't return until the next day.

"Where did you go yesterday?" I asked.

"Nowhere."

"Yes you did," I argued. "When I came out of the barn you were gone."

"I don't know," he mumbled, his head down.

"It's okay," I said, sensing his discomfort. "It doesn't matter. Want some ice cream?"

"Yeah," he answered, a bright smile covering his face. "I like ice cream."

A few minutes later, we sat the picnic table in the backyard, enjoying the sunshine. The green grass gave off a pleasant aroma all around us. My ice cream was already gone, leaving just a sticky residue in the bowl, but Bobby's sat melting in the sunshine, untouched.

"I thought you said you liked ice cream?" I asked.

"I do. I'll eat it later."

"Later it'll be ice cream soup." I laughed.

"I like it that way," he said defensively.

Sighing with defeat, I stretched out full length on the grass and left him to eat his *soup*. My skin felt warm to the touch and the soft, spongy lawn cradled my body.

When I pause to remember now, the first time I ever heard Bobby laugh, I felt good. He just had that effect on me. High-pitched, easy and carefree. I remember I wanted to laugh like that too. For months afterwards, I would often be found in front of my bedroom mirror trying to copy him, while my sister cast odd looks at me and told my parents I was weird. I didn't really care, though. Bobby was a good little friend.

If only it could have stayed that way.

He laughed hard as I tried to copy his effortless roll down the grassy hillside in our back yard. Push-starting continually with one leg, I giggled, feeling awkward.

Mom laughed heartily as she went by. Bits of grass still clung to my hair and I tousled it self-consciously. She waved as she moved off to the chicken house with a bucket full of vegetable clippings.

I smiled back and raised my own hand in reply. Bobby was grinning openly.

I remember that day distinctly. Although I was still disappointed at the lack of school-age friends in the area of my new home, I was delighted by my new friendship with this strange but cute little boy.

It was summer and I finally had a good friend. Too bad if he was younger than me! We spent time together talking about everything and nothing. Our conversations rambled from one topic to another, the way it does when you're with a good friend. I learned to avoid the topic of his family, as it seemed to always make him sad, but he had opinions on everything else, so he was easy to talk to. Mostly, the thing I liked the most about Bobby was that he liked to listen. That was fine by me; I love to talk.

My parents had been worried about me adjusting to this new country life, but I was A.O.K. as long as I had Bobby.

~~~~

I remember a significant discussion we had at dinner one night, a couple of months after I met my little friend. Mom and dad made a point of asking about each person's day at the dinner table. When it was my turn, I talked happily about the things Bobby and I had done. Looking back, I realize that their reactions were always somewhat guarded and slightly suspicious, but I was a kid. What did I know about parents and big sisters?

"Who is this friend you keep talking about?" mom had said.

"My friend, you know, the little neighbour kid," I told her.

"Oh, your Brown boy," dad said, smirking.

"Dad," I said, rolling my eyes. "Only you call him that."

"Oh?" mom replied. "Do you know this boy, Will? Why do you say he's brown?"

"Brown shirts," dad answered in his cryptic way.

"Oh," she said. "Of course. And you saw him today?"

I nodded and cast a sidelong glance at Mom. "Can we play in the house tomorrow?"

"Who's we? You and your boy in the brown shirt?"

"Uh, yeah." I laughed awkwardly.

"Alright. Does this boy have a name?"

"Sure. His name is Bobby."

A small frown had crossed my mother's brow, but it was gone in an instant. "Okay, well you and Bobby can play but no more leaving half-eaten food in the back yard please."

"Whoops," I said, making a small grimace. "Sorry. I guess Bobby didn't like ice cream soup after all."

"I guess not," she said, her tone registering disapproval. "Try not to be wasteful, Virginia."

"Someone's gonna get it," Diana said in a sing-song voice, as she passed by.

"Diana, mind your own business," dad replied automatically. He was always saying that to her.

Mom shook her head briefly. "Well, if he's coming over tomorrow, I suppose I can meet him then. What does he look like? Does he live nearby?"

"Um..." I paused, suddenly confused. "Mom, you've seen him before, lots of times. Remember?"

"I have?" mom seemed honestly confused and that scared me a little. "No, I haven't met this boy of yours yet. Have you been playing outside? All I've seen is you sweetie. Oh! Do you mean to tell me he was with you today?"

I nodded warily.

"Oh, I must not have seen him," she said. "Oh honey, it's okay," she said, noting my expression. "I'll meet him tomorrow ... now go get your pajamas on."

I was floored. Why was she acting this way? He was right there and had been for weeks already. I thought back to the scene earlier that day. Perhaps the trunk of the big tree had hidden him from view?

Yeah, but that only explained today. Was there something about him she didn't like?

When I stepped outside the next morning, Bobby was already there, standing on the path beside the pool. Waiting. It was cloudy and I glanced nervously at the darkening sky. A summer storm, the weather man predicted.

Bobby seemed unconcerned by the weather. Come to think of it, he was always like that.

Once again, he wore a brown shirt and jeans, faded black and white sneakers peeking out from underneath the hem of his pants. I smiled and shook my head. Was this all he had in his closet?

"Let's play inside today okay?" I said, walking back to the sliding glass door of the family room and pulling it open. I crooked my finger at him. "It's supposed to rain, and you don't even have a jacket. Come on inside."

"No," he said, backing away.

"What? Don't be silly. It's okay. I asked."

"Mom?" I called out into the house. "Bobby and I can play inside today, right?" I turned to him and nodded, waiting for the verbal confirmation I knew would come.

Mom came around the corner from the kitchen and stood there in the doorway of the family room, drying her hands on a dishtowel. Her gaze was questioning.

"What was that honey?"

"We can play in here right?"

"We?"

"Uh … yeah. Me and Bobby." I stepped to one side so she couldn't miss him. I smiled at him and he smiled back, rocking back and forth on his heels, uncertainly.

"Uhhh, sure sweetie, whatever you want."

Her reaction was truly puzzling. She kept looking at me with narrowed eyes as she walked back to the kitchen.

But Bobby refused to budge.

"No," he said simply. "Not inside."

Mom ended up serving us cookies and two glasses of milk, on the picnic table in the back yard, despite the gloomy weather. Her smile never disappeared, but it was a weak smile full of confusion.

I was starting to get worried. Mom had never acted this way with any of my friends before. Didn't she like him? And what was with Bobby not wanting to play inside. Something was weird, but I couldn't think what.

"What a great imagination you have," she said as she approached yet again from the house. "Bobby is a great name for a special friend."

I turned to him, feeling embarrassed, but he looked away.

"And where does Bobby live? Do we know his parents?"

Mom stood there looking around as though searching for something.

I looked over at Bobby but he shook his head.

"Uh, no I don't think so. Mom, what's wrong?"

"Nothing dear," she said, touching my face gently, before breathing a deep sigh and walking slowly back to the house.

Nothing my foot, I thought. Something was really bugging her, but what? She wouldn't even look at him!

Out of the corner of my eye, I watched him. He sat so still, it was almost eerie. Maybe he was cold. I pulled my windbreaker tighter around my shoulders.

"Are you okay?" I asked. "You cold?"

"I'm fine," he said.

"Sorry about mom."

Bobby didn't say anything, just looked past my shoulder at the house with a sad expression.

"I mean it. She's acting weird today, but she's not always like that. What are you looking at?" I asked impatiently.

"Nothin'."

I sat puzzling for a few seconds, watching him look around with a sad expression before it hit me. "Oh!" I said, jumping up. "I just realized."

"What?" he asked his eyes wide.

"This is the boy's house! The boy who died."

Bobby's eyes narrowed and he frowned at me.

"I'm sorry. He was your friend, wasn't he?"

"I don't know." His frown evaporated as he turned away and sighed deeply.

"Okay. I get it. You don't want to talk about it … no wonder you wouldn't come in."

"Yeah," he said, rising from the bench. "I gotta go."

"Do you have to?"

Bobby nodded and looked around again. "Uh-huh."

I watched him walk down the gravel path, his feet barely making a dent in the loose rock.

Why didn't I realize he would feel weird in my house? The little kid who died was supposed to be about his age, so of course they would have been friends.

What an idiot, I thought, smacking my forehead with the palm of my hand. Mom had told me so many times not to be insensitive to people's feelings, and yet that's exactly what I'd done to Bobby.

I sat there for a while after that, wondering and worrying whether I'd scared him away. I hoped not. He was so small and always alone. I felt like he needed a friend.

The Nightmare Man

6

It was on a night when Diana was left in charge that I consciously saw my first ghost. Diana was practicing with the pool cue, sinking ball after ball. I could hear the clinking sound as the billiard balls dropped into the pockets, one after the other.

"You're actually not too bad at that game," I told her.

"Yeah, thanks," she replied dryly, holding the pool cue negligently in one hand. "I never really thought I'd like it, but it's grown on me, I—."

I raised my head to see why she'd stopped. She was squinting at the glass patio door as though she'd seen or heard something outside.

She walked to the door and started to unlock it, but something about her body language told me she was being cautious. Suddenly, she gasped, stumbled backward and screamed. The sound reverberated off the walls.

I tripped and fell over my own feet trying to stand up too fast. THere was something strange in the reflection of the door, but I wasn't sure what it was. When I finally looked over the edge of the table, I clearly saw my sister's white-face reflected in the glass door, but it was the reflection that stood beside her, that dragged an involuntary scream from my own lips.

A man stood there, reflected in the glass as though he was standing between us, only no one was there.

He looked as real as we did. He was an old man, tall and thin, a black cloak or raincoat covering him from neck to toe. His face looked angry. A hat was perched on his head, pulled low over his eyes. The effect was menacing enough, but the fact that he wasn't really there topped it off for me.

Automatically I turned to my sister for help. I could feel my face flush with the heat and colour of sudden fear.

When I turned back a second later, he was gone, like a trick of the light. I remember rubbing at my eyes as though they'd deceived me, and rushing to my sister's side.

Diana was trembling all over. Her face was drained of colour and I could tell she was trying to be brave, but she clung to me as though I was her lifeline.

"You saw that … right?" She asked me at last.

"What was that thing?" I said.

"I don't know," she said, looking at me with startled eyes. "Tell me I'm dreaming."

"If you are, then I'm having the same dream."

Diana wrapped me in a tight hug and looked around the room.

"Something's going on around here," she said. "I wish I knew what."

Of course, when mother and dad returned they got the full story. I know they didn't believe us, but after that, Diana and I kept the curtains closed after dark.

~~~~

Strange books began to appear on the kitchen counter over the next couple of weeks. Mom had taken a part time job at the Library and she'd been bringing tote bags full of books home for all of us to read. I loved to read and still do, but the titles of these books left no doubt about what was on her mind.

Among the mysteries and adventure stories were other non-fiction titles that dealt with creative children, kids with imaginary friends and people called "hypnotists" who used the power of their minds to do amazing things. I screwed up my face and sighed. Obviously, mom was determined to explain our experiences away with casual references to hypnotism and the power of the mind.

In retrospect, I'd say she was getting warm.

A few days after the rec room ordeal, my parents sat me down to have a "nice long chat."

"I think it's time we talked about Bobby," mom said.

"What's he got to do with anything?" I was feeling defensive.

66

"Don't you find it odd that dad and I can't see him?"

"Can't or won't?" I asked, folding my arms.

"Now Ginny, that's unfair," dad replied. "Why would we do that?"

"Well, he's not invisible, that's just crazy!"

"Perhaps he isn't invisible ... to you. But he might be ... imaginary."

Mom folded her hands in her lap and looked down at them, letting the silence lengthen.

"Oh no, we're not doing this again," I said. "I'm too old for that, now. I'm nine." I looked at both of them, noting their serious expressions. "You mean you really can't see him at all?"

"I know exactly how old you are Virginia," mom replied. "I realize this may be difficult for you, but ...."

"Oh no," I interrupted her, my voice sarcastic and angry. "It isn't difficult at all. What you're asking me to believe is impossible! You're telling me that for some reason, you can't see my friend, who is as real as you are by the way, and so he's a, what ... imaginary friend? I already told you, I'm too old for that and we both know it. Imaginary friends are for babies!"

"Ginny," said dad sternly. "Don't talk to your mother that way. We're only trying to help you. Remember, you've been through this before. Granted, you were younger," he said, holding up his hand to forestall any more comment. "But there's got to be a reason for this; we're just trying to figure it out. And we'd appreciate your help."

I cast dark looks first at mom, and then dad. This was not going well.

"Your mind is a powerful tool, Ginny. You're a strong-willed girl and you've been through a lot, we know," mom said. "Perhaps this is your way of dealing with the move and having to leave your friends behind. We're not blaming you, sweetie. We're here to support you."

"Bull," I muttered, my eyes flashing angrily.

"Pardon me?"

Dad stood up and towered over me.

Anger had made me reckless. This was a tactical error. "Uh-oh. Uh ... sorry?"

"I should say so," he replied. "I think this conversation has run aground."

"Yes dad." Our little chat hadn't enlightened me in the least, but I knew better than to say so.

The biggest problem with my parent's theory was that it didn't fit the situation. I knew all about imaginary friends already. The descriptions in the books mom brought home only strengthened my argument. They spoke of little kids under the age of six, who were emotionally traumatized, damaged somehow by the events of their young lives, fragile and haunted by their own thoughts. That wasn't me. I was haunted alright, but not by anything the books mentioned.

Pausing for a moment outside her bedroom door, I wondered what else my mother had been reading.

The title of the book lying open on Mom's bedside table was *Hypnosis and Harnessing the Power of the Mind*. Ah-hah!

In the days following the infamous chat, I decided my first instinct was probably correct. Mom and dad didn't like Bobby. They were weird about my friendship with him, and for some reason they were determined not to acknowledge him. Maybe they hated his parents. How was I to know? Adults never told kids anything and now they were trying to dredge up some tired old idea of imaginary friends to cover their ... what? Embarrassment?

So they thought Bobby was imaginary. To them, I supposed the answer was perfectly plausible, but I knew it wasn't. I remember how it felt when they told me Emily couldn't possibly be real. They said I made her up, but I can still remember her long brown braids and her thin hands. I can still remember how sad she got whenever she looked at my parents ... but they never saw her either.

What did it all mean? The longer I thought about it, the more confused I became.

Put it away, I told myself. Don't think of it. Just don't.

~~~~

Thump.

Bang.

Clank ... rattle ... whump! My eyelids fluttered open at the noises originating somewhere behind my bedroom wall.

Clack, clack.

I rolled over and pulled up my covers. It was cold in my room again.

Clack, clack ... clack, clack ... Creak.

My sleep-filled mind tried to make sense of what I was hearing. A cupboard door? A closet? Someone walking? That last sound was definitely the hallway outside my bedroom door.

"For goodness sake!" I complained, sitting up to punch my pillow. "Diana."

A constant, rhythmic tinkling sound clearly indicated she was stirring something as she clanked around in the kitchen.

The sounds were unmistakable. Diana was up, foraging in the kitchen again. It was becoming a nightly ritual.

I rolled over and groaned aloud. It was three a.m. didn't she ever sleep?

~~~~~

"Diana, you'd better watch it," I told her the next morning at breakfast. "Dad's on the warpath."

"And just what are you talking about?" She asked, dedicating her attention to the smooth application of jam onto the toast in front of her.

"What I'm talking about is your nightly visits to the kitchen in the middle of the night," I whispered, cupping my hand around my mouth to keep our conversation private.

Diana stared at me. "You're mental," she said. "Quit trying to blame things on me."

"I'm not," I retorted, my voice growing louder. "And don't call me mental!"

Mom and dad looked over at us and frowned; my angry tone interrupted their conversation. "Girls," dad cautioned.

"It's okay dad," Diana said, smiling sweetly. "Gin's trying to blame me for stuff I'm not doing, and I'm just setting her straight, that's all."

"Oh really? I seem to recall dad saying no one was allowed to go wandering through the house at three a.m. What do you make of that, miss know-it-all?"

Dad's eyebrows had shot up and he was staring hard at Diana.

"Don't be ridiculous," she said. "At three in the morning I'm fast asleep. Teenagers need their beauty sleep."

"Nuh-uh," I said. "I can hear you. I can hear everything." I pointed at the wall that the kitchen shared with my bedroom. "My room is just there, remember."

"Diana? Is it true? You're the one making all the noise?" Mom sounded strangely relieved at the idea.

"Oh for heaven's sake! If it was me, then why does it always happen at three?"

69

"Who said it does?" I said. All eyes turned on me. "Well," I continued defensively. "I can hear it, that's all, and I have a clock."

"I think we've heard enough of this nonsense," dad said. "It's becoming a blame game. Let's settle this once and for all. No more three a.m. visits to the kitchen please. For *anyone*. We're on edge lately as it is, and this certainly isn't helping."

"Yes dad," Diana and I answered together.

"That's settled then."

As soon as my parents turned their backs to resume their earlier conversation, Diana stuck out her tongue at me. "Nice try," she muttered.

"You are so gonna get it," I said. "They'll catch you. Wait and see."

"The only one who's gonna get caught is you," she said. "Because you're the only one doing anything weird." Her expression disdainful, she flipped her hair back over one shoulder and stalked out of the kitchen.

~~~~

The next afternoon, I snuck carefully through the back yard, past my father who was very determinedly working with a long pole and a trailing hose by the side of the pool. He was vacuuming the last bits of debris off the bottom of our now beautiful, clear swimming pool, and his concentration was complete. Climbing awkwardly through the horse corral fencing, I was grateful dad was so engrossed. He hadn't noticed me leaving the yard. For some reason, they were always calling me back whenever I tried to go out into the back field.

Proceeding at a run now, I covered ground fast and soon, I settled into a steady fast-walk that ate up the distance. Five acres was a long walk when you were trying to be stealthy.

My destination at last came into view; a small patch of grass by the side of a jagged stream. That stream ran diagonally across the back of our property, overhung with weeping willows and snarls of overgrown blackberry bushes. It was a sheltered, peaceful place, but that wasn't the reason I was there.

I was missing my little friend, and I couldn't help but wonder if he would find me there. I knew he liked that spot; I only hoped he still liked me.

Perhaps, now that I knew my parents disapproved of him, he wouldn't come over anymore. I had no way of knowing whether they'd spoken to his parents. Perhaps they'd gone and demanded that he stay away? I wished for the hundredth time that I knew where he lived, but he'd never told me. In fact, I realized with a start, he never talked about his home at all.

A guilty feeling of betrayal stole over me as I wondered whether I should have just kept our friendship a secret after all. I grabbed a fistful of pebbles and one by one, started chucking the smooth, round stones into the gurgling waters of the stream, trying to let the current carry away my feelings. I wiped stray tears from my cheeks and sniffled.

"Uh-oh."

The sound of Bobby's voice startled me so badly I almost pitched head first into the stream, just trying to turn around.

"Bobby! What are you doing here?"

"Nothing," he answered defensively. "I heard you."

Heard me? What was that supposed to mean?

I looked at him closely, studying him as though, with the next breath, he'd be gone. He'd done that disappearing act on me often enough. There was a war going on inside of me as I watched him, his head cocked to one side in amusement, noticing my prolonged stare.

How could a figment of my imagination look so real? And how was he always able to sneak up on me like he did?

"I'm sorry," I said at last, anxious to ease the awkward silence. "I don't know why my parents are being so mean." This was the only answer that made sense and I was determined to stick to it.

"Oh," he said. "You're worried about that?" He sighed tragically. "I wouldn't. Grown-ups just don't see me." His simple statement tore at my heart.

"What? That doesn't ... they don't see you?"

"Nope."

"Why not?" I asked.

Bobby sighed deeply, "I don't know."

All other questions died in my throat: strange how he had that effect on me. He was so childish one moment, and so adult the next.

"I'm getting older, you know," I told him. "I'll be ten in September."

"Oh," Bobby said, his expression brightening. "You gonna have a party?"

I smiled. An almost ten-year-old and a six-year-old was a very unusual friendship, no matter how mature he seemed. My friends from school would never accept it.

"Yeah, I'm having a pool party," I said. "That is, as long as dad gets the pool ready in time. Do you wanna come?" I smiled brightly but secretly I hoped he'd decline.

"Oh," he said. "I don't much like water."

"Oh, okay," I said, wondering why. Didn't all kids love swimming pools?

In the distance, past Bobby's shoulder, I saw my dad.

"Ginny!" He called.

I looked worriedly at Bobby, but he seemed unconcerned, sitting on the grassy bank facing the stream as though he wasn't aware of my father's approach. His strange, heart-wrenching statement, "grown-ups don't see me" echoed in my head as dad approached, his face sporting a big grin that was all for me. I looked around hurriedly, but Bobby had already disappeared. The sapling trees and blackberry bushes rustled in the breeze, but there was no sign of a little boy anywhere. How did he do that?

"There you are!" dad said. "I have a surprise."

"What?"

"The pool!" He announced. "Don't frown at me like that. You've been bugging me about this since we moved in. Your mom and Diana are waiting, so let's get a move-on."

"Dad, did you see anyone else when you came out here just now?" I ventured.

Casting a sidelong glance at me, dad replied. "Nope. Was I supposed to see anyone else?"

He laughed at his own humour, and I smiled distractedly, following behind him back through the fields to the house. A peculiar sensation had settled inside me that I couldn't shake. I couldn't explain it either, just like Bobby's cryptic comment, "Grown-ups don't see me". No wonder they didn't see him if he was always running off like that, I thought. Weird.

I walked in silence behind my father. Thankfully, he didn't question my lack of conversation. He was probably relieved, I thought wryly. Dad and mom always said I was too talkative.

As we approached, I caught sight of my mother artfully arranged on a chaise lounge. She was lounging by the pool on the other side of the short chain-link fence that surrounded it. She wore a one-piece swimsuit that flattered her figure, and a fancy looking drink was held negligently in one hand. A large brimmed hat completed the picture. She looked over at me through the fence, the dark lenses of her over-sized sunglasses slid down on her nose. The picture she presented was one I'd seen in an old-time movie magazine. I couldn't help grinning.

The image I'd previously held in my mind of a child drowning in this pool was instantly swept aside. I couldn't imagine anything bad happening here.

"Hi sweetie!" she shouted as I drew near. "Isn't it grand? Your daddy's a miracle worker! Just look at it!" The oval-shaped in-ground pool was indeed beautiful. The water was crystal clear, and I could see the aqua- coloured liner for the first time. It had a shallow end closest to the house and the other end, a full 10 feet deep, sported a gleaming white fibreglass diving board.

That diving board had potential, I thought, my dark mood lifting.

"Hurry up and get your suit on," she said, her words following me as I hurried into the house.

It was late August and the air was deliciously warm. I could actually smell the leaves on our trees and the scent of the lilac bushes, strong and sweet, surrounding our house. Although my thoughts were still churning from the brief encounter with Bobby, I tried to relax. There was a nagging sense of something not quite right about that kid, but I couldn't put my finger on it. With a shake of my head, I changed gears and clothes. I'd been waiting long enough for this pool; I wasn't going to waste even one more minute!

The water sparkled enticingly as I opened the chain link gate and stepped out onto the concrete patio that surrounded the pool. The sparkling white tiles that rimmed the edge had been scrubbed clean and they gleamed in the strong sunlight. My bare foot sunk into the first four inches of cool water.

"Whoo-hoo!"

The splash that followed transferred a large amount of water up over the edge. My look of chagrin, aimed at dad was brief, but his frown quickly turned into laughter.

"Oh go ahead, you've waited long enough. A little splashing isn't going to hurt anything."

The experience was nothing short of spectacular. I'd been waiting for months for this moment and the temperature of the water, just cool enough to be refreshing, drove all thoughts of mysterious little boys from my mind. I swam down into the Mediterranean blue until my feet touched the bottom and pushing off against it, I shot to the surface like a rocket, blowing the air from my lungs in great gusts of frothy white bubbles as I went. "Excellent!" I said, reaching the side, slightly breathless with the effort. My voice took on a strange echo as the sound bounced off the surface of the water and the edges of the pool. "I gotta do that again!" I grabbed the metal rungs of the ladder and hauled myself up for a repeat performance. As I did so, the diving board came into view and I grinned with delight. As I approached it, however, I noticed something I hadn't before. A large yellow plastic milk crate sat to one side of the pool deck, against the fence. In it were some old, grubby looking children's toys. The pile was small. On top was a naked baby doll with half the hair missing from its head, a small, deflated ball, the colours faded, and a water-damaged comic book. The pages of it were mildewed and stained, rendering it unreadable. There were other items beneath and I bent down to examine it further when dad noticed the movement.

"Ginny, don't touch those," he said. "I haven't gotten rid of them yet."

"Where did they come from?" I asked.

"The bottom of the pool," he said. "They were part of the reason the whole thing went to crud. When people throw junk in the water it upsets the PH levels. Stuff like that doesn't belong in a swimming pool."

"What's in there?" I asked, craning my neck to see more.

"Uh, let me see... kids toys, some costume jewelry, a few rocks, a broken picture frame. Junk."

"Oh," I said. "Why can't I touch it?"

"Well, aside from the fact that it's garbage, the whole thing's full of chlorine. I only found all that stuff after I put a double dose of shock into the water and it started to clear up. As soon as I could see the bottom, I found that ... among other things." He waved his hand at the items in the crate. "But chlorine is corrosive and it'll burn your skin, so don't touch it," dad said, narrowing his eyes at me and lowering his chin. "I mean it Ginny," he said. "Now, are you gonna swim or just stand there, dripping?"

I jumped into the pool gratefully, mom and dad watching me with huge smiles, taking pictures that would last a lifetime. On my way to the diving board, I had to walk past the mysterious crate every time, looking, but not touching. It was killing me.

"Diana! Are you coming out sometime today?"

"Coming," she sang from an open doorway at the back of the house. Dressed in a bathing suit that made my father look away, she emerged and paused for dramatic effect.

"You look lovely dear," mom told her. "Now jump in, while we're young."

Diana ignored mom's sarcasm and sauntered over to the pool. She slipped out of her flip-flops and dipped one painted toenail into the water with a sweeping movement.

"Ooh, it's cold!" she said, frowning at my parents. "I thought you said it was heated."

"It is," replied dad, "but I'm not about to turn it up to 90 degrees just for you."

"Hmmm," she said. "I suppose it is warm enough for a quick swim." And with that, she moved gracefully to the diving board and dove cleanly into the water as though she'd been doing it all her life.

Diana's idea of a quick swim was ludicrous. It was like me saying I was going to tell a quick story.

~~~~

It was a family dinner and my cousins were all in attendance, with the exception of one who'd already grown up and moved away to settle 'up north somewhere'. Mom was serving homemade spaghetti and cabbage rolls, and the scents rolling out of the kitchen kept everyone hovering slightly, as we waited for the appointed hour.

"How do you like the new place?" My cousin Ainslie asked me, looking around.

"Mostly good," I replied warily. Ainslie was my age, but she was known not to keep secrets.

"Mostly?" Her eyebrows climbed.

"Yeah, you know, the horses need looking after and all that. Farm chores aren't fun."

"Oh," she sounded disappointed. Leaning back in her chair she eyed me for a minute more.

"What?"

"Nothin', it's just that," she trailed off and seemed to collect her thoughts. "I heard my mom talking to Auntie Liz a couple of minutes ago. Are you ... okay?"

"What do you mean?"

"Auntie Liz said you talk to yourself and you have an imaginary friend?"

"I don't know what you're talking about." My flat denial seemed to soothe my cousin.

"Good," she said, her face brightening into a huge grin. "I thought it was probably made up anyways." She rolled her eyes dramatically. "Grown-ups. They don't understand kids."

"You got that right," I told her. "Wanna go swimming?"

"You bet!"

It was a beautiful hot day, and the first of many barbecues my family hosted in that house.

What I didn't know then, was that various members of my extended family also encountered the entities we lived with.

~~~~~

—Recently, as I was preparing this manuscript, one my cousins offered further validation, as we sat in her modern living room, sipping white wine.

"I never really liked that house," she told me seriously. "I knew there were other, um, people there, that no one could see. I sensed them, but there was no way that I was gonna say anything. I saw the way the adults were treating you and I knew there wasn't anything I could do to change that, so I kept quiet. I tried to give Diana hints, but she never took them. I wanted to talk to you about it, but you and I didn't really spend too much time together, so I didn't really know what to say."

"It's okay," I reassured her. "Like you said, there wasn't anything you could have done. I know you spent most of your time with Marianne and Diana. After all, you're all around the same age. You didn't want us younger kids hanging out with you. I'm just happy we're friends now, and to hear you say this to me, even after all these years means more than I can tell you. Thank you." With that, we'd hugged spontaneously and grinned like the children we'd once been. —

~~~~~

Life in our house was as normal as we could make it, with the majority of my family firmly in denial while unexplained forces banged cupboards and doors trying to get our attention. My biggest respite was our pool. I swam as often as I could and used all my powers of persuasion on dad so he'd keep it heated as long as possible into the fall in winter months. Nothing could reach me in the middle of that calm, blue oasis and although the chlorine turned my hair an odd shade of bleach-blonde that summer—verging on green—I didn't care.

I knew my parents talked with each other and apparently to my aunts and uncles too, about my lack of socializing, and my daily walks in the back field with Bobby probably didn't help. I overheard them often, referring to my introverted behaviour as a "phase".

Mom's answer to this phase arrived in the form of library books that kept coming home from work with her. And although I glanced through them dutifully, I didn't learn anything useful.

I tried to avoid doing my barn chores alone, because when someone else was there with me, it seemed that the watcher kept his distance. Being almost ten meant that no one told me anything directly, so what I learned about mom and dad's concerns, I learned through shameless eavesdropping

Bobby's cryptic remarks about adults not seeing him still weighed on my mind, but he steadfastly refused to say anything more.

I was determined to get to the bottom of it though. However, talking about Bobby to Diana wasn't one of my better ideas.

"She's a freak!" I heard her saying to mom and dad one day. "My friends can't even come over here anymore because of her stupid imaginary friends, Bob and John! My friends all think she's crazy or possessed! Maybe she is!"

"That will do," dad had replied firmly. "Your friends had better watch their mouths, and that goes for you too." This was how dad dealt with things. Direct and to the point, but without clouding the issue by asking for our input.

I wasn't sure what possessed meant, but I knew what crazy was. And where was she getting this other guy? As far as I knew, I didn't know anyone called John. That just showed how well she listened to me, I thought in disgust.

~~~~

"I don't like being called names Mom," I said the next day when we were alone together.

Mom sighed heavily. "I expect you girls to be civil to each other," she said. "I don't like all this fighting. It brings too much stress to the family."

"But Mom, she's saying stuff about me that isn't true."

"Like?" she asked.

"Like I'm crazy and possessed!"

"Where did you hear that?" Mom squinted at me and seemed to think of a better question. "Do you know why she says those things?"

"Let's see, oh I don't know, maybe because she enjoys torturing me?" I said, only half-joking.

"Because she's worried, that's why." Mom let out a long slow breath and rubbed her temples. "To tell the truth, Ginny, we're all a bit worried about you. Since we've moved in here, you've been acting strangely."

"That's not my fault! She needs to stop calling me names! You say that people should always be fair to each other."

Mom smiled and her face grew thoughtful. After a while, she nodded. "I think I can pass that on," she said. "Well said. You're such a negotiator."

I smiled in spite of my earlier anger, a sense of pride filling me at Mom's words.

Touché Diana, I thought. Take that. I suppressed the urge to stick out my tongue at her closed door as I walked back to my room.

The Sisters

7

Our neighbours across the street lived in an old-fashioned cottage. The wooden siding was weathered, in need of re-painting long ago. There was a tiny porch on one side, which led to a substantial garden. Obviously, that was where the homeowners spent their time. Blossoms of every description bloomed there. I could smell the heady perfume of the flowers, mingling with the unmistakable scent of oregano and thyme as the plants baked in the afternoon sun. Despite the beauty of the idyllic scene, I was nervous.

I'd seen these neighbours from a distance, of course. They always waved and smiled, as they tended to their gardens and we tended our vast expanse of lawn. Their enormous dog, a sort of crossbreed English Mastiff they called Fred, bounded across the yard, playing a tireless game of fetch.

"As I understand it, they are two widowed sisters," my father had explained to me. "Relatives of the family who used to live here," he paused. "It seems the two moved in together after they both became widowed. They're in their eighties. Mom and I want to be good neighbours. We've told them all about you, so it would be nice if you went over for a short visit. They're nice old gals. You'll get along great."

"When you go over, I want you to take them some eggs," mom said to me. "I promised two dozen. They'll appreciate that and I need some room in my fridge. Those chickens we've got are laying too well! We're going to have to eat more eggs around here." She thrust the two egg cartons into my hands; that was Mom's sign language for "get going."

The gravel crunched loudly under my sandals as I walked, my steps dragging.

With the eggs tucked securely under my arm, I approached the road and made a big show of carefully looking for traffic. I crossed safely, turning to smile and wave at my parents, whom I knew were watching the whole production from the large picture window at the front of our house.

Scuffing my feet down the sisters' driveway, a small group of flowers caught my eye. Each one was like a miniature tulip, but they were snow-white, with long delicate stems. It seemed wrong somehow that something so elegant would grow so well at the bottom of a dirty, roadside ditch.

"Crazy," I mumbled, skidding down the slope. "They look like they were planted here."

At the sound of my voice, a massive dog rounded the side of the house and ran at me full speed. He was way bigger up close! His name was Fred and he closed the gap between us faster than I could think. I, with my untidy handful of ditch-flowers, tried to think of some bit of doggy wisdom that would keep me from becoming his dinner. Even the ditch I still stood in wasn't going to be a deterrent to this dog. I braced for impact, and two giant front paws landed hard against my small shoulders.

I gave a small scream of surprise as I fell backwards against the sloping ground. Fred's baritone woofs, as he 'hugged' me with doggy delight seemed to attract some attention from the other side of the house.

At least he wasn't about to eat me, I realized, but his breath, as he woofed into my face again, was horrendous!

"Fred? Now what are you up to?" A feminine voice came from amidst the blossoms. "Ah," she said, finally emerging and peering down into the ditch. "I see Fred's escorted you in." The grey-haired woman who faced me stood stripping patterned gardening gloves from her hands. "You must be Ginny. Funny you chose to walk through the ditch when we have a perfectly good driveway, though."

While I laughed sheepishly, another shorter woman emerged from the house to stand on the wooden porch.

"Well, if it isn't our little angel from across the street, bringing us more delicious eggs. Your mother said you'd be along." She turned and spoke with authority to the enormous dog. "Fred, for heaven's sake, let the girl be."

"Oh, yes, thank you," I said, as Fred reluctantly got down and backed away, his tail still wagging. "I hope the eggs aren't broken."

"And what have we here?" The taller woman said, suddenly coming forward, intent on the items held in my outstretched hand.

I'd almost forgotten the flowers I still clenched, the stems a little mangled where they'd pressed up against the hard cardboard egg carton.

"Well," they both said together, as both eggs and flowers were deposited into waiting hands. Gently, the blossoms and their stems were smoothed with a touch both professional and reverent, and the shorter woman held them out for her sister to see. "I didn't think I'd see these again," she said, turning to me. "Where did you find them?"

"Um, there by the road." I told her, pointing back over my shoulder.

"Oh my! In the ditch?" she asked, her eyes widening. "How strange. Penny! These *are* Bobby's wishing flowers, aren't they?"

The tall woman frowned momentarily, and then gave a knowing smile. She had short-cropped white hair and an air of quiet confidence. "Well of course they are," she replied, laughing suddenly. "That figures!When the house went up for sale I looked everywhere for them, thinking it would be good to take a cutting, but I never did find them. I'd almost forgotten about these little flowers. These are definitely the same variety as the ones I remember. But how did they end up here?" She scratched at her cheek, leaving a trail of potting soil and frowned. "Didn't we plant them out by the back shed?"

"Oh yes. He was adamant, I remember that very well. It had to be right in front of those windows. I remember that specifically."

"Yes. He was afraid of that nasty old shed, wasn't he? I never did understand why.." She turned to her sister thoughtfully. "Was he four then?"

I frowned at them. "I beg your pardon?"

"Always so full of energy. He loved his games and tricks." It seemed as though they were both lost in their own thoughts and couldn't hear me.

They turned away for a moment and then the one called Penny spoke in a far-off sounding voice. "It's a gift, that's what this is." She turned to me and seemed to register my puzzlement for the first time.

"Oh! Ginny."

Her sister cut in, "I'm so sorry my dear, we're a couple of old women lost in our reminiscing and you're still standing in the yard! How rude of us! Come in, come in." She smiled, hastily untying an apron and brushing ineffectively at her short, white locks. "Mind the door; it's got a wicked backlash! The spring's too tight." She held the screen door wider and moved backwards into the worn, but clean kitchen. "I'm sorry, you haven't the faintest idea what we're rambling on about do you?" She laughed and beckoned me forward.

Hesitantly, I stepped inside, chewing my lower lip.

"Well, so much for manners," the taller woman said, an easy smile on her lips. "I haven't even introduced myself or my sister. I am Penny, and this," she pointed at the shorter, white-haired woman behind me, "is Elise. Thank you for the eggs, and the flowers. What a nice touch."

"The flowers? Well they aren't all that special; they're wild. I just thought they were nice. I picked them on impulse."

"You've brought us more than a visit and some farm fresh eggs," Elise said. She seemed happy, but underneath it, her voice betrayed a strange warble that I'd only heard in people who were about to cry. The mix of emotion confused me. Her green eyes glistened as she spoke, and I looked intently at her.

"Perhaps we'll move the whole lot to the garden, hmm?" She moved away abruptly, dabbing at her eyes with a handkerchief as she went.

"That's probably a good idea," I said, not having a clue if it was or it wasn't, and why these innocent looking flowers would make anyone want to cry.

"Well then, to show our appreciation, how about we have some tea?" Penny asked. Her gait lurched a bit as she moved and I wondered if I should get up to help.

"Um, appreciation? That's not really necessary. It's just some dumb old flowers and chickens eggs."

"Dumb old flowers?" Penny blinked at me for a moment and frowned. "You may not understand," she continued. "As a matter of fact, I can see that you don't." She took a deep breath and let it out slowly. When she looked at me again the familiar smile was back in place. "It's what old ladies do. You can't tell me you don't like cookies."

Elise blew her nose behind me and I jumped at the unexpected sound. She sat down at one of the wooden chairs drawn up to their small square table, where chocolate chip cookies filled a china plate.

I grinned. "I love cookies," I replied. "But I don't usually drink tea."

"Of course," Elise answered quickly. "Milk it is. And please help yourself to some of our world famous cookies, hmm?"

"Oh yes, thank you very much." Manners matter, my mother had always told me. "They look delicious."

Elise indicated the chair next to her for me to sit on, "They taste even better."

"So, how do you like your new house?" Penny asked, seating herself across from me.

"Very much. The pool is the best part, but my sister loves the riding ring."

"Oh that's good. Very good," said Penny, turning around. "And what of your parents, they seem like nice people. Are they getting on alright?"

"Well, I think so," I said cautiously. "I wonder though...."

"Yes dear?" Elise answered.

"Do you know ... has that barn been there a long time?"

"The barn?" Elise frowned in thought. "Oh yes, a long time. Great big behemoth of a thing."

"Oh."

"Why?"

"Well," I looked at both of them, their clear gazes fixed on me intently. What could I possibly tell them about my strange experiences? Would they understand? Would they march straight over to my parents and tell them their daughter is cuckoo? So instead of confiding in them, I changed course.

"Is it an old house? Dad said the wiring's goofed up."

"Oh dear," Elise said, her green eyes widening. "I hope there isn't a problem. It seemed to work fine before."

Oops! I wondered belatedly if I should have said anything after all. I guess they knew the folks who lived there. Why wouldn't they? They lived right across the street!

"Oh," I said, blushing. "Well, I'm sure it'll be okay then. What do I know? I'm just a kid."

"It's not an old house, to answer your earlier question." Penny replied. "It was only just built a little over six years ago. But this wiring problem, now that sounds serious. What are your parents going to do about it?"

"Oh, uh, I don't know. Dad goes around with something called a meter and he holds it up to all the power plugs and stuff."

"Makes sense," Penny commented as she handed me a glass of milk. "Sounds very practical."

"Well I don't know about that," I continued, feeling friendlier towards these women with every passing second. I selected a chocolate chip cookie from the dainty looking plate. "But at least dad finally stopped blaming me for leaving the lights on."

"Oh? Why are the lights on?" Elise asked.

"Maybe that's why your dad says the plugs are goofed up." Penny commented, turning around from her tea-making ritual at the kitchen counter. The words I'd so casually used sounded funny coming from her.

"Maybe." I answered, my mouth full of cookie. "All I know is that when we go to bed, the lights are off and when we wake up they're on again."

"Uh-oh," Elise muttered.

"Well that sounds like it's quite a problem," Penny interjected, looking meaningfully at her sister. "What are you going to do?"

"I dunno," I said, wondering at the non-verbal exchange between the two sisters. What did they know that they weren't telling? "Uh, mom said that maybe they'd call somebody."

"Oh I see. Like who?"

"Beats me," I said.

"Well, I'm sure they will figure it out. Do you have any theories?"

"A couple, but I shouldn't say. Mom and dad always tell people that I have a wild imagination. This is code for 'don't believe what she says.'"

"Well, you shouldn't let that get to you. It's children who often see things with greater clarity," Elise said knowingly. I wasn't sure what to say. Her wise comment left me wondering just how much she knew. And more importantly, how she knew it.

"Let's finish our snack shall we?" Penny winked good-naturedly and leaned forward. "And then Elly, Fred and I will show you our world famous garden. We've won awards for our blossoms, you know! The local paper always photographs our zinnias! Elise and I are a good gardening team. You tell your mom to call us if she needs any help with plants or flowers. We helped select all the shrubberies on your property, you know. Turned most of 'em into the earth myself."

"You did?" Obviously these two women knew the former home-owners better than I thought.

"Yes." Penny stood up and began to pour steaming water into the tea pot, then re-filled my glass with milk. Returning to the table, she cocked her head to one side and said, "Elly, I wonder if our guest would like to bring home some flowers for her mother?"

When I returned home some time later, I had a generous prize-winning bouquet in my hand and a smile on my face. I realized that I'd had a wonderful time meeting the sisters. Fred was a cool dog, when he wasn't trying to hug me. His fur felt like a huge, thick rug.

I stuffed the bouquet into a vase on the counter and tried to arrange it the way they'd shown me. I smiled when I thought of how surprised mom would be with the unexpected gift.

It seemed I was destined to make people cry with flowers that day. Mom's response was a little over the top, but since we'd moved in, her emotions were on a roller coaster.

"This is so, so … perfect," she whispered, her green eyes tearing up. "How did you know I needed this?"

"I didn't," I replied honestly. "I brought Elise and Penny some wild flowers I found on the way to their house this morning, and they loved them too. Called them wishing flowers. They gave me these for you."

Mom and I laughed together as she dried happy tears. Turning to open the fridge, she listened as I went on talking. "It was weird mom, when I gave them the flowers, they couldn't stop going on about how they were Bobby's wishing flowers. Maybe they're special flowers, with super-powers that make wishes come true."

Mom and I laughed together as she peered thoughtfully at the items in the fridge. "That's nonsense, Ginny," she said.

"Well, I thought it was kinda cool. And sorta neat too, that the boy they kept talking about has the same name as my friend. Bobby. Do you think they're the same person?"

The fridge door banged closed with a whump, and she turned to face me, instantly serious. "Don't start," she said.

"Start what?"

"You know very well what. Let's not ruin this nice mother-daughter moment with more of this imaginary broo-ha-ha."

My eyes narrowed instinctively as the implication of her words struck home.

She still thought of my friend as imaginary. I knew that if she'd only talk to me about it, she'd see. It infuriated me that she wouldn't listen. Bobby was real.

And why was it so bad if he was the same person? A bad person wouldn't bring flowers to old ladies. They'd called the naming of those flowers 'a little boy's fancy'.

But if all that was true, why did mom react so strongly? I knew my parents didn't want me talking about Bobby, because for some reason, they couldn't seem to catch a glimpse of him. I still couldn't figure out why that happened or what to do about it. He was just a fast mover.

My eyes widened with sudden realization. Of course! Didn't that mean he had to be the same person? Elise and Penny said their Bobby was 'full of energy'. Boy, that sounded like my friend, too. I was more sure than ever that it was the same person! He was probably a neighbour kid, or a relative. Mom and dad had reasons for disliking him, although I still didn't know what they were. Now though, I felt like I was finally on the right track. Helping them plant flowers and stuff like that, he had to be a frequent visitor to the sister's cottage, and it was only a short walk to my house ... it all made sense, in a mixed-up sort of way.

Could he be Elise's grandson? That made all kinds of sense. It would be natural for him to help his grandma if she were planting stuff in my new yard. That would also explain how he knew the land and all the trails so well. And there *was* a slight similarity in their features... the same eyes.

I went off happily, pleased with my deductive reasoning.

Maybe it was absurd, but I felt a close bond with Elise and Penny, as though I'd known them all my life. I smiled and thought about my next visit. I fully intended to go again soon, and now that I knew the truth about Bobby's relationship with them, I was confident that I'd see him there too. Pausing to peer under the living room couch in search of Timothy, I wondered idly how long it would take two old ladies to consume two dozen eggs. I didn't want to look too eager.

Strange Revelations

8

"Ginny, this room is beyond ridiculous again," mom warned as she stood in my doorway.

I looked around, taking in the neatly made bed, but completely missing the fact that the rug on my floor wasn't visible for all the laundry and debris that covered it.

"What do you mean Mom?" I asked. "I made my bed this morning."

"Yes, thank you very much, however I think you missed a few items." Her gaze rested on the floor suggestively and her eyebrows shot upwards.

"Oh," I said. "That."

"Yes, that," she sighed. "What are you planning to wear to school on the first day? A paper bag?"

I shrugged sheepishly and started picking up laundry. "Must you remind me about school mom?"

"And what is it you're working so hard on? I haven't heard a peep from you all morning."

"I'm just writing," I said, returning to my small desk and leaning protectively over a nearly filled page.

"I'm glad you're getting back into that. Good practice for school."

I made a face.

Mom laughed. "Journaling is good for you. I, uh, suppose you've been writing about the new house?"

"Well, I …."

"I know living here has been a big change, honey."

"Yes." I knew there had to be more.

"And I've been thinking about the other day."

My heart leapt.

"Remember, when we talked about dreams? Sometimes things we think of and imagine, affect our dreams. I was at the Library the other day, and I came across a book called, Great Writers of the 20th Century. You know, many of those great writers have done the same thing. They all have wonderful, if not over active, imaginations." I squinted at her thoughtfully, trying to figure out if she was being serious.

"Well, I just wanted to point out that it's natural for a writer to have such thoughts. I wondered if it might make you feel better to know you aren't the only one."

Mom smiled, but her expression looked a bit forced. I shrugged and smiled back. "After all," she continued, "you don't have any friends nearby to take up your time and you don't spend hours on the telephone the way your sister does." I nodded, feeling puzzled at the direction our conversation was taking, but acknowledging that she had a point. "So you might as well create stories. You have an agile mind."

"So that's it, then?"

"What's it, honey?"

"It's all just stories?"

"Yes!" She sounded excited, as though she'd finally made a breakthrough.

"I see," I said cautiously, reaching for my duo-tang. "Do you wanna read some?"

"Absolutely!" She said. "Just not right now, it's laundry day … which reminds me, the contents of your closet and dresser seem to be on the floor. If it's not in the laundry room, I'm not washing it. You can't leave all of this until the day before, you know."

I watched her turn around and head back down the hallway, the *snick-snick* of her slippers receding into the distance.

Sighing, I folded the page where I'd been writing and closed the orange duo-tang. It was about half-full of loose-leaf paper, the pages limp with rounded, childish handwriting. I promised myself I would go back to it later, but since I was wearing bathing suit bottoms for underwear, I knew my laundry situation was already in crisis. I opened the bottom drawer of my little white student desk, the wooden drawer-glides sticking and bumping, to shove the duo-tang into its hiding place, under my current stack of detective novels.

As I tried to gather the dirty laundry into a single pile, I wondered at Mom's comments. Was it really that I was a natural born writer and I had a big imagination? Or was there another reason that I saw things other people didn't, and heard parts of conversations playing out in my dreams, while people I'd never met seemed to parade through the rooms of my own home.

I was astonished to find out that not everybody dreamed like I did. Most nights, when sleep finally claimed me, I dreamt of walking, seeing people I didn't know. They spoke, but I never understood their words. I would step through my own back door, only to fall down a huge deep hole that became a ravine, its sides covered in slippery vines. I tried to grasp at the vines but they slid away from me as I fell faster and faster. Brush and thorns slapped and snagged at my skin as I plummeted down, screaming for help, in a fight I could not hope to win. In my dream, I knew I was falling to my death, and when I could stand the terror no longer, I would suddenly awake, breathless, with tears streaming from my eyes, the remnants of a scream still echoing around me.

~~~~

I picked at the tangled mass of metallic chain with a pair of tweezers and a fork, showing astonishing patience. The old tangled necklace had languished in my pocket until that morning, when I'd gotten the idea to go for a morning stroll and grabbed my barn jacket to ward off the chill in the morning air. The bulge in my pocket reminded me of the treasure hidden there. I'd almost forgotten it, the found necklace had remained in my pocket for so long. Soon I was rummaging through Mom's cleaners under the kitchen sink for a product that would remove the tarnish and a thin-tined fork was now helping me work out the knots from the delicate chain.

I worked at it with single-minded purpose, and soon, my glistening prize hung proudly around my neck, reflecting the summer sunshine as I wandered outside. A country walk on a summer day, wearing your best jewelry and your pajamas ... ah, there can be nothing better. My sense of sudden freedom was euphoric. I was doing what I wanted without a care. Well, almost, I thought, peeking back over my shoulder for any signs of sisterly pursuit. I was going to miss this when I went back to school next week.

The old house next door set my imagination afire. Curiosity pulled me nearer to its derelict front porch. Moments later I was climbing the steps and using the palm of my hand to wipe away some of the dirt covering its windows.

"Wanna go inside?"

I jumped, my heart thumping double-time as I whipped around.

Bobby stood in front of me, grinning. His stealthy approach scared me half to death and I stood there clutching my chest, trying to catch my breath.

"Quit doing that to me!" I shouted at him in surprise. "What are you doing here anyway?"

"Dumb question," he muttered. "A better question would be: how do we get inside?" He wiggled his eyebrows and followed the porch around to the back door.

"I don't think I can open it," I said, grasping the doorknob and pulling hard.

"Nope." Bobby replied. "The doorknob doesn't work."

"Okay, so what's the secret?" I asked, brushing my hair from my face with mock superiority.

"Like this!" he said, pointing at a wooden panel that looked like Fred, the enormous dog from next door, could fit through. It was a lighter colour than the door itself, perhaps newer? Surprisingly, it wiggled at my touch.

"What is it?" I asked.

"I dunno. Dog door?" he said. We looked at each other and laughed.

"Yeah, but I doubt Fred would fit," I laughed.

Bobby's head swung around sharply to stare at me. "You know Fred?"

"I met him," I said, pleased that I'd have a way to introduce the subject that burned in my brain. "Well, are you gonna open it?" I asked.

Bobby stood back and frowned. "Uh-uh," he said.

"Can't or won't?" I said, placing my hands on my hips. He just shrugged. Giving it an exasperated push, I soon figured out that the panel swung sideways. It opened into a grimy kitchen that was rumored to be full of rats.

I held it open and pointed at him. "There you are your highness. You first." Bobby smiled and ducked through effortlessly.

Inside, sunlight filtered through the dirty windows, illuminating cobwebs and dust motes as they floated past.

"Mom would kill me if she knew I was here," I said, keeping a sharp eye out for rodents. "She hates dirt."

"Yeah, my mom hates dirt, too."

I tried not to look startled. Finally, some information about his family!

I pointed to an intricately carved staircase. "What's up there?"

Bobby shrugged.

"I wonder what it was like to live here. It's like looking into the past, don't you think so?"

"No."

I mimed punching him in the arm, which he quickly dodged. "Spoil sport … WHOAH! Did you see that?" I exclaimed suddenly. Something the size of a small bird flitted through the room behind us. A bat maybe? "Hey," I continued, walking carefully by his side as we edged further into the rotting house. "I went to visit those old ladies across the street yesterday, that's when I met Fred."

"Fred? Why would Fred be there?"

I was startled at his reply. "Why … I don't know, but he was."

"Oh," Bobby sounded as if he was bored.

"Yeah. They've got a nice garden, too. They gave me some flowers for my mom. She liked them."

"That's nice," he agreed, sounding sad. "I don't see the garden anymore."

"Why not?"

"I can't."

"Because?"

"Because I can't." The answer was firm and final sounding and I marveled again at someone so young sounding so adult. "I don't know why. I can't find the way."

"Okay, okay, don't get sore at me." I looked sideways at him, wondering how he could find his way to my house, a perfect stranger, but he couldn't go across the road.

"Can't you cross the road?" I asked.

"Not by myself," he said, staring straight ahead. "Mommy said I'm not allowed."

I wondered again at the logic behind such a thing, but I knew if I asked the question that was on the tip of my tongue, 'why don't you just go with your mom then?' he'd probably storm off and I'd be left alone. Even though he was only six, and I was nearly ten, I definitely didn't want to stay in that place by myself and company was company, after all. I watched him for a moment, trying to think of another way to get at the question.

Bobby stared back. "What?" he asked.

Ah-ha, I thought.

"Are Penny and Elise your family?"

Bobby tilted his head to one side. After a while, he nodded ever so slightly.

"They told me about your wishing flowers," I said. "I wasn't sure it was you they were talking about until I thought about it later. Then I knew."

Bobby smiled and the tension seemed to melt from his body. "That's nice they remembered the wishing flowers. But *why* did they do that?"

"Well, 'cause I found some growing in the ditch by their house and I picked them."

"In the ditch, that's funny," he said.

Encouraged by his answer, I plunged ahead. "Bobby, why you don't go there anymore? Did your folks have a fight with them or something?"

"No!" His startled gaze looked fearful more than anything. "It's not my fault!"

"Hey, don't yell at me. What's going on?"

Bobby ignored the question and, scuffing his feet through the dust piled on the floor, he walked quickly away into the next room, and I followed his trail of small footprints.

"Bobby," I called out, following. "Bobby, what's going on? I don't understand."

"Can't you help me?" His voice was quiet, almost inaudible, coming from the room ahead of me. "Help me."

"Bobby?" His change in tone had me alarmed. "Just a sec," I said, rounding the corner of the small room quickly, only to stop and stare at the empty space. "Where are you? Bobby? Come on, this isn't funny. You asked me for help, so where are you?" There was nothing in the room but a simple wooden chair. My gaze travelled quickly to a closed door on the far side of the room. Hauling it open with triumph, I was left open-mouthed and staring. A closet?

My eyes went wide. He knew another way out! I was in there alone!

"Bobby? Where are you?" Crossing back into the kitchen, I checked that room, only to find it empty too. An old window gave off just enough light to see by. Years of dust still lay undisturbed on its wooden sill.

There were no finger prints and no hand prints on the sill. "Well, you didn't go this way. How did you get past me? I was standing right ...."

Looking down, my breath stuttered and I went cold all over.

There was only one set of footprints in that house, looping from the makeshift front door, through the dusty rooms and back to where I now stood, shaking.

These footprints belonged to me.

What was happening? What about the clear set of prints I'd just been following? They were gone, erased as though they'd never been.

None of this made sense.

There was no rational explanation for any of this.

I don't remember getting out. Somehow, gravel crunched underfoot. I was nearly home before I thought about my nosy sister.

Diana was waiting for me on the back porch, her arms crossed. The expression on her face said she was pissed off, but I couldn't bring myself to care.

As I approached the house on shaking legs, I tried again to come up with a plausible explanation, but my mind wasn't working clearly. Something wasn't right, but although I knew Diana would demand answers, I didn't have any.

I made a firm decision on the spot. If she asked me anything, I was going to lie.

Lost Treasure

9

The more I thought about it, the more slippery my thoughts became.

None of this was right, yet it seemed like it should fit together somehow, like some sort of weird puzzle. My head ached just thinking about it. Help me, he'd said. But how?

"So what are you going to do?" I asked my reflection as I stared in the bathroom mirror. "Sleeping on it didn't work. Probably since I didn't actually sleep." My eyes were red from incessant rubbing. Taking a deep breath, I tossed back my long hair and leaned my palms on the counter in front of me. "So are you going to figure this out and help him, or what?"

I watched as the eyes in the mirror narrowed with purpose and determination.

"Yes," I said at last. "But I'm not sure how to do it."

Heavy footsteps stopped outside the open bathroom doorway. "Talking to yourself again?" Diana asked.

I didn't bother to look at her or even answer, reaching to clutch at the crystal necklace for inspiration.

Instead, my fingers encountered the smooth skin of my unadorned neck.

"Crazy," I heard my sister mutter as her footsteps faded.

My mouth hung open in surprise, but not at her words.

The necklace was gone.

~~~~

The house rose up before me. My heart beat double-time and I took a moment to gather my thoughts. This time, I took the time to really look. It didn't look that bad, really. Its wrap-around porch sagged on one end, and the wide stone steps that led up to the front door were chipped and broken. Stylized pieces of wood curled down from the roof's edge where the weather hadn't destroyed them yet, giving it a gingerbread look. Despite my trepidation, I smiled at the effect.

The long yellowed grass that grew beside our second driveway was once the front yard of this old brick home, but now the roof had partially caved in and it was slowly being reclaimed by nature. Blackberries grew in abundance and thistles pushed up between the bricks that made up the walkway. Towering, gnarled oaks shaded the house and grounds.

This had been a beautiful house once. More than that, it had been someone's home. I tried to keep that thought firmly in my head as I trudged on.

My necklace had to be in there.

I needed to find it. I'd retraced my every step thr0ough the yard since yesterday, when I came out through that makeshift door, with no luck. The only place I hadn't checked was back *inside*.

As I passed through the last patch of sunlight on the weed-choked path and entered the deep shadows cast by the looming trees, the leash in my hand pulled taut and I was nearly yanked off my feet.

"Rookie! What are you stopping for? Let's go." I moved to the big German Shepherd's side, but instead of following me, she crouched and laid her ears back with a faint growl.

"Rookie!" I scolded. "Come. Now." Rookie always obeyed firm commands, but not that day. She stayed crouched, her large brown eyes riveted on the house, her ears laid back against her head. The ruff on the back of her neck stood straight up as the faint growl grew in its intensity.

I swallowed hard. The dog's obvious distress was making the hair on the back of my neck stand up too. What did she see? Would rats or mice upset a dog this way? Somehow, I didn't think so. Puzzled and frightened by her behaviour, I was still too curious, or maybe too stubborn to drop the whole idea.

"Come on," I said. "You're supposed to be my back-up."

But Rookie wasn't about to go in that house.

She wagged her tail appreciatively as I led her back to her own doghouse.

"There you are, coward," I said, ruffling the fur on her head and giving her a quick hug. "You don't like that place, huh?" Rookie licked my cheek as though she understood.

The big dog gave me a last reproachful look and lay down. I felt her eyes on me as I walked away.

"Tell me I'm doing the right thing, tell me I'm doing the right thing," I chanted to myself, dredging up what was left of my courage.

As I pushed the plywood panel to one side, I said, "Okay Bobby, I'm coming in. If you're hiding in here, you'd better come out now, and give me back my necklace. I'm tired of this game."

The house looked exactly like it had yesterday. Nothing had moved. Even the footsteps created by my own sneakers were still clearly laid on out in the thick dust and I followed them eagerly, like they were a life line. The ancient staircase creaked suggestively as I walked past, beginning my search for the missing necklace.

Despite what I tried to tell myself, this wasn't a beautiful house any longer. The wallpaper hung in moldy shreds and the floors were layered with dirt. At one time they may have been finished in gleaming hardwood, but now they were dull and worn. A sharp, cool wind blew across my face and I looked up. Whole sections of the roof were open to the sky and to the punishing weather. The weather had been dry for weeks, but the dampness inside this house lingered, clinging to me.

A corridor branched off to my left, leading to a larger room. Had I gone in there yesterday? I couldn't make out the footmarks in the dwindling light. Every window in the place was clouded by dirt, effectively shuttering out the strong sunlight.

A slight shuffling noise quickened my heart rate.

"Bobby? Are you here?" The sentence slipped from my mouth before I had time to think about it. A second later, I stood staring in disbelief at the scene before me. In the center of the otherwise empty room, heaped into a pile on the dirty floor, lay several small items. An old comic book—water-stained and dog-eared—something that looked like a 5x7 photo, but it too was faded and water stained ... wait a second! Hadn't I seen this before? A naked baby doll with half the hair missing from its head; a small deflated rubber ball, the red, blue and yellow barely visible now and a few little toy cars. I *had* seen this before! By the pool? Yes! The items my dad said had come from the bottom of the swimming pool. What were they doing here?

Sticking out of the pile was something else that made my eyes go wider still: a child's running shoe. Not remarkable in shape or colour, but I knew it well.

It was scuffed and dirty. The toys that nearly obscured it still stank of chlorine, and I could see where the dried chemical had left a white stain on the floorboards. Spider's webs glistened in the half-light, seeming to fill the shoe's opening, criss-crossing back and forth like a barrier.

These spiders work fast, I thought, shaking my head and crouching for a better look.

This was proof positive that my little friend was hiding out in this place. Why, I had no idea, but it was a relief to know that I wasn't going crazy. And now, he had some explaining to do.

"Alright," I said firmly. "It's no use hiding anymore, come on out, I know you're here." I stood straight, arms folded, my heart beating rapidly as I waited for my little friend to jump out and try to surprise me, albeit with one shoe.

It would be just like him to try and scare me, I thought.

But as the seconds ticked by, and still no one appeared, I began to have my doubts again.

The tears that slid down my face only made me feel more of a fool and I dashed them away angrily.

Why was Bobby carting this garbage into an old, rotting house, and what was going on with the shoe? Better yet, why was it covered with spider's webs, as though no one had worn it in months?

My heart was beating too fast.

"Okay calm down," I said aloud. "Bobby, if you're still hiding in here, it's a very bad joke. I'm not mad at you, but just come out, okay?"

If Bobby was real, then none of this made sense.

If. There, I said it.

Was mom right? Was I using the power of my own mind to scare myself?

A new sound made me jump.

I whirled around, seeing only more empty space.

"Don't be such a chicken," I said, trying not to tremble, concentrating on making my voice strong in the reverb of the empty hallway. "Turn off your haunted house filter."

Dad would say I invented these feelings. He used words like creative and inventive, which sounded nice, but it meant the same thing. He wanted me to believe that every strange thing I saw was my own imagination.

But it wasn't. It couldn't be … and dad wasn't there.

The unpleasantly cool air in the house was making goose bumps stand out on my arms. I rubbed at them, annoyed with myself for not bringing a sweater.

"Okay, I've been in here long enough. Where's that necklace, you brat!"

When in doubt, be forceful, I told myself.

Thinking I'd backed into something, I whirled around, but there was nothing but open space.

My imagination was on overload. I had to get out. Where was that necklace? It was nicely polished, it should have gleamed amidst against all the dust and grime, but I couldn't see it anywhere.

Swallowing a lump in my throat, I realized that my treasure was gone. I was never going to find it in this place, with all of its dark corners and cobwebs. It was like looking for a needle … in a stack of needles.

All I knew was that I had to get out of there.

The staircase groaned again as I darted past, my over loaded imagination making me see things I knew couldn't be there. In the next instant, the breath whooshed from my lungs as I dropped to my knees in front of the makeshift kitchen doorway.

I've got to get out of here, I thought.

Inexplicably, the small sheet of plywood refused to budge no matter how I pushed or tugged at the edges. Panic made my body start to shake at the thought of being trapped in there …

With who-knows-what.

"Oh come on," I groaned, pushing at the wood with all my strength. A quick glance behind me revealed that same shadow, moving past the upstairs railing.

"Go away, go away" I chanted in a hoarse whisper, tears streaming down my face. Pushing with renewed desperation, I threw my shoulder at the doorway, but still it wouldn't budge.

Glancing back quickly, my eyes widened again as the patch of darkness seemed to flow down the staircase. My eyes followed it, the breath stuttering from my throat as I watched it come for me.

The air had grown colder, and goose bumps stood out on my arms once again. The chill settled over me like a blanket and I tried desperately to focus through my tears. Pressing the heels of my hands to both eyes, I drew in a shuddering breath.

When I looked again, the shadow was gone.

I stood abruptly and wiped my sweaty palms on the legs of my jeans, trying to think clearly. Okay, all of this was weird and hard to accept, but maybe there was a logical explanation. The shadow of a small animal, maybe? Reflected sunlight from the warped window glass?

Maybe.

On hands and knees once more, I forced myself to slow down and calm my racing heart. With purposely gentle fingers, I pushed gently at the makeshift door.

As I did so, a cold wind seemed to come at me from all sides, as though the windows had all been thrown open at once.

"Work this time, damn you!" I shouted, surprising myself as it gave way and tumbled me through the opening. Not satisfied with merely being out, I continued the momentum and rolled off the wooden porch as fast as I could.

When my heartbeat finally returned to normal, I was huddled up protectively on my own back porch.

I only had a moment more to collect myself before Diana's irritated face appeared at my elbow.

"Where've you been?" she asked.

"Ah!" I screamed, frightened at her sudden appearance. "Don't do that!"

"Well?" she said. "I'm waiting for an answer."

Sheepishly, I realized I didn't have one to give. "Um, nowhere. I was exploring," I said.

"You're not supposed to go in there, you know."

My eyes went wide. She knew?

"And, you left me with your big mess, plus the regular chores. What could you have been doing in that stinking place for half the day? It's three in the afternoon! I've been worried sick."

"It's what time?"

"Don't change the subject. Yes, it's three. Don't bother denying it; I know you were over there…"

"Well you never came to check on me."

"How do you know?" she said. "You never notice anything."

Oh, man, I thought. She was so *wrong*.

"Just help me get the chores done and quit rolling your eyes. Mom's gonna be home soon and I have to cook dinner. Boy, I'm gonna breathe a sigh of relief when you're back at school. "

"Okay, okay."

That night, I watched my sister carefully, waiting for her to tattle on me.

Nervously, I forked up the casserole Diana had managed not to burn, and mom turned to us, a tired smile on her face.

"Let's have a family night tonight," she said. "We hardly ever use this great big pool table. So let's shoot a game of billiards. How does that sound?"

Dad sighed and reluctantly switched off the T.V., moving wordlessly to the pool table to rack up the colourful billiard balls.

I looked at Diana. "Family night could be fun," I said, emphasizing the first word.

"Yeah, alright," she agreed, giving me a look that spoke volumes.

"Oh, you two," mom muttered, obviously wondering at our behaviour, but too weary to care.

The family room still made me uneasy. I didn't want to see that tall dark apparition again, especially after my nerve-wracking afternoon next door. I still wasn't sure what had happened, but I was beginning to think that all these things were somehow connected. They had to be.

Moving quickly to the sliding glass door, my reflection disappeared as I slid the curtains closed, determined to shove those questions firmly from my mind, at least for the time being. Diana caught my eye and jumped up to close the other window drapes.

"Girls, it's barely dark outside, what are you doing?" mom asked.

"It's dark enough," I answered, hoping she wouldn't make me explain further.

"Oh for Heaven's sake!" she said, shaking her head. "Well, who's up first?"

I had to admit, when the kitchen and family room lights were blazing together, rock music played on the hi-fi, and the curtains were drawn, the rec room was a cheery place. Ghostly visitors and strange sensations seemed as far away as the moon.

~~~~

The next day dawned cold and misty. Not exactly summer weather.

One thought stood out above the rest: I've got to get it back. My necklace was still in that house, and dad and the neighbour had been making arrangements all week to have it bulldozed. I had to go now, or lose my chance altogether. It was going to take all of my courage to go back in there, but I wasn't about to be beaten by my own imagination!

"Just two minutes in and two minutes out," I said to myself. "Two minutes in and two minutes out...." It had become a chant.

My father, the 'gentleman farmer' had gone to the local farmer's auction to buy baby pigs. Remarkably, my mom the city-girl went with him, and I took that as a golden opportunity.

"We're trusting you," mom had said.

"Diana is out," dad told me, raising his index finger in front of my nose. "She's going to be home in one hour. Think you can stay out of trouble for one hour?"

I smiled at them so hard it hurt.

They smiled back, raising their eyebrows. They knew an act when they saw it, but lucky for me, they didn't ask for explanations.

"Be good," mom called, as the truck rolled down the driveway in a cloud of dust.

~~~~

"Two minutes in and two minutes out."

"Two minutes in and two minutes out."

The plywood panel swung easily on its loosened nail.

"Two minutes, two minutes ..."

There were my footprints, confused patterns in the churned-up dust.

"... two minutes, two minutes ..."

The light was good today. Lots of sunshine. Even the darkened corners were brighter.

I can do this.

"... two minutes, two minutes ..."

The air felt heavy, like just before a thunderstorm. Imaginary beings flitted at my peripheral vision and I stumbled trying to hurry.

"... two minutes ..."

I wanted to twist around, to make sure nothing was there, but I knew that was a very bad idea.

Then suddenly, the necklace was there, the chain glinting in a patch of sunshine that pooled on one of the broken floor tiles. My fingers closed around it with relief, and I thrust it deep into my pocket, determined not to lose it again.

The all-too familiar feeling of dread and fear drove up and down my vertebrae, and I dove for the paneled-opening that would lead me out of there. My head and torso fit cleanly through the small opening and the welcoming sunshine warmed my face instantly as I pulled my legs through after me, one at a time, owing to the fact that I now had hips. My left leg was still inside the house when I felt something close tightly around my ankle. I'd been grabbed!

Screaming and kicking at the small opening, I expected to see a face, or feel sudden pain in my ankle, as unseen claws or teeth sank into my flesh! Panting with fear, I kicked and flailed, thankful that the initial grab hadn't pulled me back farther, through the opening and into certain danger.

As the seconds ticked by I realized that kicking and flailing weren't working. My foot was no closer to the opening and freedom than it had been before. Tears were streaming down my face. Part of me wondered why nothing else had happened yet. What was it waiting for?

Suddenly and inexplicably, the thing that held me let go. The force of my fear rolled me backwards, into the thorn bushes that encroached all across the ancient porch, but even this painful side effect was no match for the blind panic that raced through my body. Kicking fiercely at the vines with all the residual anger I could muster, I hit the ground running.

Moments later I stumbled through my own doorway, and screeched to a halt in front of the kitchen clock. I had to get cleaned up fast. Diana would be home any moment. There would be time to panic and sort through my feelings later. For now, I only had a couple of minutes to … My thoughts trailed off as the implication of the numbers on the clock slowly sunk in.

Somehow, I'd been in that house almost an hour.

Lights Out

10

We were a horse family, and I couldn't escape that, so even on a long weekend, the barns and chores were part of daily life. It would be ridiculous to suggest that I be exempt for any reason, especially in light of the conversations I'd overheard. But each time I went out there, someone or something watched me, and after my close call in the old house, I had a pretty good idea of what it was capable of.

I spent extra time looking behind me and illuminating dimly lit corners with a hand-held flashlight, so my chores tended to take twice as long. With Diana gone so much of the time now, it had become my job to feed and water the animals in the evening.

Dad was obviously getting tired of accompanying me. "Humph," he grunted. "Avoidance tactics, that's what this is. I know you don't relish the thought of cleaning stalls and feeding the horses, Ginny, but it has to be done and your mom and I are busy." He stopped talking abruptly and folded his arms in a way that made him look like a stern lawyer or a doctor delivering bad news. "You enjoy riding your horse, don't you?"

There really wasn't a response to that, and he knew it.

It was a clear night, the moon and stars shining brightly as I made my way to the barn. My mind was occupied with thoughts of my extreme bravery in retrieving the necklace without my parents or Diana being any the wiser. That had been close.

I still wasn't sure what had grabbed my ankle, and to be honest, I didn't want to think about it too much.

I was surprised when my parents had arrived home that day with the news that our neighbour was finally tearing it down. Now, it stood as a sad pile of bricks, mortar and splintered wood. The huge pile of rubble stood as the only reminder of my terrifying experience. I frowned at it, grateful that whatever had lurked there was finally gone, trapped under all that debris. I was sure it couldn't find me now.

Swinging my arms by my sides purposely, I entered the barn. The frown on my face was one of fierce determination.

"Va-doo-da-doo-dwee-e-ee, va-doo-doo-doobee-dooba-dwee-ee," I sang, practicing a jazz song I'd learned from the radio, almost dancing as I walked, stomping my feet hard onto the concrete floor. "Doo-ba-da-dwee-dap-do-ba-doo-wah ... it's gone, it's gone, do-do-do-do-wee, it's gone, it's gone, do-da-dwee-do-do," I sang.

I knew these chores so well by now that I proceeded on autopilot, intent on returning to my favorite T.V. show, the Dukes of Hazzard. My head was filled with images of car chases, cute boys and slapstick humour, as I bent to fill up one of the horse's water buckets from the inside tap in the centre of the barn.

All thoughts of the hero's bright red car were chased from my mind however, as that same familiar frisson ran up my backbone, turning my blood to ice.

No.

All reasonable thought went right out of my head in that instant and fear gripped me so completely that I found it hard to breathe.

I tried to resist the urge to turn around to look—I knew there would be no one there—but instinct is a hard thing to control. As I began to turn, all the overhead lights in the barn went out. I stood, rooted to the spot in shock and fear as the unmistakable sound of the heavy sliding door echoed through the empty barn. It slid shut, cutting off even the faint glow of moonlight. I hoped for a sign that it was merely my sister pulling a joke on me again, but this time there was only silence.

Acutely aware of my own heartbeat, my legs turned to rubber and I stumbled into the bucket I'd been filling, dousing my leg in icy water.

There was nothing else to do but get to the door. Maybe the power was out. That happened in the country, didn't it? Sure, it did.

So why was I so convinced that wasn't the answer?

Shying away from the obvious, I kept moving, knocking over heavy rubber buckets and lead ropes. I lost my balance and fell down painfully on my hands and knees, scraping the exposed skin so it stung with every movement.

"Damn! Great idea to wear shorts idiot," I mumbled. "Just get to the light and everything will be okay," I thought.

My groping hands slid over the rough wood, picking up slivers, but I hardly felt them now. The bare wall went on and on, as the outline of stall doors slid past my searching fingers.

Heart hammering with fear, I couldn't help thinking of my experiences in the old house and my fall from the hayloft months earlier.

I was exposed and alone; I knew the unexpected could quite easily happen again. My eyes watered but I forced down the panic and tried to reason myself into a sense of calm.

Everything is fine, I thought. This is a power failure, nothing more. Don't panic. Just breathe.

I would, no doubt, find the switch still in its 'on' position, and then I'd carry on to the door and get some light.

This brought me to the thought that completely burst my bubble.

So if this is only a power failure, who closed the door?

Shying away from that thought, I kept moving and tried not to think about the answer to that question.

At last, my trembling fingers felt the cool plastic of the light switch, which meant the door was close, but my searching fingers did nothing to calm my nerves.

It was down. Set in the 'off' position.

How could that be?

Swallowing the sudden lump in my throat, I realized that it could only mean one thing.: I was alone in the darkness with the Nightmare man!

Pulling down the old house hadn't done anything at all to stop this thing. If anything, it seemed angrier.

I pushed at the switch desperately, hearing the tell-tale "click" as it snapped into place, but instead of comforting fluorescent light, the overhead tubes remained dark. My eyes darted back and forth, straining to make out anything in the deep shades of grey around me.

Why was this happening? I needed to get out now!

I groped forward with one hand on the plywood wall and the other out in front of me. With the door ahead of me closed, no air moved.

In the darkness, all I could hear was my own heartbeat and exaggerated breathing.

How far was the door? It should have been right there … did I get turned around in the darkness? There were no sounds to go by, no landmarks to prove I was still traveling the right way.

Irrational thoughts crowded my mind, and I fought hard to keep them under control, talking to myself in an effort to stay calm.

"Come on, you can do this. Don't think about it. It's just dark, that all. No big deal. It'll just take another minute, and then my eyes will adjust. Okay, I think that's the door, just a little farther now…." My shaky voice sounded odd in the darkness.

To my left an unmistakable sound clanged with the ring of metal on metal. A moment later, I began to breathe again. This was a sound I knew. A heavy bridle had slid off its hook and clanked to the floor. But it shouldn't have. Those bridles were anchored in place with heavy straps.

Coincidence?

As that thought formed in my mind, I took a step back and bumped into another water bucket, soaking my other foot. Pressing my shivering body into the wall, I squatted and tried hard not to throw up. I wasn't being ridiculous; something was going on here.

"Is someone there?" I whispered, praying that I wouldn't hear an answer.

My senses were on fire and I hugged myself hard while gritting my teeth to keep it together. One awkward step at a time, flinching at every sound, I inched forward again. I had to keep moving.

Almost like a wall, the air I came up against was thick and cold, like stepping into a sudden winter. An overwhelming feeling of dread repelled me and instinctively I backed up again. I was shivering. My cotton t-shirt was no protection. I was so cold now that when a tiny breath of warm air spread across my face, I noticed it immediately. Far from being pleasant however, my tortured mind leapt to unfortunate conclusions. It was warm, *like human breath*.

Whimpering in fear and desperation, I pulled away, wind-milling my arms as an electrical sensation raced across my scalp.

"Bobby?" I whispered into the night. A second later, a harsh, grating sound seemed to come from everywhere at once.

It sounded like laughing.

"GET AWAY FROM ME!" I screamed into the darkness, scrambling forward, hands out in front, sweeping through the open air in wide, frantic arcs. Alternately lurching and running, I hoped I was going in the right direction, toward the door and the safety of the moonlight.

"Safe in the light, safe in the light," I chanted to myself, hoping the mantra would help me somehow.

Don't be locked, please don't be locked," I whispered as my groping fingers at last discovered the handle I could not see. Clumsily I fumbled with the mechanism, until at last, my cold, stiff fingers triggered the catch and the unlocked door slid open with a loud, metallic roar.

Stumbling out into the night, I paused only to slam the door back into place with a bang. Staring at the closed door, the wood glowing silver in the moonlight, I backed away, the muscles in my legs pulsing.

After the absolute darkness and the pervading chill of the barn, the moonlight seemed overly bright, the night air mild and comforting to my frazzled senses.

I didn't waste time hanging around. With my muscles twitching, I ran jerkily back to the house as quickly as I could go. Logic tried to reassert itself as I slowed to a walk just outside the back door. Was there a reasonable answer for that strange, guttural laugh? Could it have been another sound, and maybe my paranoid senses perceived it as human? Yeah right. Like what? My clumsy excuses were as ludicrous as the truth. I only knew of one thing that would make that sound: a human being.

My thoughts returned to the moment when I had lain, panicking, on the porch of that old, rotting house, kicking at something that I couldn't see. Ridiculously, as I stood at the back of my house, inane laughter bubbled up inside me and I found myself giggling nervously, trying to come up with a way to convince my doubting parents things were definitely not alright on this farm. This place was haunted. It was time they faced facts.

"There," I said triumphantly. "Haunted."

I should have felt better for saying it out loud, but I didn't.

My chores forgotten, all I could think of was getting back into the house with my family. I guessed they would already be lighting candles and waiting out the power failure, but I didn't care. I just needed to be with people.

"What the heck?" I asked, standing in the doorway, my mouth hanging open. "The power's on in here?"

"What honey?" mom said, working on something at the counter, the kitchen light blazing around her.

"The power, it's on in here?"

Mom looked at me questioningly.

"The barn" I answered, my confusion cutting away the words. "Power's off."

Dad rounded the corner and looked at me. "What's this about the power being off in the barn? What did you touch?"

"Nothing," My frightened eyes found his. "The lights just went out. The switch…" Now what could I say about the switch? I searched frantically for the words that would explain my terrifying experience but nothing came.

"Well we better get out there then," dad answered, his tone resigned.

"What? We?" I squeaked. My pulse raced anew, and I could feel my palms begin to sweat. I really didn't want to go, but how could I tell him that?

"Just a second," mom said. "She's soaked! And look at those skinned knees! Ginny, what were you doing out there?" Shaking her head, she propelled me back through the house to the bathroom, where I was subjected to iodine and band-aids, dressed up with new socks and shoes, and hurriedly pushed back in the direction of my patiently waiting father, who tapped his cowboy booted toe as he stood there, waiting for me.

It felt as though lead weights were tied to each ankle as he placed a powerful flashlight in my hand and held the door.

I followed him back outside, down the gravel path and into the darkness.

I had no choice. But at least I had light. And my father.

"Okay we're here, let's test this thing out." He hauled the door open and strode forward into the darkened interior while I hung far back willing myself not to run away. With one negligent flip of his hand, the offending switch clicked into place and all five 60 W bulbs came to life, bathing the interior of the barn, and my astonished face, in light.

"Hmmm…" It was a credit to my father's patience and quiet demeanor that he didn't say anything. He didn't really need to; the look he directed at me said it all. As he turned around to face me, I felt my cheeks grow hot. Profound disappointment was etched across his features.

There was no way he would ever believe me now.

"I don't know," he said slowly, picking up and re-filling the upended water bucket. "Sometimes that switch can be hard to move. Maybe you just didn't push it hard enough."

I stared at the bucket in his hands and felt hot tears spill down my cheeks.

"It turned off by itself, dad. I can't explain ..." I whispered.

Dad placed the handle of the full water bucket into my palm. "Lights don't usually go off by themselves Ginny; let's just finish feeding the animals so they can come in for the night, okay?"

Daddy, please believe me! I wanted to scream, but I breathed deeply instead, trying to stay calm. "Stay with me?" I asked.

"Sure, I'll stay right here by the light switch in case it happens again."

Dad grinned, as though it were all a big joke, but he stayed right where he said he would. His arms folded, he leaned back against the wall and watched me as I worked. Water buckets and feed troughs filled, dad left the switch long enough to open the far doors and let the horses in.

By the time we walked back to the house, I knew there were no 'magic' words I could come up with. If I couldn't even discuss the possibility with my mother, there was no point in wasting my time with dad.

The Photograph

11

"Stop fidgeting and hold still," mom said, trying to talk while holding pins between her teeth.

"Mom, is this really necessary?" I whined. For the past half-hour, I'd been standing on a bench, wearing a new skirt she'd bought me for the first day of school. As usual, everything we bought in the store was way too long on little me. Mom pinned it in fourteen different ways while I tried to think of ways to escape. I had to admit that the fabric had a nice way of 'swooshing' when it moved, but then, I wasn't allowed to move just now.

"For Heaven's sake Ginny, quit jitter-bugging and let me finish."

"Okay, I'm sorry," I said, wondering if I really was. "Do you think the sisters are finished their eggs yet?"

"Well, I'm not sure," mom replied. "They do a lot of baking, so perhaps they are. Did you want to go and see them?"

"Yes!" My voice sounded louder than I'd intended and I felt my face grow hot. "I mean, uh, yeah I think that would be a good idea. We don't want them to run out."

"No, we certainly don't want that," my mother agreed, closing one eye and tilting her head as she stood back to look at me in my new dress. "I think that about does it," she said. "Off you go, and take it off carefully. I don't want any of those pins falling out."

"Okay," I agreed, happy to be finished with the endless sewing project. "So can I go after that?"

"Sure," mom replied. "I'll go with you. I haven't seen those dears in quite some time."

My heart sank. How could I possibly talk with the sisters about stuff I really wanted to know with mom there?

"Oh, you want to come too?" I asked.

"Absolutely."

I knew that tone.

~~~~

A short time later, mom and I walked up the driveway to the sister's cottage.

Once we'd crossed the road, I went to take a shortcut through to the side yard, but mom caught my arm.

"The front door is this way," she said. "Manners matter."

"Yes mom," I'd replied, wondering what the big deal was about front doors. I had yet to see the sister's front door but I didn't think I was missing anything.

I couldn't have been more wrong.

"Elizabeth, Ginny, how nice of you to come," Elise greeted us as she opened the door to our knock. "Come right in. Penny," she called over her shoulder, "we have guests. Put the kettle on dear."

Oh great, I thought. More tea.

Standing in the foyer of the small house, I smiled at Elise and she smiled back.

"What brings you over today?" Elise was saying to my mom.

"Well, we just thought it had been awhile since we saw you and Ginny thought you might need some more eggs."

"And so we do, perceptive young lady. So we do!" Elise moved ahead of us into the tiny kitchen and indicated we should follow her, but a framed photograph on the wall caught my attention like a super-magnet and I stopped.

"Bobby," I whispered.

There, hanging on the wall in front of me was a framed portrait of my friend. The photographer had caught his likeness in the midst of one of those characteristic giggles. A slow smile spread across my face as I stared at the photo. Here was even more proof! Mom couldn't deny this!

"Mom, look," I said, pointing. "Look at this. You have to see this!"

In my excitement, I pulled her back from the kitchen while the two older women just stared, puzzled looks on their aged faces.

"What's got you so excited, Ginny?" mom responded, allowing herself to be led. "What am I looking at?"

"This," I waved my hand at the photo. "It's Bobby. My friend. See? I told you! Now you can't say you don't see him. He's right there. That's him." I planted my hands on my hips firmly and nodded for emphasis.

The adults had all grown quiet.

The silence stretched on and on, and I started to worry. Had I said something wrong?

Suddenly, Elise gave a stifled sob and hurried from the room.

Penny stood up from the table; the puzzled look was replaced by one of shock. Tears glistened on her cheeks. Her mouth hung open in the shape of an "o".

"Mom?" I said wonderingly. Something was wrong and I knew it, but I honestly didn't realize what it could have been, so deep was my naiveté. "What's wrong? What did I say?"

"Nothing, it'll be alright, but we have to go. Now." She took my hand firmly and turned me around. In seconds, we were over the threshold. "So sorry my dear, I don't know what to say." Her voice was full of emotion as she spoke. Penny merely nodded silently at my mother, as she edged me back towards the door. Penny had a strange expression on her face as she closed that door behind us.

"Mom, I don't understand, what did I say?" I repeated, as she and I fast-walked down the driveway.

Still, my mother didn't answer. She just propelled me home as fast as her feet would carry her.

It wasn't until we were back inside our house that she whirled to face me, her face a carefully controlled mask.

"Why did you do that?" she said. I'd never seen mom look so intense.

"I don't know. I just wanted to show you."

"Sweetheart," mom began, running a frustrated hand through her curly hair. "When people lose someone, it hurts for a very long time. It's rude to ignore that."

"Mom, I—"

"I've raised you better," she interrupted. "What I don't understand is *why* you would do that?"

"Mommy!" Exasperated, I enunciated every word carefully. "I-don't-know-what-I-did."

Mom stared at me, her mouth hanging open. "How could you not know? The photograph?" she prompted. "The picture on the wall. Surely you knew that was Elise's grandson."

"Her grandson? Yes, of course, his name's Bobby." I struggled to make the pieces fit. "Mom, don't you see? I found his wishing flowers last time. He must go over there a lot." For the third time that day, I failed to notice the obvious.

"What? Flowers? What has that got to do with anything?" Mom frowned at me like I was never going to get the point. "Bobby is dead, Ginny. He died months ago. We've been over this."

I felt my face grow hot and the smile slid from my face. "No, you're wrong! That's impossible! I just saw him. And what do you mean we've been over this? Bobby is fine."

My mother simply turned abruptly and walked away, her arms folded tight against her body.

"Mom?" I called to her, my voice sounding small and afraid. "My Bobby is fine. He's not dead. I just saw him ... this is a big misunderstanding."

"I know you don't understand honey," she said. "I do, but it's true none-the-less." When she turned around to face me again, there were tears in her own eyes and I knew at once that everything would be different from then on.

My mind shrieked against it, but I knew my mother would never lie to me.

"But how can that be?" I asked.

"I don't really want to talk about it now," she said. "Later. I need some time to think. Can you go to your room please?"

Still confused but worried at Mom's response, I shut my mouth and went to my room.

Dear Journal: (I wrote in my battered orange duo-tang)

I don't know what to think. Mom isn't making sense. She told me Bobby is dead! She said he was hit by a gravel truck of all things??!

What's going on? Why didn't I know this? My poor little friend. He wouldn't have known what happened, would he?

I can't even write the words, journal, I'm sorry. I'm crying as I write this.

My tears fell, onto the loose leaf paper and I wiped them away, creating a blurred out spot on the page. Skipping a couple of lines, I continued to write, hoping that somehow, getting the thoughts down on paper would make it easier.

There's something really weird about what mom said, I continued. *When did this happen? She said it was months ago, before we moved in, but she must have gotten that wrong. How could that be? Grown-ups don't always tell the truth about some stuff. Mom is totally wrong. I just saw him a couple of days ago! Maybe it was a different kid. I want to believe it was someone else. Maybe the boy she's talking about isn't the same one. Maybe he only looks like Bobby ... yeah, that has to be it. That's why Penny and Elise looked like that. I know there's more to this story, but I can't get any answers. Diary, I'm so confused. I don't know how much more of this I can take or what to believe.*

Looking for Clues

12

"Mom," I asked the next day, on the drive to my new school. "When did that boy die?"

"What boy?" She turned, darting a startled look at me before turning her eyes back to the road.

"The one you told me about," I said. "The one who used to live in our house."

"Oh! That boy. Uh, as near as I can figure out, it was March. Why?"

"March?" The word squeaked out. "What do you mean as near as you can figure?" I held onto the slim chance that she could still be wrong.

"Well, the realtor said it had been three months when we first came to look at the house. Do you remember that couple?"

"Yeah," I said, trying to remember. "The crying lady?"

"Uh-huh," she answered. "That was the boy's parents. Why do you want to know this?" She was watching me carefully but all I could do was sit there.

My mind was whirling, trying to put the pieces together. Half-sentences, veiled hints and all those puzzling reactions piled up on each other until I started to draw conclusions I wasn't ready for.

"Could have been a different boy from the one in the photo, you know."

Mom looked at me sharply. "No," she said. "It was the same boy. We purchased our house from his parents."

"You mean ... he lived in our house?"

115

"Ye-es," she said slowly, watching me.

It couldn't be.

"Are you okay?" She asked.

I nodded again. I needed time to think.

I stared at the car's dashboard, and tried to understand.

It just didn't make sense. Ghosts were invisible and Bobby was real like me. That was proof right there, wasn't it?

People see what they want to see, my sub-conscious suggested.

The memory of Bobby's pitiful statement came back in a rush.

He hadn't said, "nobody notices me." He'd said, very specifically, "grown-ups don't see me."

That was something else entirely.

I was breathing hard. Heat and emptiness combined in the pit of my stomach to make me feel sick. Something Elise said to me before was circulating in my head, making my pulse race.

Children see things with such clarity.

"Do you remember his name?" My question, coming out of the extended silence obviously startled my mother.

"His name? No, I-I don't believe I was ever told." I watched my mother grip the steering wheel harder, her knuckles turning white with the effort. "All I know is he'd just turned six, poor little thing. It's very sad."

Six? I was either going to scream, or I was going to be sick. Maybe both.

"Ohmigod, ohmigod ...," I chanted.

"Ginny?" The country landscape flashed past the windows. "It's just first day jitters, don't get yourself so worked up."

"Huh?" I asked.

"School. First day jitters. You'll be okay. Remember to breathe."

I don't remember getting out of the car, but all of a sudden, I was aware of gravel underfoot, and, like a robot, I turned in the direction of my new elementary school and walked forward.

Somehow, the first day of school came and went. I've searched my memory repeatedly, but the introduction to my new school in Grade five is still completely missing. About all I do remember is my teacher's smile and a vague sense of size.

My new school was massive compared to the last one.

Kids in the hall stared at me, but then they always did that when a new kid came along. Why should this time be any different?

Because I'm different.

The thought wasn't a helpful one, but it followed me. Probably another reason that the particulars of that first day are lost in a blur of colour, sound and unfamiliar faces. The only thing that mattered to me was keeping safe the terrible secret that existed in my house.

No one must ever guess.

~~~~

"Mom, can I go to work with you today?" I asked.

"Today?" She said, frowning as she tried to guess my motive. "Let me see ... it's Saturday. I'm not going to the mall."

"I know."

"Did you do all your chores? You're trying to get out of those, are you?"

"No Mom, I'm all done. I even did the lunch dishes, see?"

My mother turned and her eyebrows climbed high on her forehead.

"So you did ... so why the sudden interest in the Library?"

"I need to get some books for a project at school."

Mom looked puzzled. "Already? They're getting you off to a roaring start aren't they?"

"Well, it is Grade 5."

Mom looked across the table at my dad, who had tweaked down the top edge of his newspaper to peer at me. They were always so suspicious.

"Well," she answered. "I suppose your dad will be busy working on the house. Diana, of course, is out again."

"I promise I won't bug you," I said. "You won't even know I'm there."

"Oh for Heaven's sake, Ginny," mom said, smiling. "You don't have to make promises like that. Okay, sure you can come, but you'd better get a move-on, I'm leaving in half an hour. And bring yourself a snack; I'm doing a four-hour shift this afternoon."

The Library in our town had just finished a major renovation and the new improved layout was L-shaped, with lots of nooks and crannies where people could curl up and read, plus a second floor just for the vast collection of children's books. It still had the hushed ambiance it always had, but the new ceramic tiles in the front entryway and the serviceable but stylish wall-to-wall carpeting lent it a sophisticated look that was said to be very "modern." Although it was still only 1979, the forward-thinking architect had designed the building to boast an '80's décor, with clean lines and mono-tone colour schemes.

Later, with the "introduction rounds" all done amongst my mother's co-workers, I saw her settle down onto a high, leather upholstered stool behind the library's Returns desk, which was more like a long, high counter. She began to choose books from stacks piled high on the counter, rhythmically stamping each one and setting it aside on a pushcart to her right. Within minutes, she was absorbed and I took the opportunity to begin my search in earnest.

Very quickly, I too was absorbed in the material I found in front of me. The 'alternative philosophy' section had some very informative books. Coincidentally, I found it by accident, as I wandered into the non-fiction section. The tall, metal shelves my mother referred to as stacks loomed over me. Those stacks were jammed with serious-looking leather-bound books on the world of the paranormal. I'd already taken time with my pocket thesaurus, writing down all the synonyms for "ghost" and now I walked the aisles looking for the words on my list. I felt like a spy, hiding out from prying eyes while I examined the shelves for books I knew mom and dad wouldn't approve of.

As soon as I started reading, I was fascinated. Pulling one book after another and leafing through them at a rapid rate, I soaked it all in. A surprising amount of people, it seemed, lived in houses that were considered by some to be haunted. It was interesting to me as well, that the Library had a special section for these books. Not fiction, not non-fiction, this was a small area in the "research" section, that shared space with the old newspapers and a machine called a microfiche, where people could look up documents stored on strips of film, like photograph negatives.

The other interesting thing I learned was that there were two camps of people: those that wrote these books and those who laughed at the writers. But I soon learned that there were just as many people to laugh and call them names as there were to encourage, agree and launch scientific investigations. The public, it seemed, wasn't about to make up its mind on this issue.

All too soon, an announcement came over a muted speaker system. A bored-sounding voice piped through the little round speakers in the walls, one located directly above me.

"The Library will be closing in fifteen minutes."

Fifteen minutes? What? Four hours already?

The time raced by as I continued reading. Just one more sentence, one more sentence …

"The Library is closed; please bring all materials to the front counter for check-out."

Oh perfect.

Mom's shift was over, and as I peered through the stack at the counter where she'd worked all afternoon, all I saw was an empty chair! My heart raced as I literally ran between the stacks, slipping the books back onto the shelves, not caring if they were in the correct spaces, only hoping I had enough time to put them all away before she found me and discovered my secret.

I was just shoving a particularly large book into place on the shelf in front of me when the lights overhead went off, and then on, then off again.

My skin went cold.

Not here too!

I left the section at a run, nearly bumping into her as I rounded the last corner.

"Whoah there!" She said, catching me by my arms.

"What's going on?" I asked her, breathlessly. "Did you see that? The lights!"

"Calm down," she said, her tone low and her eyes furtive. She reached out to smooth down my wild-looking hair. "People will think there's something wrong with you. We always flick the lights on and off when we're closing the library. It's our way of warning people that the doors will be locked soon, that's all. No one wants to get locked in a Library overnight."

I sagged against her, my energy suddenly gone.

"Let's go home," she said. "You look worn right out. That must've been some research … did you get what you wanted?" I nodded and smiled at her, hoping she wouldn't notice my distinctly empty hands.

"Great." She turned and waved to her co-workers, hitching her cloth shoulder bag higher on her arm. "Goodnight everyone, we're off!"

"Goodbye Elizabeth! Goodbye Ginny!" They called, as they looked up from other areas of the library, tidying up piles of papers and locking office doors behind them.

Arm in arm, mom and I crossed the ceramic tiles and went out the front doors to the car.

"You're going to get some extra sleep tonight," she told me. "You're a nervous wreck."

I managed a small smile and slumped down in the seat, playing the part she expected, but internally my mind was whirling.

At dinner that night, I was forced to lie about my afternoon of research. I wondered which one of them was going to see through my story. I am a notoriously terrible liar.

"So, mom tells me you went to find some books today. What did you find?"dad asked.

My body stiffened. Here it was: The moment of truth.

"Purramyffs," I answered, my words garbled by the mouthful of mashed potatoes.

Truth probably wasn't the best idea, after all.

"Ginny!" said my mother. "Don't talk with your mouth full."

"Mmff. Forry." I said. Mom sighed and rolled her eyes. Turning to my father, she translated. "Pyramids. She's researching ancient Egypt for school."

And just like the perfectly normal household that we weren't, everyone returned their attention to the meal before them.

I finished my dinner, relieved that no one had any more questions. Absently, I listened to my sister as she planned an activity for the weekend with her friends, to my dad as he puzzled over the lights that *sometimes* worked and how it had to have a logical explanation and to my mom as she cautioned us all to remember that the butter didn't belong in the fridge.

"When I want to use it, it's hard as a rock," she complained. "Someone keeps putting it in there."

I shook my head. It was all so remote. None of it really interested me. It was like a record that kept skipping, repeating itself over and over, waiting for someone to lift the needle.

I was counting the seconds until my family would be asleep.

Full of the information I'd gleaned from the alternative research section that day, I fidgeted through the rest of supper and was positively squirming when mom announced she'd baked a fresh apple pie.

"Ginny, you love my pies!" she'd said, obviously disappointed in the expression I couldn't keep from my face. "What's wrong? You're acting so ... nervous. Just calm down."

The words paranormal, telepathic, mystic, entity, poltergeist, manifestation and medium swam through my brain. Good thing she didn't expect a real answer to her comment. I did my best to breathe deeply and plant my butt firmly on the kitchen chair, while mom served pie. My feet just touched the floor in front of me—that's the problem with being short—and, predictably, my family turned to me again, their faces irritated.

"Must you do that?"

Dad set down his fork with a clatter.

"What?"

"That incessant banging," he said. "Keep your feet still. Dinner's almost over. You can sit still long enough to eat this gorgeous pie your mother made. And then you and Diana can take care of the horses."

"Yes dad."

"Make sure you give them fresh water when you bring them in for the night."

"Oh, uh…"

"Yes?" He asked suggestively, wiping his mouth with a paper napkin. "You have something to say?"

"Well, I, um…"

"We'll go together, dad." Diana interrupted unexpectedly. "I gotta check on Koko's hoof anyway. She's been favoring it lately, and I wasn't around to check it today."

The look I directed at my sister probably contained everything that was in my heart at that moment: relief, surprise and a little bit of suspicion.

With my sister at my side, the chores went quickly. The atmosphere was strangely, but happily benign. The scent of pine shavings was strong in my nose as I hung up Chuck's lead rope and swung the door closed on the tack stall.

"Well, that's it for the night," she said. "Happy I came?"

"Yeah," I said, breathing out the word with relief. "Thanks."

"You're really scared in here, aren't you?" I nodded, relieved she was being so nice. "It's just a building though. Once you realize that nothing can hurt you in here, you'll feel better. Honest."

She was expecting an answer, I knew, but I didn't have one.

~~~~

Dad was snoring.

Mom's breathing was deep and even.

My sister's door was firmly closed and although I strained my ears, I could hear nothing past the solid wooden barrier.

The coast was finally clear. I wiped at my eyes, which had become heavier and heavier as I waited in the dark, feigning sleep.

With my heart pounding, I slipped out of bed and reached in between my mattress and box spring, pulling forth an old book, its binding was worn and frayed.

I'd taken it from the Library, but if mom knew I hadn't properly checked it out, but smuggled it home under my jacket, she'd skin me. And then she'd notice the title and I'd get it again.

With my heart hammering anew at this latest mental image, I crept to my door and listened again for the comforting sounds of my sleeping family.

The cover on the book was bluish grey, and it looked like it was made of some sort of rough-textured fabric. The title was stamped deeply in large black letters. "The Sleeping Prophet: The Life of Edgar Cayce"

I had taken this book in haste, sure that it contained something to help me. In truth, it was a sentence that I'd read before, written by a man named Shermer that was responsible for my sudden interest in Edgar Cayce. His words, while written as an attempt to discredit Cayce's work, had instead drawn my eager attention.

Shermer had written that, "Cayce was fantasy-prone from his youth, often talking with angels and receiving visions of his dead grandfather."

Bingo!

Could it be angels that whispered to me in my sleep? Didn't Pastor Smith say that they were with me always? Protecting, watching over me? That sounded a lot better than ghosts.

My heart had been beating double-time when I'd been at the library searching for answers. Now, with my family safely asleep, I could begin my research in earnest.

Am I Different?

13

I woke up with a start. I hadn't remembered falling asleep. Had I been in a trance?

No. That was stupid.

I was just thinking that way because of Cayce. He claimed to have psychic episodes, all while practically asleep. It was fascinating, but I was quickly losing hope that there was anything similar between his situation and mine.

Stashing the book again under the mattress, I blinked rapidly. Morning sunshine flooded the hallway when I opened my door and ventured forth. No one was up yet.

Pausing to stretch at the threshold to the kitchen, I contemplated going back to bed, but decided instead to grab a banana and play with my Barbies until my family got up for the day.

~~~~

I hadn't been back to the sister's cottage since that day when I'd seen the photo. I knew they were probably hurt and my silence didn't make it any better, but it was all so confusing. If only I could put this aside, stop thinking about him. But I couldn't. I needed to talk to someone. Someone who understood, but I didn't know who that was.

Deliberate footsteps took me where fear could not. I found myself standing poised at the edge of the crumbling asphalt, while memories of past encounters cycled through my head. Before I'd even reached their front door, the image of his face flooded my mind. I remembered the first time I'd seen him. A little kid, alone by the side of the road, watching the passing gravel trucks. I shuddered.

That was where he died.

He'd come to me for friendship, that much was obvious. A lost little boy missing his family, unsure of what had happened to him …

"He must be so scared," I whispered to myself. But was he *able* to be my friend? Was he even aware of what it did to me, being friends with a … ghost?

No. I couldn't think of him that way. He was my friend. It always came back to that. He deserved my trust and my loyalty and my help. I desperately wanted to confide in someone, but I wasn't eager for another 'chat' about the 'power of the mind' and how tricky the human brain could be. That was always mom's slant. And dad's answer wasn't much better. "… anything can be explained if you take the time to really look at it," he would say.

That's how I found myself standing on the sister's doorstep, eager for answers.

I knocked at the door and waited. It seemed like forever that I stood there on the porch, waiting.

Why don't they answer? I wondered. I couldn't even hear Fred barking. Maybe they weren't home?

Better luck next time, I thought. Just then, a slip of paper stuck in the doorframe caught my eye. Unfolding it, I received a shock. It was addressed to me!

But I'd only just decided to go over there, hadn't I? How could they have known?

"Ginny," it read. "Sorry we missed you."

What?

My hands rested on my hips in a pose I'd copied from Diana.

As I stood there, the wind rising to make my long hair stand on end, I backed down the steps awkwardly and stood kicking at the loose rock in the driveway for several long minutes.

I stuffed the note deep into my pocket with a puzzled frown and headed back to my house. What did it all mean? I would have to wait to find out, apparently.

~~~~

The next day was Sunday and our family prepared for Church. Diana was excited; she was going to talk to our pastor about her wedding plans.

I tried to concentrate on the homily, as Pastor stood behind the lectern and talked about Jesus. Usually, I found stories from the Bible very interesting, as they spoke of Jesus' life on earth, but that day, all I could think of was the strange inconsistencies I'd been finding in my own life. Were they proof of the paranormal or that I was slowly losing my grip on reality?

That evening, as I undressed for bed, the rumpled note fell out of my pants pocket, reminding me of my thwarted visit. Had they been expecting me today? I hoped not. I was having enough trouble keeping my thoughts together without adding pounds of guilt on top of it all.

~~~~

September 1979 was a hot one. Too hot! It was nice swimming weather though, and for that reason I was secretly delighted. My Birthday pool party grew nearer with each passing day, and I knew the heat would make for a wonderful party, but it was terrible for everything else. Mom loved swimming as much as anyone, but she'd been irritable and moody ever since our brief visit to the sister's cottage where I'd discovered Bobby's picture.

Was it the heat or was it still the scene surrounding that picture? Maybe both.

Mom, to her credit, had tried to talk with me about it.

"It was very hard on the family, you see," she'd told me. "The death of a child is devastating. Eventually they realized they just had to move away and start fresh."

"And that's when we bought the house," I answered, trying to connect the dots. "Yes. So you can see why it would be rude to say you've seen this boy when you couldn't possibly have..."

"I just don't understand how you can say that," I'd said hotly.

"It's common sense," she'd replied. "Things like that simply don't happen."

"Well, they do to me!"

"Well I don't believe in ghosts, and that's final!" Mom's voice had grown louder and more forceful. I backed up a pace. Had she really just said that? Had she really just used the "g" word?

I narrowed my eyes at her and stormed off down the hall. What a joke! She didn't believe in ghosts, huh? Well, if living there wasn't doing it, I wondered just what it would take to convince her?

"We'll just see about that," I'd muttered when I was a safe distance away.

And now, it was the day before my birthday and Mom's mood was steadily going downhill. She snapped at everything, her shortened temper being blamed on that crazy heat wave.

I hoped that inviting the whole class to my party was going to work out okay. They would be kids from my new school and I was nervous about it already. Mom's temper wasn't helping. I could only hope that her 'hostess training' would come to the fore and hide her bad mood.

~~~~

"Virginia, what are you playing at?" mom called to me from the kitchen.

"What?"

"This fridge was left wide open again!"

"Well I didn't do it. I wasn't even in there!"

"Oh really? Somebody keeps leaving it open and I'm sick and tired of it!"

"Liz, calm down," said my father. "I'll take a look at the hinges. That fridge came with the house; it's at least six years old. Maybe it's not closing properly."

"Everything in this whole damn place is falling apart!" she exclaimed. "I'm so tired of it, you have no idea!" With that, she threw her dishcloth onto the counter as hard as she could and stomped out of the room.

It was happening all the time now. Lights randomly went on or off as we walked past, things were misplaced and tempers grew shorter by the day.

"It's the heat," dad complained. "We're all grouchy."

It was hot, but there was more to it than that. Even at nine years old, I knew it.

I also knew the other members of my family witnessed mysteriously open doors when they should have been closed, strange drafts and telltale 'touches' when no one else was near. But unlike me, they steadfastly refused to talk about it. I was a persistent kid back then, but even I got the hint eventually. Mom's firm statement to me about "not believing in ghosts" made it clear that she wasn't interested in a discussion on the paranormal.

I was still the new kid at school, but I hoped that the pool party would win over a few of my classmates. I had a handful of kids whom I could more-or-less call friends, but I didn't dare tell them anything important, like why I stayed after school to do my homework so it wouldn't mysteriously disappear, and why, even at the brightest and hottest part of the year, I still slept with the lights on and an extra electric heater by my bed, just in case. There wasn't anything I could do about it, I reasoned, so why bother painting a target on my back.

Kids are cruel, mom had told me. It sounded like a warning.

And so it was that the most interesting part of my life remained hidden. It was a terrible burden for a kid barely into the double-digits, but I didn't see it like that. I just … managed. My greatest comfort was that battered orange duo-tang where I wrote down my most private thoughts and craziest ideas.

Pool Party

14

Twenty kids gathered around the gate by our pool, the sparkling clear water looking like the Mediterranean Sea with its deep blue liner and the white tiles that marked the edges helping to complete the feeling that we were stepping into the warm ocean. A sun-kissed breeze tugged at my long hair and I tossed it for effect. I knew the kids were all watching me, knowing this was my house and they were thrilled to be invited, even if it was only to swim in that glorious pool.

"Please observe the pool rules," my dad was saying to the group. "No rough-housing or running on the deck." Blank stares registered on their young faces.

"Umm, that means no fighting and don't run around the pool. We don't want any accidents," dad clarified.

Heads bobbed up and down in mute agreement and the anticipation was ramped up a notch. Dad stood back a moment later in astonishment as my classmates flowed through the open gate and into the water in one movement, squealing with delight and splashing each other. I hung back, trying to fix the moment in my mind forever. This was my first pool party and I wanted it to be perfect. I hoped nothing would get in the way but already a couple of the kids were making problems and I made my way over to them, determined to set things straight.

"What's going on?" I asked.

"None of your business!" Rhonda snapped. She had beautiful golden hair, but any beauty she had was marred by the nasty expression on her face. "If I want to talk to my boyfriend I can. There's nothing you can do about it, Ginny!" I was taken aback by her venomous tone. She was a guest in my house and in my pool, had she already forgotten that? I narrowed my eyes, thinking briefly about throwing her out, but in the end, I merely shook my head and sighed. Invite the whole class, huh? What a great idea.

I looked Rhonda in the eye with what was known in my house as the "stink eye". Rhonda returned the look at first, but as the seconds wore on and I didn't look away, some of the venom left her gaze.

Determination was making me bold. This girl infuriated me and I wasn't going to let her ruin my party. She was probably just jealous.

"Hey, Ginny let's not start fighting. Rhonda's worried because there are so many bikinis, and not enough time. I'm irresistible!" Joey turned and winked at me and I felt my face redden. Joey was the cutest boy in the school, but he had the inflated self-confidence of an Italian male model.

"Look, if you two need to talk, go somewhere else. Don't stand here shouting at me. I invited you here for a swim party. So swim!" With that, I stalked over to the diving board and dove cleanly into the deep end of the pool. I was well aware that most of the class was watching me, and I felt an adrenaline-rush as I sliced deeply into the water, grateful that I'd practiced endlessly through the summer. Gentle pressure pushed on my ears as I reached out a hand and caressed the bottom, some nine feet down, before pushing off to surface like a rocket. The dive was perfect, and pulling it off at such a timely moment made it unforgettable. When I surfaced, I wiped the water from my eyes and took a moment to look around for Rhonda and Joey, but they'd disappeared. I narrowed my eyes at the house.

"Good riddance to bad rubbish!" I muttered, resurrecting my grandmother's phrase. A moment later, my classmates excitedly gathered around, teasing and splashing. I returned their banter, happy to be the center of attention. This was my day.

As I swam to the ladder to prepare for another dive, something else caught my eye. Another classmate? It was only the briefest glimpse, but it seemed to me that he was too small to be Grade 5. It seemed as though a small figure had disappeared past the edge of the fence and my heart lurched. Bobby?

I struggled up the ladder only to slip backwards, playful hands pulling me back, the water splashing violently around me. By the time I gained solid ground once more, I knew I wouldn't find him. He was gone, if he'd ever really been there to begin with.

I continued to stare for a moment, lost in thought.

Why was my mind playing tricks? Today of all days?

The thought came unbidden and I rubbed my face with both hands in an effort to banish it.

"Hey, Gin! Watcha doin'?" A boy called to me from the shallow end of the pool.

I turned to look, shading my eyes against the brilliance of the sunshine. The shallow end was already cloaked in the shadows thrown by our house. Many of my friends were now gathering by the smoking barbecue, anticipating lunch. "What? Who said that?" I called.

"Come over here and see," the voice said teasingly. As soon as I crossed into the shadows, I could see it was Gary. He was big and blonde and I secretly had a huge crush on him. Just talking with him in such a casual, friendly way was making me blush to the roots of my hair. He was calling me, 'Gin'? How was I going to live that down? Who else was listening?

"Uh, hi," I said. "Having fun?"

"Yeah, this is great," he said. "Nice of you to invite the whole class, too."

"Yeah, well…"

How could I tell him that my parents and I had fought for days over the guest list? I grinned at him sheepishly and he splashed me, a great whoosh of water enveloping my head.

"What the-?" I shouted, coughing and spluttering, but managing to splash him back, which of course, alerted the other kids that a water fight was underway. Two minutes later, we were surrounded. The noise level rose, the water splashed and the sun shone down. It was a perfect day for my first pool party.

Even Joey and Rhonda managed to put in another appearance, smiling in a bad imitation of nonchalance. Even so, they seemed to rally in spite of themselves and I watched them talking animatedly and swimming with the other kids.

As smoke rose from dad's barbecue, I grabbed a towel and left the pool area, determined to put space between me and Rhonda. She laid herself out by the pool, sun-tanning with her friends, pretending not to see Joey clowning around with the other guys while shamelessly flirting with every girl there.

"Hey birthday girl! Over here!" My friend Meridee called from the picnic table in the backyard. She and I had become great friends since my arrival as the new kid and I was pleased to see she'd saved me a seat right next to her.

"Thanks Meridee, I'm starved!"

"Yeah, me too. Your dad said 'hot dogs', so I ran over and sat down! The way I feel right now, I could eat ten!" She giggled and I joined in quickly.

"Hey, this is a pretty good turn-out, huh?" Mentally, I counted heads, but came up two short. "Oh great, where did they go now? They were here a minute ago, but I don't see them anymore." I swiveled my head, looking around, but didn't catch sight of either one of them. "They'd better not do anything stupid."

"Who?" Meridee asked.

"Joey and Rhonda of course. Who else."

"Oh who cares?" Meridee said. "It's not like either one of them is much of a loss … oh! Here comes your dad with the food! Let's eat!"

The scent of mustard and ketchup filled my nostrils as I dug in with the rest of my school friends.

"Ginny, shove over!" One of the other girls, Judy, playfully nudged me so she too could sit at the table. "Great party! I think you're the most popular girl in school now."

"Yeah," I agreed, laughing. "I'm having fun."

"Yeah, us too!" A group of kids I knew only casually overheard us talking. "Great party! Happy Birthday!"

Soon the tables, littered with crumpled up napkins and discarded paper plates were abandoned in favor of the cool, soft grass. We sat in a rough circle while I shredded open presents. The next gift was equally admired.

"Blondie!" I called out, holding it up to a scattering of applause.

The soundtrack to the popular teen movie 'Grease' on a full size vinyl LP appeared in my hands amidst shreds of wrapping paper. I smiled ear to ear.

"It's Systematic … it's Hy-dromatic … it's greased lightning!" The boy beside me sang in a mock impression of John Travolta as I laughed along with my friends, pleased at the gifts, but secretly already wondering how I was going to play all this great stuff when all we had was an ancient record player with touchy buttons that *sometimes* worked.

131

"I think you might want to use this right away," dad said, grinning as I stripped off the ribbons and paper from the last gift in the pile. It was the biggest box yet.

"My own record player!" I screamed, almost not believing it. "Thank you, thank you, thank you!" Excitement made my voice overly loud.

Dad immediately set it up with a long extension cord snaking over to the umbrella table on the edge of the lawn, and two over-large speakers were quickly wired up. Obviously he'd prepared this surprise well in advance.

Soon, other albums were produced from nowhere—or so it seemed to me—and we started dancing on the grass with the wild abandon of children given over to total bliss.

Let's face it. When you're ten and 'Emotional Rescue' by the Rolling Stones fills the air, you just become a rock star. That's all there is to it.

A while later, we were still up and dancing like fools, leaving remnants of birthday cake and a few melted candles strewn through the grass. Everyone was doing their best impressions of rock stars mouthing the phrases committed to memory, as they boomed out from my new stereo.

Suddenly, Joey came pelting up the gravel path into the middle of our impromptu dance-floor, with Rhonda hot on his heels. They were out of breath and clearly terrified.

"What's going on?" I said as they crunched to a stop on the path before the group. "Where have you been? You missed everything!"

A few people had stopped to stare at them too, but most kept dancing and talking, oblivious to their arrival. Mom and dad had fortunately gone back inside.

"A man, b-back there!" Rhonda said, jerking a thumb over her shoulder. The gravel path they'd traveled was empty.

Joey stepped forward, his eyes wide and his arms waving in front of him for emphasis. "Some creepy old guy told us to leave. Said we'd regret it if we didn't!"

"What? Where?" I asked, suspiciously. Somewhere behind me, one of the guests shut off the music. "Were you in the corn field? I told you, that's not our property."

Joey looked at Rhonda but she glared at me.

"We were not in any nasty old field," she said. "We went to see the barn … and don't try to make this our fault! What kind of person threatens kids?" She yelled.

"Yeah, well since you were probably slurking around where you shouldn't have been, it serves you right for being caught!"

Snickers and muffled laughter sounded behind me as more and more of the group turned to watch the drama unfold.

"Yeah Joey, you pervert!" One guy yelled from the back of the crowd.

"Atta boy!" yelled another, who was promptly smacked by a redheaded girl to his right. "Ow!"

"Look, let's talk over there." Joey jerked his head in the direction of the house.

"No. Whatever you need to say you can say right here," Meridee interrupted, linking her arm through mine and nodding with emphasis.

I nodded too, albeit hesitantly. What was he going to say?

"Fine." Joey took a steadying breath. "There's something going on here. That was no farmer and this is no joke." His face was more serious than I'd ever seen it. "I'm telling you, there's something sinister about a farmer in a long black coat on a day like this. It must be a hundred degrees out here!"

"Wh-what?" I asked, embarrassed that my voice was shaking.

Letting him talk in front of my friends was such a bad idea.

"I told you, we went into the barn, to uh … investigate." Rhonda pointed behind her.

"What were you doing in the barn? The party's here." My voice had died to a frightened whisper.

"We just wanted to see the horses," Rhonda answered defensively.

"We were all the way through to the other end and figured we'd go through the side door to that paddock there," Rhonda jerked her thumb back over her shoulder. "That's where we saw this weird guy. He just appeared, right in front of us. Right there!" She stabbed one finger at the ground in front of her. "He was this close to us! He started yelling 'You don't belong here!'"

I must have been gaping at her like a fool.

"I swear! That's what he said." Rhonda seemed out of breath.

"Are you sure?" I asked, aware that my voice was shaking. "Who would do that? Where did he come from?"

"That's just the thing," Joey said. "We didn't see him come from anywhere. He was just there one minute and gone the next."

"Gone?" Meridee interjected.

"Yeah," Rhonda answered. Her voice quivered. "He was so creepy, we took a step back and I almost tripped on all that muck out there."

"I caught her," Joey said, managing to sound proud.

"Yeah, but when we stood up to tell him off, he'd disappeared."

"Into thin air?" Someone else in the crowd asked, their voice in awe.

Uh-oh. I couldn't help looking around at the other kids. This was dangerous territory now.

"Practically," she said. "I'd only glanced down at the ground for a second, while Joey caught my arm so I wouldn't fall. We only looked away for, what, three seconds?" She looked over at Joey for confirmation. His answering nod was firm.

"At the most. Nobody's that fast," Joey added.

"Oh I see where this is going!" Meridee said angrily, folding her arms. My eyes were wide as I stared at her. What was she going to say? "Nice ghost story. This is Ginny's party, not yours."

"Who said anything —" I faced the two of them, my embarrassment in full-flower.

"About ghosts?" Joey squinted at Meridee and I, confusion and anger spreading across his face. "Look you guys, obviously we don't know what's going on. If we did, we wouldn't have … oh never mind. Your neighbours must be crazy! The barn belongs to you, doesn't it?"

I couldn't see what was going on behind me, but I could hear. Confused chatter and whispers made my eyes sting with tears. Deciding to put on a brave face, I ignored the calculating look Rhonda directed at me, and tried to appear nonchalant.

"Of course," I said. "That old guy's … um, he's probably the pig farmer next door. He's a little … unstable." It sounded like an extremely unbelievable tale to my own ears, but thankfully, I wasn't dealing with adults.

The record player was within easy reach and I breathed a sigh of relief as rock music once again poured out, effectively cutting off any further conversation.

Music soothes the heart, right? So why was mine about ready to burst through my skin?

With my back to the crowd, I dashed the tears from my eyes with a napkin.

Stupid, stupid, stupid. I was stupid to invite them.

Behind me, the music slowed down and so did the mood. Several of my classmates, now changed into shorts, halter tops and other summer wear, sprawled out on towels, soaking up the hot afternoon sun, while they talked and laughed.

It looks okay, I thought; please let it be okay.

It wasn't long before cars began pulling up in the driveway, and I breathed a sigh of relief. The party had come to an end.

Rhonda was, ironically, the first to leave. Surrounded by her friends and pointedly ignoring everyone else, I saw her smile and unexpectedly, she lifted her hand in a friendly wave.

What? Was she human after all? Perhaps she wanted to be friends. I took a hesitant step forward, but just then, Joey saved me from true embarrassment as he rushed past, obviously in response to her wave. I turned away in disgust.

"Never again," I said to myself through clenched teeth.

"Hey! I had a good time." The voice came from my elbow and I looked up to see one of Joey's friends smiling at me. His red hair seemed to glow in the late afternoon sun. "Really. Thanks for inviting me and happy birthday."

I smiled back as he climbed into his dad's pick up. "Thanks for the awesome gift. I'm glad you could come."

Mom had trained me well in the art of entertaining. "Sure, see you at school."

"Happy birthday, Ginny." Meridee said next, in a sing-song voice. "Don't worry about those jerks. We all had fun." Ever the optimist, she grinned and waved as she got into the long green Mercury that waited in the driveway. Her big sister sat behind the wheel. "Bye!" Her face took on a tragic expression as she leaned out the window. "Pray for me, my sister's driving, aaah!"

Her natural good humour restored mine at little and I smiled as they drove away.

One by one, cars pulled up the driveway and my classmates shuffled past, swim bags and wet towels clutched in their hands.

"Cool pool party!"

"Thanks for the great time!"

"Thanks for the invite! See you at school!"

Judy, another of my new friends appeared beside me. "Next time, don't invite Rhonda," she said, giving me a quick hug. "She's always looking for attention." That comment made me feel better and I felt more like myself as they drove away and I waved energetically.

"What was that about 'ghost stories' Gin?" This last phrase was spoken by Greg. He'd stepped close to me and my heart fluttered. "You're a story teller? No way! You've been holding out on me."

I realized all at once that my mouth wouldn't work. All I could do was grin foolishly and nod.

"Look, Joey's a show-off, you shouldn't let it bug you, but me? I love a good ghost story. Share one with me next time?"

"Uh-huh," I managed.

Now why had I said that? I was better off grinning.

"This was fun," he said. "Thanks for the invite. I'll see you at school Monday."

I nodded again. Taking a big breath, all that came to mind was the rote, never-fail phrase that mom used at all her parties. "Thank you. It was nice of you to come."

Greg grinned at that.

Oh great. Nice of you to come? Oh boy, what an idiot!

But instead of turning away in disgust and laughter, he moved closer. "Happy Birthday," he said quietly. His brown eyes held mine with an intensity I'd never experienced before. His voice suddenly pitched lower, so no one else could hear. "Don't be scared. Joey thinks he's a big deal, but he'll make up anything for attention."

I felt my eyes narrow in spite of my fluttering heart. How much did this guy know?

"Sure, yeah it's okay, I'm on to him," I said, trying not to trip on my tongue.

"Good," he responded, suddenly leaning in closer, he brushed his lips against mine.

My eyes flew open in amazement.

The next thing I knew, he was walking away. He went with an easy grace; his hands plunged deep into the front pockets of his cut-offs.

"See ya," he said, tossing the words over his shoulder as he climbed into the waiting station wagon.

When had that pulled up?

I let out the breath I was holding and I felt like my face was in flames. "Yeah, see ya. Thanks, uh, for coming!"

Shoot. I said that already.

I stood there for long moments afterward, staring at the empty space when Greg's ride had been. Wow. What was going on with this guy? I never even knew he liked, me!

When the last car pulled away with the last guest inside, the glow from that kiss made me feel warm all over again. As I wandered back through the yard, replaying my day and smiling, thoughts of Rhonda and

Joey's breathless claim rudely interrupted. I couldn't dismiss the possibility that their story might be real.

I knew that man, or at least his image. Had they really seen the specter that haunted me?

Later on, as I lay in bed, my mind was afire with questions. Thoughts whirled at top speed through my brain. Did Greg really care about me or was that kiss meant as a joke? Why couldn't I control the stream of words coming out of my mouth? I'd sounded like a moron. And if anyone saw Greg and I, then how would I ever be able to go to school on Monday? And what was up with Rhonda and Joey? What if they knew more than they were telling? I knew my flimsy excuses weren't likely to fool anyone for long. But if they knew about the ghosts, then how? I'd been so careful.

There were too many questions and not enough answers. The last coherent thought I had as I drifted off to sleep with my light still burning comfortingly beside me, was how I could possibly get out of telling ghost stories to Greg the next time we met.

~~~~

About a week later, I was in the family room watching T.V. with my sister and her boyfriend. They were supposedly babysitting, but it looked more like making out to me.

Their smooching reminded me of Greg's overt display of affection at the pool party. My face burned at the memory of it and I wondered again if it had been some sort of cruel joke. I'd gone to school on Monday with all sorts of ideas swirling in my head, but he'd been ignoring me all week! Boys. Diane could have 'em!

Thinking about Greg put me in bad mood, and I put all my energy into being creatively willful against my sister. My anger at the callous way they were treating me, as though I was some sort of irritating rodent, flared anew. Determined to be the pest she'd already labeled me, I disagreed with everything they told me to do.

"Oh just shut up and watch T.V. then!" my exasperated sister finally said, throwing her hands up in despair. "When mom and dad come home, YOU can tell them why you're not showered, you didn't brush your teeth and you're NOT in bed!"

"I'm getting a snack!" I announced loudly, and flounced out of the room.

"Whatever." Diana rolled her eyes and settled down with Rick, intent on enjoying the television show, and her boyfriend, in relative peace and quiet.

Being a determined sort of person, I wasn't about to let my sister have the last word, and I'd already decided she wasn't getting off the hook that easily. Flouncing out to the large, country-style kitchen, I began opening and closing cupboard doors, intentionally making lots of noise.

"What are you doing in there?" she called to me. "Don't make a mess or you'll be sorry! I just cleaned up."

Knowing she couldn't see me, I stuck my tongue out at her anyway, pausing with my hand on the fridge door. On a whim, I got down on all fours, crawled to the doorway and peeked around the corner. Their heads were bent close, with no light between their profiles …

Settling back on my heels, I decided to just hide on them. Soon, they'd wonder where I'd gone and it would be great fun to put that kind of joke over on my controlling sister and her irritating boyfriend!

I'd only just crawled in under the kitchen table however, my heart pounding with the threat of imminent discovery, when I heard a sound that didn't belong.

Running water in the kitchen sink. The tap was on! The forceful stream hit the few dishes still piled in the sink, and I could see the faint glimmer of water droplets as they sprayed out onto the floor. A moment later, the dishes began clanking together louder and louder, as though they were actually being washed with vigor. I tried to swallow the lump in my throat and failed. This couldn't be happening. It wasn't possible. I had a clear view of the kitchen from where I crouched and there was no one there!

The television switched off, and a pair of legs walked slowly towards my hiding place.

"Ginny?" My sister's voice called hesitantly as she approached. Knowing there was nothing I could do, I stayed frozen, uncertain what, if anything, we *could* do. The kitchen was in shadow and the hem of the tablecloth hid her face from my view. "Mom? Dad?" After a moment, I could see my sister's jean-clad legs and striped socks standing by the table now. She stayed still, waiting.

So did I.

I was worried Diana would blame me for the noise since I was already in a compromising location, but all I could do was hug my knees to my chest and keep still.

"Is someone here?" she called. There was no response. I certainly wasn't going to own up to anything. I heard Diana walk to the front door of our house. Then, I saw her jeans walk past me into the T.V. room again.

"Rick, you heard that, right?" she asked.

"Sure," I heard him say. "Your parents came home?"

"N-no," she said.

"Then it must your brat sister. What's she up to?" His voice sounded suspicious and I narrowed my eyes in his direction.

"She's not there either. Must be in her room."

Silently, I stuck my tongue out at him. *So there*, I thought. *I am not a brat.*

"Then who was it? Somebody turned the faucet on."

"And off," she said. "It's not running now. Wait a minute, when did it go off? Did you hear it stop?"

"No," he answered, coming to join her in the kitchen. "I thought you turned it off."

"No," she answered. "Am I going crazy?"

"Not unless I'm going crazy too. I definitely heard it, although none of this makes sense. At least, not the kind of sense I'd like to have." I heard my sister let out her breath explosively. I could picture her running her hands through her hair in frustration. "I know what I heard," I heard her whisper.

"Wait a second..." Rick said, as though he'd just thought of something. "Where's Ginny? I don't trust her."

"Oh for God's sake, Rick, now you're blaming my little sister? We both know there's something going on in this place. You stay here, I'm gonna go check on—" she began, but her words were cut off suddenly when I heard a sharp click, and the lights in the rec room, the only lights on in the whole house at that point, were suddenly doused. With the kitchen lights off already, everything was thrown into darkness.

I think I screamed. Well, someone did, so it was probably me.

I burst from my hiding place and bumped my head in the process.

There was confusion and noise, a blinding pain in the top of my head and my sister's voice in my ears.

"Ginny? Is that you?"

Clutching my head with both hands, I stared at the shadow in front of me, hoping it was Diana.

"Hey look, what's going on? Who turned out the lights? You?"

"No," I sobbed.

She watched me carefully, probably deciding whether to believe me or not.

Rick stepped to the switch and flicked it back on.

"The light -" I started to say.

"So it was you," Rick said. "I thought so."

"What? No!" I protested. "No, it wasn't me."

Diana was having a hard time. She just stood there, silently watching me.

"Why would I scream if I was the one who put out the lights?" I replied, trying to reason with them.

"I don't know...none of this makes good sense," she said, her voice small in the oversized room. "But why are all these crazy things happening? And why to us?"

Diana was clearly upset. Rick just looked at me, irritated and bewildered. He didn't know what to do any more than we did, but it was clear that he understood and he wasn't going to waste time trying to deny it.

We stood by the kitchen table, not brave enough to go back in the room, and certainly not comfortable enough to make eye contact with each other. In the silence, a tell-tale click sounded again and for the second time, the overhead lights went out.

This time, there was no one else to blame. We stood frozen, in confused silence listening to the darkness.

Suddenly, I heard Rick's voice burst out in an angry bravado.

"You cut that out!" he yelled. Almost leaping across the room, his long legs made huge strides, his tall form shadowy. Rick threw the switch to the on position and the lights flared into brilliance once again, illuminating our shocked, frightened faces.

"This is ridiculous!" He yelled at no one in particular.

My eyebrows inched up my forehead and stayed there. Diana and I sat staring at him, both of us trying to figure out what to do next, when a small creaking sound refocused our collective gaze. With Rick only an arm's length away, we watched in horror as the light switch slowly and deliberately pivoted down with an audible click.

Someone was playing with us.

In the darkness I could hear my sister crying.

Rick's voice shook as he tried to comfort her, carefully switching on the lights for the third time.

When mom and dad arrived home a few hours later, they must have been a little shocked to find me awake, sitting at the kitchen table with Diana and Rick, playing a serious board game of *Sorry!*, while every light in the house was ablaze. Diana's Confirmation Bible completed the picture, having been placed on the table like a talisman. When Rick left that night, he had a meaningful look on his handsome face.

Do we say anything or keep it to ourselves? Not one of us knew the answer.

The next day, the sunshine made me brave enough to want to talk about it, but even to myself, I came across sounding weak. In the light of day, I could almost convince myself that it hadn't happened at all, and yet, there were far too many incidents to be ignored.

I knew Diana was wrestling with herself a little too. It was a shared experience and she seemed just as eager to get it off of her chest as I was. In light of everything I'd experienced, there was no more doubt in my mind, but she was having a hard time believing, even as I filled her in on all the things I'd seen and heard. We talked in hushed tones over breakfast, but all we could do was agree that there was no possible way any of us could have manipulated that switch, or made all those noises in the kitchen. Whatever was happening in our new home was definitely paranormal. Diana was having just as much trouble with the concept as my cynical parents, but I found solace in the fact that we were finally working on the same problem, pooling our ideas, neither one scoffing or teasing.

We must have sat there for an hour or more, comparing notes and trying to figure out our wild experience of the previous night. Our theories became wilder and wilder as we talked.

"Little sis," Diana finally said. "We're not getting anywhere. I say we just tell mom and dad and let them figure out what to do."

"They won't do anything, though." I said. "They don't believe in ghosts. You know that."

Diana seemed to wince at the word 'ghost'. "Well," she anszwered. "We've got to try."

Later, my sister and I sat down with our parents to have a chat.

"Mom, dad," Diana began. "Something strange happened last night."

"Define strange," mom said.

Dad strode up behind mom and fixed his calm blue-eyed gaze on both of us.

With a courage and openness that surprised me, Diana related the whole absurd story, while I interjected my own thoughts and feelings.

"And you think something other-worldly turned on the kitchen taps? And the light switch? Is that what you're saying?" My father's tone was sarcastic. He shook his head and sighed. "I don't know what's gotten into you girls. We leave you alone in a new house and all of a sudden you think it's haunted!"

"I told you," I muttered to my sister.

"Now listen to me you two," said our mother. "This is a new house for us and there are bound to be lots of noises and things to get used to."

"It's not like we moved in last week!" Diana spluttered. "Things have been happening for months! You weren't there! You don't know."

"That's enough Diana."

"Mom–."

"And you swear this wasn't a trick?" dad asked me for what seemed like the hundredth time.

"No dad. It was real." I paused and hung my head, gauging the situation before I spoke again. "I don't know how to make you understand."

"Mm-hmm, and what would you *specifically* like us to understand?"

"Well, Bobby for instance."

"Bobby?" My mother, sister and father all turned to stare at me.

"Well, yeah I can't help feeling like he's part of it somehow."

My family was still staring at me, so I went on.

"When he's around I can kinda tell. It's a familiar kind of feeling –"

"Let's not have any of that," mom interrupted, placing her hands firmly on her hips. "I think we've spent enough time on this. We all need to get on with our day. We've got evening service at the church tonight, and Ginny, your room looks like a bomb went off in there. Perhaps we'll talk about this later."

I wished fervently that the mere mention of Bobby's name wouldn't shut them all down like that. I wasn't going crazy and the worst part was, they all knew it, but no one would say the words out loud. It was the definition of frustration and it was threatening to tear our family apart.

Cabin

15

I went to church expecting that my paranormal problems would stand out like some sort of mark on my skin, obvious to all who looked at me. I sat down, avoiding eye contact with the other parishioners, and tried to be extra attentive to the Pastor's homily, resisting the temptation to squirm or even clear my throat, lest I attract unwanted attention.

Pastor Smith stood at the altar, joyously celebrating the Eucharist and as a parish, we responded with phrases committed to memory.

Lord, why is this happening to me? I asked in the silence of my mind. I found myself staring hard at the wooden cross that adorned the front of the church, standing just behind the beautiful marble altar. The prostrated representation of Jesus made me feel sad and mad all at the same time. What was happening to me and my family? Didn't He care? How could He let this go on? Questions raged inside of me even as my lips uttered the formulaic prayers. The unofficial 'meet and greet' began at the back of the church after the final hymn, but by that time, I'd had all I could take. Making excuses that sounded lame to my own ears, I begged the car keys from dad and left the church alone to hide out in the car and wait for them. Looking out at my family, as they talked easily with the other parishioners, I envied them. How could they simply pretend this way? I wished fervently that I could do the same, but I knew in my heart that I would never be able to.

~~~~

"Okay, there's nothing physically wrong with the lights, the electrical checks out and no wires are broken. Hmmm," dad said the next day as he stood by the breakfast table, coffee cup in hand, an electrical meter hanging on his hip. He seemed to be talking to himself, his tone thoughtful and quiet. "What haven't I thought of?"

I was tempted to tell him right then and there that he would never discover the answer with electrical meters and logical thinking, when the meter inexplicably lit up.

"Dad, what does that thing do?" I asked, pushing aside my cornflakes and pointing at the meter, which had a tiny gauge at one end, with a red needle that seemed to have a life of its own. It seemed to jump up and down the spectrum of numbers as though it were dancing to some inaudible rhythm.

"It's a meter I borrowed from work. I've taken measurements with my own meter, but I thought I'd borrow a more sensitive instrument in case mine is—." He looked at it as he spoke, but suddenly he stopped and stared at in silence. The slow click, click, click of the machine had suddenly begun clicking faster and emitting a small hum, although neither of us had moved.

"Why is it doing that?" I asked. The space in front of me felt like a wall of solid ice. Tears sprang to my eyes in reflexive fear. I *knew* that feeling. Instantly on my guard, I looked around, but everything was just as it should be. Still, the air itself felt thick, heavy and cold.

The rest of my body was warm, but the cold air touching the end of my nose hovered there, feeling like a touch of winter. Was it possible that the air could be electrically charged? I wasn't sure, but it sure felt like it. Dad's meter obviously thought so too.

"What the –? This thing shouldn't be doing that." Dad was staring at the meter.

"Dad? Does the air feel funny to you?"

"Mmm," he muttered, tapping the device and frowning. "Yes, honey I know…"

I watched my father wander back down the hallway, device held firmly in his hand as he swept it back and forth, holding it out from his body in a wide arc, tracing the edges of the walls, tapping the device with his finger and muttering. He paused briefly at the thermostat in the hallway and tapped that with his forefinger too.

"Feel cold in here to you?" he called out to me.

I nodded. Mom and Diana were never going to believe this one, I thought. Good thing dad was going to be the one to tell it.

~~~~

As time went on, I came to realize that my parents didn't want to believe these things were happening, and that was why they stayed steadfastly in denial. They looked for logic, but the paranormal events in our home defied logic. There was no rational explanation, and therefore they weren't willing to discuss it—at least not with me. Thanksgiving was always spent at our family cabin in the mountains and a profound sense of calm usually descended on my parents as they prepared for the short holiday, and this time was no different. It was as though no one could get into the pickup truck fast enough. Diana and Rick were driving up together, and they'd already left, causing dad to stand in the driveway scratching his forehead in wonder.

"That girl is never early for anything, but did you see her take off out of here?" Dad faced mom with a puzzled frown. "Like she had rocket boosters on her feet!"

"I know," mom said. "I've got another one right here." She'd stood to one side so dad could see. Nestled in amongst sleeping bags, pillows, shopping bags full of groceries and one big dog, my small form was tucked in and ready to get started. There was lots of room for me and Rookie in the back seat without Diana, and they could see I was packed and ready, so why was dad wasting time?

Mom blinked at me in surprise. "I can't believe you're ready. It's not even ten."

I nodded happily. "Yup."

"I'd better not find out that you forgot anything young lady," mom warned as she walked back towards the house for a last look around.

"If she forgot, she goes without," dad called to her, eying me carefully from the driver's seat. When I made no move to run back inside, dad grinned and pushed the brim of his battered cowboy hat back off his forehead. "You really didn't forget anything? You must be excited to go huh, kid?" I nodded. "Me too," he said.

Our cabin was and still is referred to as our *private decompression chamber*. It's located in the middle of a ten acre parcel in a wooded area about three hours' drive from our family home. There are no phones, no electricity and none of the usual distractions. The only source of heat comes from two wood stoves that require constant stoking, and the water comes through a gravity feed from a meandering creek that runs through the property.

When dad first built the place, mom, being a city girl at heart, insisted that indoor plumbing be installed, and that included a system for drawing wash water from the creek. Dad, ever the ingenious inventor, acquiesced happily. He was always very relaxed at what he jokingly referred to as *the ranch*. My parents embraced their traditional roles in that environment, and as they chopped wood and stoked fires and cleaned up after us kids, they somehow managed to do all of this with good humour. Whatever stresses we faced at home, it always seemed like it couldn't touch us there.

Thanksgiving was quiet that year, as it tends to be when you leave all your electricity behind. We labored to stoke the antique wood stove, and the rule of "no shoes in the house" was never heard up there.

Ah yes, life was always good at the cabin. We all relaxed, joking around and singing silly songs on the front deck, taking long walks beside the mountain stream, marvelling at nature. Even on the way home, our good mood seemed like it would never end. But as we neared our house and all of its problems, the jokes and the easy-going attitudes seemed to stop. The singing faded and a somber mood descended over us.

What would we find waiting for us when we opened that front door?

Would there be a mess of broken dishes on the kitchen floor? Or would there be a heavy odour hovering in the air with no discernible source?

The unlocking of our front door was always prefaced with a giant sigh from my father, and whether he realized it or not, he was bracing for the worst.

As usual the house did not disappoint.

It seemed that "someone" had left the refrigerator door wide open and the smell of spoiled food filled the house.

Great.

Welcome home family, it seemed to say.

Thanksgiving occurs mid October in Canada when the leaves start to change colour and it's a beautiful time of year. By the end of the month, however, it's usually raining, just in time for Halloween. I don't remember ever having a costume that wasn't plasticized somehow, to protect me from the rain as I ran from door to door, collecting my candy.

When my parents saw that the time of ghosts and goblins was drawing near, tempers grew short once again.

"A lot of bother if you ask me," mom said. She climbed up on the kitchen step-stool to reach high into our hall closet. "I think your red hat should suffice," she told me. "You'll make a very nice cowgirl."

I sighed. "Again mom? I was a cowgirl last year."

"You could be a dead cowgirl," my sister quipped as she wandered past, a cheeky smile on her face.

"Yuck!" mom protested, pausing in her search. "Not funny, Diana."

"Yeah, thanks a lot," I said. "A lot of help you are."

"How much candy do we need?" dad asked.

Mom continued to rummage through the closet. "How should I know? I have no idea if kids actually trick-or-treat in this neighbourhood or if everyone drives their kids to the city. I'm opting for the city, but then, that's me."

"Yeah, you can take the girl out of the city..." dad began, letting the rest of the sentence speak for itself.

"Hardy-har-har," mom replied. "Aha! There it is." She pulled forth a rectangular–shaped box and brought it down to the table. "Your hat, madame."

And so, Halloween 1979 saw me as a cowgirl ... again.

~~~~~

"Look, these doors do NOT have a mind of their own!" Mom's angry voice carried throughout the house and it wasn't hard to tell they were having another fight. Lately, the strain on the family was putting their relationship to the test.

"I've told you I don't know why it's happening, but you just can't let it go, can you? What do you want me to do about it?"

"I don't know... fix it!"

"If I could, I would. But I don't appreciate it when you hurl these things at me the second I get in the door. I've worked hard all day and I'm tired."

"I can't live like this anymore," she said. From the tone in her voice, I knew she was on the verge of tears.

A second later, I heard the front door slam.

Alarm shot through me. Who was leaving?

"Honey, come here …" dad's voice was muted, and I could tell he was standing outside. A moment later, I parted the curtains and saw him standing with Mom. The harshness had left his tone somehow, and his demeanor reversed in the blink of an eye … or perhaps in the closing of a door?

He held her tenderly in his arms. "This is ridiculous … what are we fighting for?" I heard him say. "What good does it do?"

"I don't know, Will, but we've got to try something … anything! I can't even talk to anyone."

"Well, there's Julia," dad said.

"Surely not," mom answered, but her tone wasn't as sure as her words.

"It might help to talk to someone who can keep their mouth shut and give us some friendly advice."

Dad looked around then, as though worried that someone would hear. I let the curtain fall back against the sill.

At least my parents were still okay. Still together. My friend Jessie said her parents were getting a divorce.

Dad's voice still carried through the closed window. "Friendly advice couldn't hurt."

"Failing that, we could all go on vacation or something," mom said as they walked back in the house through the front door.

I jumped guiltily in the hallway, my bare feet and pajamas mute testimony to the fact that I should already be in bed.

"Virginia, eavesdropping is a nasty habit," mom told me.

"Sorry," I replied. "But I was worried. It wasn't like you were trying to be quiet or anything."

"Oh for goodness sake." mom sounded tired.

"Well, let's hear it, what have you got to say for yourself?" dad asked, his hands on his hips in a pose I knew well.

"I like the idea of going on a vacation," I said brightly.

"Yeah, don't we all?"dad's answer was sarcastic but he managed a small smile anyway. "Well as long as you're up, you can help your mother clean up from supper."

"Yes dad." I put my hastily scooped up cat down on the floor again where he meowed at me in a disgruntled sort of way. "Dad? Are we gonna have to move?"

"What put that into your head?" he asked.

"Well, I …."

"No," he interrupted. "Don't listen to your sister."

~~~~

I rarely saw Diana. My sister usually made plans with her friends so she wouldn't have to stay in the house alone. I knew she was scared but I wasn't sure whether to be frightened or fascinated. I'd already decided I was destined to be a writer, and so I suppose I learned to look at things differently because of it. Apparently, I still do.

"There's a logical reason for everything," dad calmly explained one Sunday afternoon when we'd returned from church. "We just have to find the answer. I'm going to ask some other technicians at work about this meter. The readings I'm getting don't make sense."

We couldn't explain these things away, but my family tried none-the-less.

Julia

16

I heard them arguing from inside my bedroom. The sounds of their raised voices carried through the house like they each had a microphone. I would have been happier if I couldn't hear them at all. Mom and dad were arguing about me.

I stood motionless in my bedroom, and re-closed the door.

"Well what are we supposed to do?" mom asked.

"I don't know," dad answered. "Grounding her doesn't work, we already know that. If we take stuff away she'll probably just start talking to herself again."

"That's assuming she can control it."

"Well, on some level, maybe she can ... wait a minute, is she up yet? I don't want her to hear this," mom said, pitching her voice lower. I missed dad's response as I carefully opened my door again and inched down the hall.

"... could call somebody," mom was saying.

"Like who? Oh hell, I don't know what to do."

"Well, maybe I should talk with Julia. We've got to do something. We've been putting it off for weeks now."

A long pause followed and I wondered if maybe they knew I was there. I started to back up slowly.

"Maybe not." dad replied. "Maybe it's a phase?"

"Well –." mom seemed to consider it. "I'd love to call it that, but I don't think that's it. There's truth in what she says, Will. I mean, how did those lights go on and off by themselves? You know it's still happening.

And then there's the issue of running water in an empty kitchen. There are only so many times we can claim 'active imagination'." She sighed in exasperation. "Even I don't believe my own excuses anymore."

"Look all I know is what I can see and hear. I can put a meter on a switch and if the numbers are right, I know it's working. How do I fix this? There's no meter I can use to test my own daughter!"

Dad fell silent and I could hear his shuffling footsteps as he paced the kitchen. "Look, I'll check the switches again, maybe we'll get lucky and it's a slight short in the wiring. Not enough to register on a meter, but if I can visually inspect the switch, you never know. As for the kitchen sink, well, plumbing's not my thing, but I can check for leaks. But as for Ginny ... I'm at a loss to explain."

So they thought it was me! My parents were faced with stuff they didn't understand, and their only answer was to blame me. I felt my face grow hot with indignation and betrayal.

"Look, what Ginny sees or doesn't see is something I can't wrap my head around, but what I've seen ... I don't know what to think about that."

I had to clap both hands over my mouth to stifle my sharp gasp.

"I'm surprised you haven't experienced anything. Or have you?"

I froze then, my heart thrumming wildly in my chest.

"I'm not going to jump to conclusions, if that's what you're getting at," dad said.

"So you have? And now you're trying to change the subject by saying I'm jumping to conclusions?" Mom's voice had begun to climb the register and I knew this was about to turn into a bigger fight.

"I didn't say that Liz ... let's just try to be reasonable and cautious about this, okay?"

"Hmm, reasonable ... what a unique idea," mom answered. Her statement was followed closely by a metallic clang. Soon, I heard the distinctive ring of metal, as I envisioned pots and pans banging forcefully onto the surface of the stove and countertop. "Yes." Mom's voice could be heard over the din. "Let's just be reasonable. That'll work." The sarcasm was heavy in her voice. Cupboards opened and closed, creating a rhythm that signaled the beginning of another emotional baking session that would soon fill the house with delicious fragrance.

At least there'd be cookies.

It was also an obvious clue that their enlightening conversation was at an end. I backed up slowly and returned to my room before I could be discovered. I had a lot to consider.

~~~~

It was cold, but not snowing as I walked reluctantly back down the sister's driveway. I'd received a second summons, this one asking me to "come see us at Julia's house." Squinting at the gathering clouds, I wondered just what Penny had up her sleeve. It sounded like she had a definite reason for inviting me over. I still felt weird about the invitation, though. This was Julia's house. I'd never been there before, and the invitation had not even come from her. I hoped this was going to work out, but doubt and worry crept into my footsteps.

I remember that the two storey house looked a lot like a tall box, and the peculiar shade of green it was painted made it clearly visible from my own driveway, though it seemed bigger than I thought as I trudged up the hill.

The note from the front door of the sister's cottage still clutched in one hand, I marveled at the way the huge picture windows seemed to stare at me, as though I was suddenly on display.

I hated being watched, but in truth, it was the only reason I didn't turn around immediately and run straight home.

As I neared the big, intricately carved front door, I caught a glimpse of something familiar and paused to stare in disbelief.

For a moment, it looked like a little boy had ducked in out of sight behind the big green house.

I thought Julia's kids were grown up. Didn't they have cars and girlfriends and jobs?

This was no grown up. So who was it that now hid behind Julia's greenhouse? My mind screamed the obvious, but stubbornly, I refused to believe it. He's not real. He never was.

My memory flashed back to that day in the old house, when he seemed to disappear from a room with no doors.

I shook my head. Mom and dad said it wasn't possible.

My little friend who had played with me in my own back yard, sharing stories and ice cream, I still didn't want to think of him as a *ghost*.

I could barely even say the word.

That picture in Elise's front hall, though. There was no getting past that. He was a real boy. And he'd been killed on the road I'd just crossed by a speeding dump truck.

Months ago.

That was reality.

Water sprang to both of my eyes. Our time together, our adventures, those long talks and walks out by the stream …had any of it been real? Could I trust my own eyes? Could I trust my own ears?

Apparently not. The sound of giggling seemed to float through Julia's yard and I took a step back. Unable to see clearly, and thoroughly confused, my steps faltered and I slipped on a patch of ice, almost landing with a splash in a half-frozen pot hole. The muddy ice-water sloshed into my shoes as I wind-milled my arms in a frantic effort not to fall.

When I looked up a moment later, I could see Julia watching me calmly from her front door. The door was open wide and she stood framed in her doorway. A small smile played on her lips. I flushed with embarrassment.

"Hi," I said. "Uh. Puddles." I pointed behind me. "Is, um, anyone staying with you right now?" I asked, thinking of the child I'd seen.

Julia stared at me, not comprehending.

"Um, I thought I saw a child...uh, there was … a note?" I finished lamely, holding it up for her to see

"Oh the note! Of course," she smiled warmly. "We've been expecting you. Wondering if you were going to come in or do some more, uh, gym exercises." She laughed at my surprise and her laughter was warm and friendly. "Come in, Penny and Elise are here."

So they *had* been watching … what else had they seen?

"Come, come," she beckoned. I'd seen this woman a few times volunteering at the church on Sundays with Mom, and of course I knew of her, but I didn't *know* her. Caution made me pause. Were Penny and Elise really in there?

She was short and plump, with very black hair and a pleasant face. Her skin was the colour of chocolate ice cream. Her brown eyes danced with good humour as she stood back and invited me in with an elegant wave of her arm.

"We're just in the kitchen. Join us."

She walked ahead of me into a spacious kitchen, leaving the door wide open, obviously expecting me to follow.

Overcome by curiosity, I peeked my head inside. I caught a glimpse of leather bar stools arranged beside the long counter, where I was relieved to see Penny and Elise perched, smiling at me, their hands wrapped around ceramic coffee mugs with multi-coloured flowers on them.

It all looked so normal. I felt my shoulders sag in relief at the sight of them.

"Ginny," Penny said pleasantly. "Do come in and shut that door. It's chilly today. Winter's on its way."

"Yeah," I replied remembering the ice. "I think it's already here."

Bits of stainless steel interrupted the otherwise avocado theme she had going on in that kitchen. I closed the solid front door behind me and removed my shoes. The spotless linoleum was white with little gold squares: very 1970's.

"Hello Ginny, I'm so glad you could join us," Elise commented. "This is our good friend Julia Rossi. We thought you two should meet."

The sight of her familiar face helped me to relax and smile a little, although my body still trembled.

Julia stepped forward and took my limp hands in hers. "Welcome to my home, Ginny. Your mother and I are church volunteers together. Elise and Penny are my very dear friends. They've told me so much about you, I feel like I already know you."

I smiled politely. "Thank you Mrs. Rossi."

"Oh bother that, you can call me Julia like everyone else."

Her smile was contagious, and before she'd finished speaking, I was grinning widely. I liked this woman.

"Soda pop?" she asked.

"Yes please," I replied, surprised at the offer.

"Good," she said. "A healthy response!"

Penny and Elise refrained from comment, although their raised eyebrows seemed to indicate that children in their home did *not* drink soda pop.

Julia was an excellent cook. She was part Native Indian, and the rumor was, she had married an irascible Italian. Mom and dad often talked about people when they thought I wasn't listening.

How little they knew me! I *always* listened.

According to my parents, Julia and Paul's arguments were legendary, but so was her cooking. She was a wise and creative woman, but most surprising of all was her gift. Julia, the rumours said, being Native herself, had been educated in the ways of the Shaman.

"Julia," I asked shyly, looking deep into my drinking glass, studying the patterns of swirling bubbles.

"Yes?"

"People say you know Indian Magic. Do you"

Julia laughed, a warm, rich sound and Elise and Penny looked embarrassed.

What can I say? I've always been blunt.

"My people had a way of knowing about someone by reading their soul," she answered at last.

I was startled and must have shown it.

"Oh don't worry, it doesn't mean what you think." She chuckled again and went on. "The eyes are the windows to the soul. That's how they judged character back in the old days. Makes sense if you think about it. I wouldn't necessarily call that *Indian* magic, but I suppose it's magic of a sort."

"Oh, yeah I guess that makes sense. Can *you* do that?"

"All the time," she laughed. "Makes people mad sometimes." Her succinct pronunciation made me smile. "But they either get over it, or they don't. Those that don't aren't worth bothering over."

Her simple way of sorting good people from bad sounded like sage advice. "I wish I could do that," I told her.

Julia smiled and looked at me silently for a while. Uncomfortable, I started to look away, but a small sound from her made me stop. She held me there with her gentle, but penetrating gaze for a few more seconds, but it felt longer. I guessed she was sizing me up the way she'd sized up those others she'd mentioned. Although her gaze had grown intense, her smile never wavered.

No wonder people didn't like it, I thought, aware that I was holding my breath. It was creepy.

"Aah," she said at last, drawing the word out. All at once, she broke off her gaze and turned her attentions back to the kitchen and to the pot of something that was simmering on the stove. "That's good."

"What? Something's good?" I asked lightly.

Julia laughed. "Oh yes."

I laughed too, albeit nervously, casting uneasy glances back at Penny and Elise. "So what did you see? Am I a good person?"

"You don't need me to tell you that," she said. "There's no problem with goodness, but you are troubled. Am I right?" Julia turned to her friends and received two very serious nods.

"You can tell all that from looking at me?"

"More or less," she said. "Now, all this talk of Indian magic intrigues me. You have an agile mind. I wonder now, what should I divulge? Hmm, perhaps we should speak of spiritual gifts?"

"Gifts?" My voice squeaked a little and I looked quickly at Penny and Elise. Elise was looking down, but Penny met my gaze and gave an almost imperceptible nod.

"Yes, you will come to realize yours in time, when you're ready," Julia said cryptically, beginning to hum to herself as she stirred the bubbling pot on the stove. "Now you come on over here and stir this so it doesn't burn; we're making lasagna today."

Julia was like that. She would dip one toe into the mysterious but that's all you got until she was ready to give you more. No matter how many times I asked her tell me more about these "gifts" she just smiled, gave me another kitchen task and said, "when the time is right; not today."

I learned how to make real Italian lasagna that day, but I yearned to know more about the strange and wonderful gift she seemed to have. I couldn't shake the feeling that maybe Julia was my answer after all.

~~~~

"Why can't they see it?" I said to my sister one afternoon a few weeks later. I was helping her pack her things in boxes. Dad had finally finished the renovation of our carport and Diana was wasting no time moving in to the new, spacious back bedroom. I would be moving into her old room, and dad would finally be able to claim my small bedroom as his home office. The boxes were heavy, but our parents were out at a volunteer function, so the task of moving fell to us. They seemed to spend a lot of time away from the house in those days.

"I don't know," she replied. "But Rick and I have seen stuff you don't even know about."

"What stuff?"

"You don't want to know," she said firmly, in a tone that I knew not to argue with.

"Maybe it only appears to kids."

"I'm not a kid," said my sister. "Hand me that scarf over there."

"I know," I said, my fingers lingering on the filmy material before she yanked it free of my hands. "But I've seen stuff too, you know."

"Yeah, I know. Look, I don't know why mom and dad can't see this stuff, or why it doesn't happen when they're around. Maybe it does and they just aren't telling us. Wouldn't be the first time they've kept things to themselves. Believe me, it frustrates me too."

156

"Yeah," I replied. "Do you think I should ask them about it?"

"Again? Do you really think this time will be any different from the last? You can do what you want, but don't expect any real answers," she said. "There! That's does it, now give me a hand with this dresser, would you? Then we can start moving your stuff."

Crazy

17

"I don't know what to think anymore," mom said. She and Dad were talking together in the kitchen over breakfast the next morning, and I froze in the act of coming down the hallway. Hardly daring to breathe, I listened carefully to what they said. I seemed to learn a lot more by listening in, and I knew I should feel guilty about all this eavesdropping, but considering the information I was gathering, I figured it was worth the risk.

"Just this morning when I was making breakfast, I could've sworn I caught a glimpse of a small child running past me through the kitchen doorway. I only just barely caught the edge of it, but …."

I caught my breath and held it, clamping both hands over my mouth to stifle the involuntary gasp that threatened to break free. Pressing the sleeve of my pajama shirt against my lips so I could breathe undetected, I stood, willing them to believe.

"Liz, it was probably the cat," dad answered. "That cat lives for reaction."

"Maybe, but …" my mom didn't sound too convinced "… what about the doors? You know I don't like it that they're swinging open on their own!"

"I'll get around to fixing them," he said. "Hinges wear out."

"Humph, hinges now? Okay. Well, as long as we're on the subject, there's something else that's bothering me."

"What is it now?" He answered, "Does this one end with me taking another trip to the hardware store?"

A long pause followed.

"Be serious, I'm getting scared okay? The day before yesterday, I was standing right here, facing the table when I felt a tugging at the hem of my skirt. You know, the way Ginny used to when she was small and wanted something. But when I turned around there was no one there. And I didn't just catch my skirt on something, Will. The edge of the table is smooth. There was nothing there."

Mom fell silent and I could hear dad clearing his throat several times.

"What do you want me to say? I don't have all the answers ... hell, I don't have any!"

"Look," mom began. "We're jumping at shadows around here and that's not good for any of us. I just want to figure this out, or ... be done with it!" I could hear the edge to her voice and I wondered suddenly whether she would cry or storm out the front door again.

"Be done?" he asked. "What do you mean? Sell? We've just finished renovating it!"

"Oh I don't know! I don't even know what I'm saying anymore. All I know is I can't take this much longer."

"I know honey, but let's not be hasty. The market's not good enough yet. We can't open that can of worms until there's no other choice. We're likely to have a fight on our hands with the youngest. You know how she feels about this place."

"All she loves is the pool. We can find that anywhere! It's for her own good."

"Elizabeth," he said, projecting an unspoken warning in his tone.

"I know, I know. Okay, we'll just wait and see, but honestly Will, I don't know how much more of this suspicion I can take. I mean, let's face it, there's something odd going on around here."

"We've gone over this," her husband replied.

"I know, I know, but look, we've lived here for how long? Months! And how many neighbours do we know? Just the sisters across the road, and now Julia, but that's it. Where are all the people? Don't get me wrong, Julia is sweet, and she's a good person and all , Lord knows I wouldn't let Ginny go over there so much if she wasn't, but I need *people*! You've always said I'm a city girl at heart. This place *still* doesn't feel like home to me."

"Give it time," dad said.

"Hah!" The sarcasm in her voice was evident.

"Alright, then let's introduce ourselves to the neighbours," he said.

"Oh yeah, and how do you propose we do that? These people are farmers. They keep to themselves. That's just the problem."

"Well, what can it hurt to ask them over?"

"What do you want me to do, throw a neighbourhood party?"

"Well, why not?"dad said.

"Wait. You're *serious*?"

Mom went silent for a few seconds, obviously pondering the idea. "Well, okay," she said at last. "I'll think about it. You may have something there." She didn't sound convinced, but I knew my mother loved parties. In twenty-four hours, she'd be in full swing.

~~~~~

My new room was a lot more cheerful, with its big, bright window and billowing white gauzy curtains. Little by little, I claimed the new space as my own. It was November, and the air outside was getting colder, so it made sense that there was a chill to the air in my room at night, didn't it? I was sure Diana would say it was no big deal. She'd probably say it had always been like that. Decisively, I listed off the reasons that the unexplained cold of my old room couldn't possibly be paranormal in nature. I wrote down my list with gusto in my battered orange duo-tang.

1. It was ridiculous. Reality had no room for ghosts.

2. Things like that only happened in movies—*Poltergeist* was coming out in the theatres soon. Great story but no basis in fact.

3. Any house with windows and doors was going to be a bit drafty from time to time.

4. People will think I'm crazy if I go around talking about this kind of stuff.

By the time I'd written down the whole list, I wasn't feeling that confident anymore. At the risk of sounding crazy, I decided to ask my sister about it. What could it hurt? She certainly wasn't going to rush right out and tell anyone.

"Have you ever noticed how cold it gets in that room at night?" I asked her, the next morning.

"Nope," she said. "It was always toasty for me. That must be you."

"Oh yeah, thanks," I replied drily. "I feel so much better."

"Hang on a sec, you're serious?" she asked, squinting at me.

"Yeah I'm serious. Seriously freezing." I rubbed my arms for emphasis. "Feel my hands." Diana reached out and grasped both my hands. Hers were deliciously warm.

"Whoah!" she said, her eyes betraying her concern even if her words did not. "Crazy!"

"That's what I thought you'd say," I told her, jerking my hands from her grasp and walking away. Chalk another one up for me and my failed experiments, I thought drily.

~~~~

"Yes, that's right ... at our house ... yup ... uh-huh ... oh, I don't know yet, I'll probably just serve sandwiches and finger food, you know, munchies." I heard Mom's side of the conversation as she stood stirring something at the counter, phone pressed up against her ear, the long spiral cord curling dangerously around her ankles as she shifted her stance back and forth. It sounded like she was talking about a party.

"Sure," she said into the phone. "Yup, it's just casual. You come as you are, all the neighbours are invited." She mouthed the words thank you to me as I unwound the cord from her restless legs and smiled. As I'd predicted, the party planner was in action. I wondered how long she'd been on the phone to get tangled up like that. Mom was a telephone wanderer. She couldn't seem to sit still when the phone receiver was pressed to her ear.

Sensing a massive re-organization and cleaning spree coming on at any moment, I shrugged into a windbreaker and went out the back door before I could be pressed into service.

~~~~

It was a crisp day in mid December when I made the short walk to Julia's. A dusting of snow covered the ground.

A tall man met me at the door as I entered.

"Who's this?" He growled.

I froze in my tracks. It had become customary for me to simply knock while entering, but until that day, the only person I'd encountered inside had been Julia. Now this great bear of a man faced me, his dark eyes boring into mine. I shrank under his gaze.

"Oh Ginny!" Julia sang out from behind the man. "Come on in. Paul, step aside. This is our neighbour, Ginny. She's come to help me with the baking for the party on Saturday."

Paul thrust out his bushy black beard at me and squinted. "Liz and Will's daughter?" His pronounced lisp seemed out of place for someone so huge.

"Yes, that's right, now move aside, you great, burly man! We've got women's work to do and you're in the way." Good naturedly she slapped his shoulder and the huge man moved sideways to allow me entry into the home.

"Uh He-hello," I said to him, keenly aware that manners mattered, especially in a situation like this. "Nice to meet you."

"Humph, Ginny is it?"

"Yes."

"Well, get in here, then. I'm not heating the outside. Next time you'd better knock."

"Yes sir."

Paul grinned unexpectedly. His face took on a foolish cast; his wide grin showed he was missing his left canine. "Sir," he commented. "I like that. You can call me that any day. You're okay kid."

I wasn't sure what to think. I was certainly on my guard when it came to Paul. He was a very unpredictable man.

The Party

18

"You don't get it!" I muttered to myself, my tone argumentative, as I carefully dried and put away the evening dishes. "Stop!"

"Stop what?" Diana asked her hands busy in the sink full of soapy water. "If I stop, this isn't getting done."

"I'm not talking to you, just thinking out loud."

"Weird-o," Diana responded.

I'd spoken the words aloud as they formed in my mind. I often did this when I was alone. It was the only way to interrupt the endless repetition that I assumed was the plague of creative people everywhere. Diana only shook her head and glanced sideways at me, continuing to move the washcloth rhythmically around in circles over the dirty plate. Sure, I knew it bothered her, but she'd survive.

"It can't be helped," I continued, my mind only half registering the mundane task at hand. "Perhaps it will play out." The tea towel looked odd in my hands as I stood gazing down at it. A flutter of words filled my head and I shook it in a vain attempt to slow them down.

"Slow down, slow down," I muttered. "It's too much."

"And you're not talking to me at all, right?" Diana said, her voice cut through the clamor sharply, and I smiled at her with relief.

"Nope," I replied, grinning suddenly. "But thanks."

"What's wrong with you … *really*?" My sister said her tone heavily sarcastic.

"Nothing. It's just pretend, don't get so worked up."

"Yeah, well, shut up and finish the dishes, you're creeping me out."

"You could stop listening," I offered.

Diana faced me, her face becoming pinker by the second. She advanced on me, her dishrag all but forgotten in one clenched fist. I felt my eyes go wide. Maybe I'd gone too far this time.

With a swiftness that shocked me, mom strode into the room, her eyes dangerous. "Ginny, stop torturing your sister. Keep it to yourself for a change!" And to my sister, she said, "Diana, you're older, I expect more of you." She faced us both. "Enough said? It's almost Christmas and here you are at each other's throats."

Diana turned her back on me and muttered something under her breath.

"Ooh, you girls," mom sighed as she rubbed her temples and walked slowly back the way she'd come.

~~~~

"Sure, it'll be great to see you. William will be thrilled! Oh no, I can't possibly surprise him; you know how he is. Gotta know everything … uh-huh, yeah. No, he certainly hasn't changed with the years. But you do realize that he's going to show off the renovations, don't you? He's quite proud, and I have to admit, it does give us a lot more room."

Mom was talking on the phone about our upcoming party. What had started out as a simple neighbour-meet-neighbour get-together had grown in to an impromptu birthday party for my shy father.

"Oh yes I can hardly wait to see you too. It's going to be fabulous!" she said enthusiastically. "We'll have family, friends and neighbours. It'll be a house full!"

Just the way she liked it, I thought, gloomily. Dad was certain to be showing off the house. I could hear it all now: "Well now, most people would have hired someone…"

I'd heard the story before, but I did have to admit, it was great seeing dad so happy. My smile faded as I wondered how all those people would react when the weirdness that was our life began to intrude on mom's carefully planned celebration.

The day of the party, it looked anything but festive. The black winter pool cover now had a thin blanket of snow and ice on its surface, and it was still lightly snowing.

I'd been staring out at the flakes, enjoying the sight of the softly drifting snow, when I heard mom come through the doorway.

"Come and help me move the kitchen table will you?" She asked. "And then, let's drape it with this fancy tablecloth."

Dutifully, I helped her maneuver it into place. Wordlessly, she then handed me a corner of the white lace creation, which we spread across the imitation oak. She stood back, smiling, to admire our handiwork.

"Dinner will be served buffet-style, I think," mom said thoughtfully, touching fingertips to chin and continuing to murmur, as she reached out for my hand, lest I stray. "I'm glad I planned for that. A sit-down dinner for that many people would be ridiculous."

"Mm-hmm," I agreed, wondering how many other chores she was going to volunteer me for and precisely how large this guest list had become.

Mom continued to stare at the empty table, frowning slightly. "Pastor's coming," she announced suddenly.

"What? Who?" I answered, startled.

"Pastor Frank."

"Oh," I tried not to sound as rattled as I sounded. "That's nice."

"Yes, I hope so," mom said mysteriously, thrusting a piece of paper into my hand and casting a quick look at me before turning to hurry away, muttering something about napkins.

Great, I thought, looking down at my own hand and the list of chores printed in block letters on the crisp white paper.

With my volunteer list in hand, I skulked through the house with eyes narrowed, waiting for something weird to happen. My day was starting out badly enough, I reasoned. But as the minutes ticked past and I dutifully swept floors and dusted surfaces, wiped away fingerprints and cleaned mirrors, our house was just that: a house. The clock on the kitchen wall, an Alpine knock-off, chimed five times.

"Five o'clock already?" Mom's anguished cry carried through the house. "Ginny, how's that list? Have you fed the horses yet?"

Mom appeared briefly in the dining room before hurrying away. "I still have so much to do!" she cried, the crisp 'snick, snick, snick' of her slippers receding back into the kitchen.

"Well it's show time once again," I muttered, pulling on my cowboy boots and flinging open the back door.

A few minutes later I swung wide the barn door on its long, metal track. "At least the lights work." The fluorescent glow of the ceiling fixtures bathed the deserted barn in eerie white; it seeming to bleach the colour out of the new wood that covered surfaces here and there. Even the hay looked somehow colourless as I heaved great chunks of it into the horse's stalls. By the time I opened the other end of the barn to let Koko and Charlie back in, I was seriously suspicious.

Something was different.

What was it waiting for? No shudder rippled along my backbone. Not one goose bump stood out on my arms. Now, when we were sure to have more eyes than just mine to validate my claims, the world of the paranormal had gone quiet.

"Figures," I muttered as I slid the lock home on Koko's stall. "Nighty-night Koke."

It seemed like my barn boots were barely back in the closet before the doorbell started ringing. The party guests had arrived.

"Ginny, put the coats on my bed," mom told me, handing me an enormous pile of wool and faux suede as I tried to sneak past. Mom's face was smiling, but there were lines of tension around her mouth and her eyes darted from side to side as she stood there.

She looked tired. And worried. She too, was waiting for something in explicable to put in an appearance.

As the night wore on and the food kept coming, I was amazed at the grown-ups that ambled past me. They made silly faces at each other, and said things that didn't quite make sense.

And these people were supposed to notice a little paranormal activity? Fat chance, I thought, relaxing a little.

Giggling suddenly erupted from under the edge of the lace tablecloth and I jumped sideways. Peeking out from under the kitchen table was a woman with bright red hair and slightly unfocused eyes. She giggled again and lurched to her feet.

"Dropped my napkin," she said.

"Uh … right," I answered, as though her statement had made perfect sense.

I smiled pleasantly at her as she wobbled past. In the other room, dad was serving homemade wine from his leather-upholstered bar.

"Hey Lizzy, you got your party house!" a man's voice that sounded like my dad announced, from the other room. As he swaggered through the kitchen with a party hat on sideways, I was startled to see that it *was* my dad. Obviously, he was blowing off some steam. Lizzy? No one called mom that.

I saw her stiffen, but she lifted her wine glass in a toast and laughed anyways. "And you finally got your farm, *Billy*!"

Touché.

"You bet," he grinned. "Hide the car keys from Pedro! I might want to go for a spin later."

Mom's smile disappeared in an instant and she stiffened.

"Who's Pedro?" somebody asked.

"No one," mom answered tersely. "He's drunk."

Nervous laughter followed the remark but dad didn't seem to notice.

As sometimes happens at parties, there comes a time when the noise level dies down and people become thoughtful and quiet. But my Mom, ever the hostess, seemed to know exactly what to do. She sent me out into the living room with cups and an announcement of freshly brewed coffee. People were strewn everywhere, on sofas, chairs, low tables, crowded into the conversation pit, and even just sitting cross-legged on the shag carpeting. They cradled coffee mugs and highball glasses in their hands, complimenting my mother on her sweet cakes, her cookies and even her strong coffee.

I circulated through it all, armed with napkins, extra spoons and dessert forks. I felt like a waiter, minus the tips, but at least I could eavesdrop without shame.

Most of the guests had formed small groups and were deep in conversation, their tones too hushed for the casual ear. Those that didn't stop speaking when I came in sight merely grinned at me and helped themselves to the things I offered. The conversations I'd overheard so far had been decidedly boring.

Dad and our shy neighbour Julia were seated together on a couch in the living room, their heads bent together in earnest conversation. There was no sign of Paul. She didn't like talking about herself usually, but she did enjoy homemade wine, and dad was a very proud amateur vintner. His prized wines were arranged in crystal decanters on a silver tray, each one hand-labeled with little folded place cards.

After the first decanter ran dry, Julia revealed a side of her that she'd only ever hinted at before. I remember being awe-struck and more than a little dubious.

"All the girls in my family are sensitives," she commented as she seized the hand of a woman next to her.

"You're looking for a man," she said. Her eyes took on a far-away look as she continued to hold the woman's hand. It was one of our furthest neighbours, a petite woman named Anne, who loved every second of this unexpected entertainment.

"Isn't every single woman?" She giggled, her heavy English accent lending her speech a musical quality. Others sitting near her joined in on the joke, but Julia's voice grew harsh.

"He's wearing a cashmere overcoat. His name is … t-t …'t' something … I can't make out the name."

The laughter died down in a rush and all heads turned.

"… ooh, he's handsome. Tall. A snappy dresser. Gorgeous blue eyes." She patted Ann's hand again but still held firm. "You lucky girl, he's quite a catch isn't he? But he's far away, I think. Across water." She touched her temple with her free hand, continuing to stare off over Anne's shoulder as though lost in her own thoughts. "Who is he talking to? " Julia narrowed her eyes for a moment, then seemed to re-focus on the woman in front of her all of a sudden. "Sorry, that threw me for a moment, she looks a lot like you, doesn't she?"

"I'm sorry?" Anne seemed perplexed.

"Your sister?" Julia turned to Anne with new excitement. "He's talking with your sister, isn't he? They're both planning to come here." The authoritative way she said it made me draw in a quick breath.

"Cooh!" Anne exclaimed, clasping Julia's hands excitedly. "It's Tom, it has to be! Look!" Excitedly, she rushed to the foyer and pawed through the shoes and handbags until she found what she was looking for. Drawing a black leather wallet from her handbag, she removed two photos from it and passed them to Julia.

"Yes," she said simply.

The photos were passed around.

When it came to me, I seized them excitedly and blinked in surprise. Julia's description had been so accurate, it was like she'd been looking at the photos in my hand.

But she hadn't.

One photo depicted a woman who resembled Anne very closely.

"That's my sister, Mayra," Anne said, leaning over my shoulder.

The other photo showed a smiling, tall gentleman with piercingly blue eyes.

"That's Tom" she told me affectionately.

"Nice parlour trick!" A man in a three-piece dark grey suit ambled over to Julia and shot out his manicured hand. He was one of dad's long-time work friends. The woman took his proffered hand, and held onto it, gently turning it over, eyes half-closed. "Oh," she said, her eyes widening slightly. "Well, I …." She stopped and looked at the man carefully. "You already know what I'm going to say, don't you?" The man merely looked at her, and the smile left his face. He withdrew his hand with a snort and walked back to the table where my father stood pouring drinks. "Better load me up again, Will."

Julia's watchful stare turned into an apologetic laugh.

"Ta-da," she said, sarcastically. "Hidden talent." The usually shy woman hoisted a half-full glass of deep red wine to her lips and drank thirstily, as she avoided the puzzled stares of the other guests.

"Well I think it's fabulous the way you did that," another voice cut through the stillness. Curling up at Julia's feet and looking up eagerly at her was the woman I'd recognized earlier under the table. "C'mon Margie, come join us." She beckoned to another dark-haired woman, who came over and seated herself close by. In seconds, the three women were deep in conversation and the decanter was rapidly emptying. I closed in to hear more. This was decidedly not boring.

Mom chose that moment, however, to call out: "More napkins."

Rats!

A few moments later, just as I was placing another tray of baked tarts on the table, Julia looked up and leaned suggestively towards Pastor Smith. Having definitely consumed too much wine, she was no longer shy and withdrawn. Pastor looked around, his eyes mutely asking for help as Julia tried to maintain her balance and failed.

The heavy-set woman knocked into him, and Pastor gingerly pushed her back into her chair.

"Oh, I remember the first time," she said, nodding at him owlishly. "My father wouldn't have any of it." She wagged her forefinger back and forth like a disapproving parent. Pastor Smith, for his part, just sat there, nodding agreeably. "He understood, of course," she continued. "But he would never talk about it." She chuckled softly, and her eyes shone. "Mama used to say, 'that girl's got *ssssight'*. That meant you knew things." Her words were slightly slurred, but I got the feeling that Julia was about to reveal something significant. I saw some of the other guests looking at her with a mingling of confusion, interest and humour.

"People know more about that sort of thing now than when I was a girl." She seemed to be addressing a growing crowd. Edging closer, I could see I wasn't the only one captivated. Julia leaned her head back and smiled. "Now I just find water for people. Water Witch they call me!" She laughed so deeply that she began to snort. "Oops! Pardon me! But you know, there's truth in those words too, I suppose. But when there's no

169

water, there's no water! I get blamed for damned near everything!" Julia twitched suddenly and covered her mouth. "Oops, sorry Pastor," she apologized. "I think it's the wine."

"Yes, probably," Pastor agreed.

Water Witch? I was puzzled.

The Hendersons, mom and dad's "proper" friends, shook their heads and smiled indulgently. Pastor seemed to be looking for an escape route, but I was fascinated, mostly because this was the first person I'd ever seen talking openly about ghosts and psychics. Wasn't she?

Now, as I watched this strange woman try not to fall on our Pastor, I smiled eagerly. This party was heating up!

"Julia's pickled, isn't she?" I asked Mom. Putting a hand over her open mouth to contain her laughter, mom led me away to the kitchen for more cups. As I left the room, a mingling of laughter and loud comments drowned out what was being said. Reluctantly, I took down more cups from the kitchen cupboard, spying Diana and some of my cousins in the recreation room, shooting pool as I went. "How come they weren't being used as servants?" I thought bitterly.

But even as the thought formed in my head, I smiled at them knowing not one of them would appreciate the stuff these adults were talking about. I didn't waste time catching anyone's eye. This was way more exciting than an ordinary game of pool. I fairly bolted back across the linoleum, cups clenched in one hand, eager to hear more.

I could see that some of the guests were turned away, but their faces told me they were still listening. Others spoke in whispers behind their hands.

Julia, obviously very relaxed, was standing by the time I returned, leaning heavily against the wall by the fireplace. In a voice that sounded tired, she was telling a ghost story.

"Of course, my father couldn't see the, ahem, *gentleman* already seated in the chair and he sat right down on top of him!" She laughed and the guests laughed with her. "And you'll never guess what he said."

"Tell us," a woman next to her prompted.

Julia smiled. "My Dad stood up and said: Why is it so cold in here?"

Polite laughter interspersed with a few warm chuckles filled the room. My parent's guests obviously weren't believers.

It was Julia's next statement, however, that caused everyone in the room to stop what they were doing and stare. Someone dropped a teaspoon onto a saucer and it clattered in the sudden silence.

"Of course you know this house is quite haunted." The words were proclaimed in great ringing tones. Then, her legs seemed to buckle and Julia pitched forward in a dead faint, to land, unceremoniously, across a very startled Pastor Smith.

The clergyman managed to lever himself into a more dignified position, and started gesturing for help. Soon, the buxom woman was being gently carried from the room.

"Uh, William, about that wine of yours. Maybe a bit too powerful?" Pastor's voice was hesitant. Dad managed to blush as he helped my uncle relocate Julia to the adjoining room.

"Ah, no harm done," he said. But despite his cheery comments, it was only a short time before he made his exit. He was naturally followed by a handful of other party-goers, also parishioners, most of them proclaiming the lateness of the hour and yawning.

Was 11 p.m. late? For a ten-year-old, sure, but for grown-ups?

Our guests dribbled out the front door, some still chuckling to themselves. Julia had since awakened from her fainting spell and sat on a kitchen chair, while mom plied her with black coffee.

"Good party you guys," said my Uncle Ted. "We'd better get back to the babysitter. Take care of yourselves."

"See you soon, baby brother," said Aunt Phyllis. "Great party!"

Uncle Jim was red in the face from laughing as he pumped dad's hand. "You sure know how to liven things up, don't ya? You can't pay for entertainment like that!"

"Oh Jim," his wife said, dragging him out the door.

Dad's friend Bill, a northern Englishman, clapped dad on the back and laughed heartily as he shook his hand. "You ought to put a warning label on that homemade hooch of yours! Ha-ha!"

The Hendersons were the next to leave, and they did so quietly and with as much dignity as they could manage, which was the same way they did everything. The man and his wife were reserved, upper class types, very interested in politics and I didn't much like them. Mom looked embarrassed as she handed them their coats in the foyer.

"Dora, Fred, so happy you could come," she told them. "Thank you."

They smiled at mom and dad. "Thank you for the invitation," Dora said. "It was, er ...." she seemed at a loss for words.

"Unforgettable," her husband finished.

After the last guest filed through the front door, mom returned to the kitchen and to the recovered but still shaken Julia.

"Well, I don't think I've ever seen a house empty so fast," dad commented, hands on his hips.

"Julia, should we call your son to come and get you? Or perhaps I can walk you home?"

"No, no dear. I'll be fine," she said. "I can't think how that happened. I'm so embarrassed. I fell on him, you say?"

"Well, it's not like you did it on purpose," dad assured her. "Your legs just seemed to give way. Pastor was quite understanding about it, I assure you."

"Well, none-the-less I shall be especially attentive during service on Sunday. The poor man." Julia seemed to think about that a moment, and then with a small sigh she continued. "Paul will be back by now. If you would just give him a telephone call, and tell him I'm on my way."

"Oh no. Ginny will walk you home." Having registered the obvious hint, I left the room at a jog to gather my shoes and coat. Maybe she'd say something more when we were alone.

"Oh, William, how kind," she responded, smiling at my father and dusting a few stray cookie crumbs from her black skirt, while patting her hair into place. "If I could just get my coat?"

Mom hurried to take care of the request. "Will, where's Julia's coat?" I heard her call out from the bedroom. Dad joined her with an apologetic smile, leaving Julia and I alone in the foyer.

I leaned forward without delay, but Julia beat me to the question.

"Did you learn anything?" she asked.

"I—uh, what?"

"Did I say anything, just before the, er incident? I saw you listening tonight," she answered me with a gleam in her eye. "So my question is natural enough. Did you learn anything?"

"Um," I replied, thinking fast as I heard my parents returning to the kitchen. "Yes. I think so."

"Good, very good," the older woman responded. "Come and see me, I think we have much to discuss."

Startled, all I could do was blink at her, as she shrugged into her coat that my father held for her. Julia carefully buttoned it up tight.

"I feel so much better now, I'll manage from here." She held up her hand to forestall any objections. "Now, you've done enough. I'm quite all right. Thank you for your generous hospitality, William, Elizabeth," she said. "Perhaps next time I shall stick to coffee!" My mother and Julia laughed nervously together and briefly embraced.

Dad intervened, his expression stern. "Now Julia, there are pot holes all up and down these driveways. You could turn an ankle. Ginny is quite prepared to take you—"

"William, you worry too much." Julia's tone was friendly, but firm. "Thank you for your concern, but I'm not in my dotage yet." She smiled at all of us, her gaze resting on me for a moment longer, before she turned and went out the front door, as composed as ever.

My parents stared after her in amazement while I tried hard to hide my smile.

Possessed

19

"Mom, do you ever hear voices in your head?" I asked one morning a few days later when we settled into the car together. We were going to do some Christmas shopping at the local shopping mall.

Mom's eyes flew open in shock and her hands, instead of starting the car and putting it into drive, slid from the steering wheel to fall into her lap. I immediately realized I'd said the wrong thing.

"No, no," I corrected myself hurriedly. "Not like that. Like, well, I don't know, like people talking, but a long way off. Like you can only hear some of the words, and not very clearly?"

Mom continued to stare straight ahead as I stumbled my way through the awkward description.

"This is happening to you?" she asked, without looking at me.

"Uhh," I stopped. This really wasn't a good idea, but it was too late.

"Well," she said, looking thoughtfully at the headliner of the car, the fingertips of one hand pressed to her chin. "Maybe I do."

It was my turn to be shocked. "You do?" *Halleluiah*! I wasn't crazy after all.

"Sure," she said, turning in her seat to face me at last. "Your subconscious is telling you things."

I squinted at her. Subconscious?

"Daddy always says that he doesn't know how I keep all the details straight with everybody's schedule, but that's my subconscious. It's just helping me out." She smiled at me and nodded her head in affirmation. "You just have to learn to trust it, that's all."

Rats! This wasn't the same thing at all.

I must have been frowning, because mom reached out and gave me a spontaneous hug.

"Makes sense, right?" she said.

"Sure," I answered, feeling more bewildered than ever.

~~~~

The disjointed pieces of dialogue that seemed to float through my head constantly, was something I'd begun to accept, so it came as a surprise when I heard Diana talking to my mom about it.

Diana's raised protests piqued my interest.

"I mean, it's bad enough she goes around talking to herself all the time, spending hours in front of any mirror in the house, now she has to do it in her sleep too? That's the last time I'm babysitting, mom, I mean it."

Mom muttered something I couldn't hear. I crept closer, my bare feet making almost no sound in the plush carpeting.

"...and then up she pops, like she's wide awake and says a bunch of crazy stuff I couldn't understand. Rick and I were freaking out! Rick said she was probably just teasing us, you know, trying to play a joke or something. So we checked her over to see if she was faking, but her eyes were closed and she *looked* asleep, only strange words were pouring out of her mouth! It sounded like Spanish. She doesn't know any Spanish, does she? I realize people talk in their sleep, but this was creepy! It scared us half to death! When you said we had to babysit you didn't warn me about that."

"How could I have warned you? I didn't know," mom said, her tone was soft and wondering. "Spanish you say?"

"I think so. It sounded kinda like that. A friend of mine at school speaks Spanish, and this sounded the same, but if she was dreaming, that was one intense dream!" Diana sounded scared. "What's going on with her Mom?"

"What happened right after that?" mom asked.

"Nothing. She turned her head as though to look at us, but her eyes were still closed. She said something but I couldn't tell what, and then she fell backwards, as quickly as she'd sat up. I rushed back over to her, but she was sound asleep."

"Definitely odd."

"Yeah, you're not kidding. Creepy."

"Don't say that," mom warned.

Diana babysat for several families in our neighbourhood, but I knew instinctively that she was talking about me. For the past several nights, the voices in my dreams had been louder. Although I hadn't realized they were speaking in Spanish, it wasn't impossible for me to have mumbled something back to them. I often got lost in my dreams, the conversations sometimes seemed more real to me than the ones I had when I was awake.

The implications, however, were the farthest thing from my mind, which was why my sister's next sentence came as such a shock.

"Mom, do you think it's possible that Ginny is, well..."

No!" Mom's response came out like a gunshot and I jumped. "Absolutely not. That's ridiculous. I won't hear it."

"You don't know what I was going to say," Diana said defensively.

"You would do well not to say any of this. Not to anyone."

"Okay, forget I said anything."

"I certainly will," she said. "You're misinterpreting a bad dream, that's all. Ginny's fine."

Tears slid down my cheeks as I backed down the hallway to my room.

What was going on?

Possessed.

I knew that was the word Diana had been about to say. She'd been saying it for months.

~~~~~

Somehow, I began detecting changes in the *feeling* of a room. Upon entering the kitchen, I often paused, testing the air around me. It sounds silly now, but I could sense it in the air. It was like an electrical charge, a science experiment. And it seemed to happen most often in the kitchen.

One Friday afternoon when I returned home from school, anxious to turn on the T.V. and watch my favourite Scooby Doo cartoon, I felt the environment shifting as I crossed the room. The change hit me like a wall, and I sped up instinctively, covering the last few steps to the rec room at a run. Whirling around, I stared hard at the empty kitchen, its wooden table and chairs innocently arranged on the thick, braided rug. My heart thudded wildly as I scanned the room for anything different.

Just because it was empty, didn't mean nothing was there.

I took a step back, noticing all at once that it was unusual for all of the cupboard doors to be standing open.

I was only a kid, however, and Scooby-Doo would be starting any moment. Rolling my shoulders to shake off the strange feeling, I continued back into the rec room. Kitchen cupboards just weren't that important to me. I switched on the T.V. set and flopped down on the couch.

Dimly, I heard the front door slam and knew my sister was home. Mom and dad were at work and wouldn't be home for hours.

Diana's arrival, however, was coupled with a resounding wooden crash and an ear-piercing scream!

I sat, frozen, heart pounding, before my feet caught up with my head and I ran back to the kitchen to find my sister, her face white with shock, both hands pressed firmly over her ears.

"Go ahead, tell me *that* was nothing," she yelled, pointing at the closed cupboard doors. "Something in this house hates me!" She turned suddenly and bolted down the hall.

I wanted someone to explain what was going on, but who? My parents didn't want to talk about it, and my sister already had experiences of her own that she wouldn't share.

I hastened to follow her down the hall, only just rounding the last corner as she slammed her door and locked it. "Diana, what do you mean something hates you?" I asked her, speaking to her from the other side of her door.

"You don't want to know," she said to me, her voice barely audible through the wooden door. "You really don't."

"Come on Diana," I wheedled.

She opened her door to face me directly Red hair fanned out across her shoulders but it was her eyes that held my attention. They were frightened and on the verge of tears.

"I already told you I do not want to talk about it." Her careful enunciation was slow and deliberate so there would be no chance of a misunderstanding. "You think mom and dad are suddenly going to let us do … what? Move away? Talk to ghosts? This is 1979. People don't believe in this crap! Do you know what would really happen if we tell them our house is haunted?" She stood there, staring at me. I stared back, wondering if she really wanted a reply.

"They'd call us crazy," I said, my voice small.

"Exactly."

"I just want everything to be okay," I told her.

"Then keep your mouth shut," she said firmly. "It'll be okay when this is behind us." She took me into her arms unexpectedly and gave me a fierce hug. "You're so naive, you know that?"

Premonition

20

I wanted to tell Diana about my strange dreams, but in light of our conversation the day before, I knew it wasn't a good idea.

She wasn't going to believe me any more now than she had before. Besides, I already knew what she'd say. She'd shake her head and tell me that it was my subconscious mind at work

Whether it was real or a dream, nothing made sense anyway.

Even worse, my family was acting so maddeningly normal!

I understand now, what they were doing. I know now that the seemingly normal behaviour of my family was a coping mechanism. A way of tolerating an intolerable situation. I wish I'd realized this when I was a kid. I might have had an easier time.

But back then, I only saw my family turning away, not listening, and not believing. It made me so mad, I often cried myself to sleep at night, pretending the tears were for another reason. Secretly I held onto the hope that one day mom or dad would stop putting one foot in front of the other, stop going to work, volunteering for 4-H and doing chores. I wanted them to look me in the eye just once and say "yes", "we know", "we believe you."

Diana didn't spend much time at the house. She worked for a plant nursery down the road during the week and spent the rest of her time with her boyfriend or driving around in her car.

I guess all of us were pretending to be normal.

"Mom, do you think Heaven is a place?"

She turned to look at me sharply, and then returned her eyes to the road before answering. "I think, um, Heaven is real. But not a place like we would think of," she said.

"Oh," I said. "So you don't think it's a physical place ... up there somewhere?" I looked at the sky.

"No," she said. "If it were up there, explorers would have found it already, wouldn't they?" She looked at me out of the corner of her eye as she spoke. My gaze was riveted on her profile. I knew we were getting close to the subject she avoided, and I was determined to be careful.

"What about Purgatory," I asked. "If Heaven's not a physical place, then neither is purgatory, right? But we believe that our souls will go there anyways."

"Yes," she said. "Go on."

"So do you think people in Purgatory can reach back? Like maybe ... asking for help?" I was trying to remember what I'd learned in Catechism classes and how the situation with Bobby's spirit would fit in with that.

"Oh," she said, sounding startled. "Well, it's an interesting thought, I suppose. I guess I would like to believe that someone could ask for help if they needed it, even in Purgatory, but Ginny, what's brought all this on? We're preparing for Christmas, not a funeral."

"Nothing," I said. "I was just curious."

"I see. The things you come up with," mom said, shaking her head. "I swear...."

~~~~

"No one believes me; they all think I'm making it up. Even now. But then again, even I don't know if I believe me anymore," I spoke into the semi-darkness of my room. I looked searchingly at the large mirror that reflected half of my bedroom back at me, wanting so desperately to see something.

"I still don't understand how can you come here and roll down hills, climb fences and skip rocks if you're just a ghost. I mean, aren't you supposed to be like ... mist or something? But then I'm the only one who can see you, so I guess ...." I broke off and raked both hands through my hair, regarding my reflection critically.

Crazy.

"Geez," I whispered, picking up the thread of the odd, one-sided discussion once more. "They can't believe, or maybe they just won't.

Either way, I'm the only one who knows you're really here. When you're knocking around in the kitchen at night, they won't admit it's you, even though I know it. And when I'm sitting in here talking to you, they just roll their eyes and say 'imaginary friend', even though nobody really believes that tired old story anymore. Not since the photograph." I jumped off my bed and opened my door a crack to make sure my sister wasn't listening in again.

Good. No one there.

"But what really gets me," I continued as I returned to my bed, "is that dark man. He scares me." I closed my eyes, hoping to patch up my scattered thoughts. "Whatever," I muttered. "Maybe Diana's right and I *am* cracked in the head."

That night, I didn't sleep well. I lay in bed waiting to fall asleep, but for some reason, sleep didn't come. At first, I thought it might have been because of something I ate, but my tummy felt fine.

As I lay there, listening to the quiet, all I heard was the distant sound of our Grandfather clock ticking away in the front hall. The silence was unnerving.

That was it! Suddenly I realized why I couldn't sleep and the thought made me laugh out loud. All these months listening to the sounds of a ghostly kitchen helper that rattled pots and pans, clinked glasses and sometimes even turned on the kitchen faucet had me conditioned. Even though I should have felt secure, the silence had me off-balance, like a city person moving away to the country. It was all the sounds that should have been there, and weren't. It was a long time before I slept.

When I got up the next morning, I realized three things right away. One was that I'd had a poor night's rest, two was that my room was undeniably warm and three, my kitten Timothy was curled up at the foot of my bed, tucked into my discarded quilt, where I'd obviously pushed it during the night. I smiled affectionately at him and stroked his fur.

"It's nice to share my bed with you," I said to him. Timothy stretched languidly and his mouth opened in a huge yawn.

"I know how to feel buddy," I said, swinging my legs out of bed. The unexpected warmth was like a Christmas present, as the usual temperature mimicked a frosty winter day. I wiggled my toes happily. I was warm … so deliciously warm. I rose languidly from the bed and stretched. Was I feverish? I didn't think so. Although I was sandy-eyed and groggy, I didn't feel sick, but I passed a hand over my cool forehead just to be sure.

When I entered the kitchen that morning, I passed by the mudroom door twice, backing up and trying again when the thing just sat there, half open, the way doors are supposed to.

I smiled at the strangeness of normalcy. "I could get used to this!" I commented, humming a Christmas carol happily.

"Hi there, sweetie!" mom said, rounding the corner from the rec room with an extra swing in her step. "Beautiful day, huh? Six sleeps 'til Christmas!"

Was it possible that mom felt it too? There was a definite change in the air.

As we wrapped gifts and baked cookies, it seemed that as quickly as it had started, the paranormal activity was gone. At first, I worried that it was only a sign of worse things to come, but as the days went by, I started to relax, feeling braver and more confident. My room was warm, even a bit hot. My parents and sister noticed it too. I noticed that they lingered in doorways and stared, their expressions perplexed as the doors remained closed; tilting their heads with wonder at the lights that stayed lit. They walked through the quiet, comfortable house with increasing confidence and still, no one said a word about it.

Four days had gone by, and *normal* was feeling pretty good. I'd even stopped complaining about my barn chores, unable to sense that dark, forbidding presence in the barn.

It was two days before Christmas Eve and I was spoiling my pony with some sugar lumps. He nibbled at the sugar half-heartedly, as though he really wanted a carrot and was settling for second-best. I shook my head.

"What a character you are!" I told him, ruffling his mane.

Charlie stood crossways in the center of the barn, his halter tied to a lead rope, while I worked the curry-comb diligently through his shaggy coat, determined to "shine him up" for the holidays. Both horses had developed their winter coats from being outside in the cooler weather. I sighed to myself. It felt warm and...nice. There was just Charlie and me, with a crisp coldness in the air outside, promising snow, and Jingle Bell Rock on the radio.

I was working on a particularly nasty knot in my pony's mane when, inexplicably a lone tear escaped my eye and rolled clumsily down my cheek. It surprised me, that tear. Hadn't I just been humming along to the music?

A second later, out of the corner of my eye, I saw a black shadow dart to my left. In the same instant, overwhelming emotion engulfed me, like a massive wave. I felt a sudden, crushing depression pull me down with a physical weight and my knees began to buckle.

Obviously, it wasn't gone after all. The thought weighed me down further.

"What's going on in here?" Mom's voice floated into the barn a second before she appeared at the open doorway. "Ginny? For heaven's sake, get up off that filthy floor!" She rushed to me and helped me back to my feet, noting my lack of energy with concern. Strange. I didn't remember falling.

"Are you alright? Look at me."

"Mom?" I replied weakly. "What happened?"

"You tell me," she said, looking around with concern. "I just came in and found you on the floor. Did you fall?"

"I don't think so, I feel so … strange."

"Well, you don't look good. I'm taking you back to the house. You're probably coming down with something. You can finish Charlie's grooming tomorrow. You just sit here while I put him back in the paddock."

I sat on the bottom step of the loft stairs as mom unhooked the ropes and led Charlie away, patting his tossing head with her free hand. I eased my hands onto both of my knees. It was all I could do to stay upright. It was like I'd suddenly run a marathon and the muscles in my legs simply wouldn't respond. Heaviness had settled in my chest making it difficult to breathe. I coughed once and felt my head swim with sudden vertigo and a fierce headache.

"Mom …" I cried out, my voice weak.

"I'm here," she reassured me, sliding one hand around the small of my back and moving my arm up over her shoulder. "Let's get you tucked into bed. You'd better be okay by tomorrow!"

I wasn't aware of anything else until my eyelids fluttered open once more, and blearily, I turned my head to read the digital numbers on my clock radio. It read 3:45. I was tucked into bed. Apparently, I'd fallen asleep … or had I collapsed? I'd only been asleep for an hour, but it felt longer. I got up and walked through the house, realizing at once that the weight on my chest was gone and with it, that sudden, crushing sadness that had driven me to my knees. There was no sign of the exhaustion that had plagued me only an hour earlier. What did it all mean?

One thing was certain, the physical sensation I'd experienced wasn't normal. My brief respite from the madness that engulfed my life was gone. I should've known it would stay banished.

"Oh!" mom said, rounding a corner and nearly running right into me. "You're up. Are you feeling better? You look better."

"I feel fine," I said. "Perfectly normal." I hope Mom didn't comment on the heavy sarcasm I couldn't keep out of my voice. "What happened anyway?"

"I haven't a clue. But whatever it was, it seems to be gone now. If you're sure you're alright, how about helping me with the Dobos Torte?"

Chocolate has a way of re-setting my brain like nothing else.

I licked my lips in anticipation and went to wash my hands quickly. I didn't have to be asked twice to help make my favourite dessert. My Hungarian mother only made that 7 layer chocolate cake once every year. Christmas was special for a lot of reasons but that cake was and still is my best holiday memory.

Christmas has a way of making people forget things they'd rather not think about.

I was good at that, I supposed, in my own way. I was proof that if a person tried hard enough, they could forget anything.

For a while.

Christmas 1979

21

It was Christmas time in the country, which was infinitely better than the traffic clogged cities.

Christmas Day was the most welcome distraction ever and I looked forward to it with eager anticipation as we completed the last preparations. The house was festooned with red and green ribbons, a red velvet-backed wall hanging spelled out "Merry Christmas" in large *papier mâché* letters hung vertically on the wall in the foyer, greeting all who came in. Mom had her apron firmly tied behind her back as she removed yet another batch of shortbread cookies from the oven. The smell was heavenly.

Dad strolled in through the laundry room door and plugged in the strand of lights strung across the top of Mom's hutch. I looked at him in surprise.

"What," he answered. "It's December 23rd. We can turn these on *now*. Lights are festive."

I chuckled and shook my head at him. *Oh Dad.*

Our house was filled with Christmas carols, and as a child, I loved every minute of it. Rosemary Clooney and Bing Crosby made the holidays bright for all of us, and when the music suddenly and inexplicably cut out, dad simply sighed and went back into the living room to press the power button on the stereo again. It was proof that we'd grown so accustomed to these paranormal interruptions that we took them in stride.

Preparation for the big day infused the whole family with good cheer and an almost single-minded determination that seemed to sweep away any worries.

Even so, strange things continued to happen as they had since moving day, so long ago. Sometimes, things simply disappeared as though they'd never existed. Car keys and important papers went missing and then, a few days later, they'd appear inside the refrigerator or under a bed.

But now, as we raced towards Christmas Day, mom and dad's responses, although consistent, had changed. They no longer tried to make sense of the bizarre things that happened daily.

Dad snatched a cookie from the cooling rack on the counter and leaned down to open the fridge. Peering inside, he withdrew a piece of paper and chuckled; he walked to the table and set it down.

"Chilling your homework for extra credit now?" he said. "School's out for the holidays, you know."

"What?" I said, peering at the page. "My Socials project? That's where it went!"

Mom sighed softly as she stirred something else on the stove.

The last Sunday of Advent fell on the 23rd that year, and our family prepared for an evening service at church. Moments before we were to leave, however, it was discovered that the car keys, dad's wallet, and Diana's purse had all completely disappeared. Although we searched the house top to bottom, none of it was recovered and our Church plans had to be cancelled.

Predictably, no one talked about it much. We just took it in stride.

The next day was Christmas Eve. Mom and dad were busy in the kitchen together, preparing a pancake breakfast when I got up. From his post at the cast-iron griddle on the stove, dad pointed vaguely over his shoulder with a spatula.

"Placemats are in the drawer."

But instead of quietly setting the table for our Christmas Eve breakfast, I let out a yell that brought my family running.

In the drawer that contained the placemats, all three previously missing items lay jumbled together.

The car keys, Diana's purse and dad's wallet lay innocently on top of the woven mats.

"Huh," dad commented. "Well, it looks like I can go get your mother a Christmas gift after all."

Oh dad. How anticlimactic.

Trust my father to be cynical at a moment like that.

It was maddening. Dark circles had appeared under the eyes of my family members and I wasn't all that surprised to see them under my own as I got ready for the Christmas Eve candlelight service later that evening. At least they won't see my haggard face, I thought.

The Christmas candlelight service has always been my favourite. During the final hymn of the service, each parishioner lit the small white candle they clasped in their hands, bathing the whole church in the soft light of a hundred or so candles. As we join together to sing the last line of the traditional Christmas song, Silent Night, all of those candles are held high over our heads and the moment is pure magic.

It was precisely that kind of magic that sustained me. In the car on the way home, I was trying to hold onto that feeling, when I suddenly wondered if moving really *would* make my life normal. The prospect of living with *only* the living was enticing.

~~~~

Christmas Day was a much needed respite. Relieved faces peeked into the front room on Christmas morning, where everything was as it should be.

The happiness of such a special day overshadowed even my paranoia and I barreled into the room at full speed, flanked by my sister, who was just as eager as I. Dumping out our Christmas stockings onto the rug in the conversation pit, Diana and I talked and laughed as we went through our pile of goodies, stuffing chocolates into our mouths and looking longingly at the presents that lay undisturbed under the tree.

It was a hard and fast rule in our house that we were not to open the gifts under the tree until we were breakfasted and dressed. It was a bummer, but we didn't dare break the rule. Still, it seemed like an eternity before mom and dad emerged from their room, completely dressed and ready for the day. Christmas breakfast was also part of our family tradition, and my parents allowed no shortcuts. Eggs and bacon, fruit, croissants and fresh pastries were laid out in due course. It's a tradition that I have carried on with my own family, although I'm not as strict about the "no presents 'til you're dressed" thing, as my candid Christmas photos display all too well.

It was hours before we were all once again seated in our festive living room, the lights on the tall, albeit fake, Christmas tree winking and blinking while Christmas music played in the background. While mom snapped pictures, Diana and I tore into the gifts with fervour.

The biggest present in the room happened to be for me.

Heart thudding, I peeled the paper away like the peels on a banana, soon revealing a picture of a boy and his dad playing with an electric race-car set.

I couldn't have prevented the scream of triumph that flew from my mouth even if I'd been gagged.

"Alright!" I screamed. "Mom, dad, I wanted this!"

My parents laughed. "We know!"

Dad reached over to stay my hands as I began wrenching the box open on one end.

"Whoah there, partner," he said. "We'll set it up later."

Hours later, our colourful living room had grown wild, as ripped wrapping paper, curled ribbon and shiny new items lay everywhere. When the largest pile of crumpled paper suddenly gave a lurch at my mother's feet, she screamed and the rest of us went still with shock.

Moments later, we all laughed as Timothy's small, striped cat head emerged, followed by a playful white-mittened paw. He pounced on ribbons and shuffled through the torn paper with kittenish frenzy, and the fright was forgotten, or more accurately, it was pushed aside.

That Christmas was filled with favourites. The next gift I shredded open bore a label announcing it was "from Santa". I smirked as I read the card. To this day, my mom and dad still wrap a gift for my sister and I, bury it under as many presents as possible, and label it the same way.

It was a package of brand new Nancy Drew detective stories. I began reading almost immediately, making up encoded messages with the code book located in the back of one, until my father's extended throat-clearing brought me back to reality.

Later that day, as I waited for dad to get the contents of the race track organized, I pretended to dust for fingerprints with talcum powder—much to my mother's horror, when the windowsills and door handles became covered in the fine, white powder—and skulked through the house while looking through the large, round magnifying glass that accompanied my gift. The package also contained a Nancy Drew

Cookbook and I listed off recipe after recipe until my mother, no doubt already tired of my enthusiasm, wrote down "larkspur lane sandwiches" and "blackwood hall muffins" on the family calendar, promising we would make these delights on the days indicated.

Smart lady.

Dad, lying on the rec room floor with the contents of the race set, joked that the living room looked like a "crime scene" and that a certain "lady detective" was on the prowl, while Diana light-heartedly complained that I was gonna leave a trail of talcum powder everywhere I went. She even went so far as to suggest that I would spy on her, recording her phone conversations, in code of course.

Hmm, not a bad idea, I thought, warming to the subject.

Mom laughingly told me that with all our fingerprints *on file* she was starting to feel like she was living with the FBI.

"Okay kid, come help me with this," dad called. "We're gonna put it on the floor here, between the legs," he said, indicating the space under our massive pool table where he'd set out the pieces of track and the little cars on the low-pile carpeting. "That way no one can inadvertently kick it or step on it. You'll be lying on the floor to use it anyhow."

The T.V. show Dukes of Hazard was very popular and the style of the cars was modeled after the "General Lee", the car that really was the star of the show.

Lying on my stomach beside dad, I was confused in a matter of minutes, as I tried to help him by reading the directions from the manual out loud.

"Tab B slides into slot C," I said.

"What slot? I don't see a damned slot! These things would go together a lot better if they were labeled," dad grumbled. "Directions must've been written by 'Frick and Frack.'"

"Okay, that's enough help for now," mom interjected. Helping me to my feet, she led me away. "Leave your father alone for the time being, the language in there is going to get worse, I think, and you don't need to learn those types of words."

I hid my smile as I went off down the hall to immerse myself in the world of girl detective, Nancy Drew. Mom was right, dad was determined to put my gift together—he was as anxious to play with it as I was—but for some reason he never wanted to read the directions first. It was going to be hours before the thing was set up, and I knew it was in my best interest to stay clear.

"Dinner's almost ready," mom called in a sing-song voice later that afternoon, while I carefully set plates at each place and Diana set out the good silver and crystal glasses for our Christmas Day supper. "Will, are you done with that yet? Your mom and dad will be here soon."

Dad finally stood up from where he'd been working on the racetrack, pressing both hands to the small of his back. "Great timing, it's finally done!"

Dad pointed his index finger at me from across the room. "I challenge you to a race after dinner!" He said, smiling broadly.

It was a great Christmas, made even better by the presence of my paternal grandparents. Even the threat of the paranormal couldn't break the spell of happiness that swept us along.

Four days later, the brief respite of the holidays was a happy memory.

Given everything that had happened in that house, I still wonder why I didn't see it coming.

The phenomenon happened gradually. I'd been dusting for fingerprints again; the mystery stories in my new books seemed as real to me as anything, and just as credible as the six o'clock news. In my imagination, I followed a group of crooks that would stop at nothing to elude my superior detective skills. I particularly enjoyed being "Nancy," bringing my favourite stories to life.

"Isn't it wonderful," said my mom as she watched me playing that day. "You're so creative."

"Dad thinks I live in a world of make-believe," I said, sadly. "He doesn't like my stories."

"Oh honey, your dad's a serious person, that's all. He expects the rest of us to be serious too, but you know he loves us. Anyways, as long as a person can tell the difference between what's real and what's not, there's nothing at all the matter with imagination. Remember that."

"Okay."

That evening, as I got ready for bed, a strange whirring sound reached my ears.

"What's that?" I wondered aloud. Walking out into the hallway, I peeked in my parents' open doorway. They were both in bed, reading lights on and engrossed in their books.

"What is it honey?" mom asked, catching sight of me.

"Do you hear that?" I asked her. "Where's Diana?"

"Not home yet. Rick said he'd have her back by midnight. What should I be hearing?"

The whirring noise seemed to have subsided.

"Nothing," I muttered. "I thought maybe I left my racetrack on."

"What?" dad said, lowering his book and frowning at me.

"I know, I know, I'm going," I said. "I'll turn it off."

As I made my way down the hall, I heard it again. A dull, electronic hum.

A moment later the sound changed again and as I listened, I couldn't help but pause. A strange sound, like paper shuffling, hurried my steps. Something was wrong with my track. Had I left it on too long and now it was overheating? Dad warned me that might happen. As I neared the family room, I could see the green power light casting an eerie glow over the room. Whew! Still intact!

Intent on switching it off and returning to bed, I didn't notice the change in air temperature until later when I replayed the event in my head. All I knew in that moment, when I threw the light switch on the wall, was that strange whispering sound was one I knew. The track was not only on, the cars were moving too!

"That shouldn't be happening," I muttered.

In the instant the light went on, the cars and the sound stopped. The green power light had gone dark.

Cold fear slid down my back.

"Wh-who's in here?" I asked, my voice shaking. I was trying to be brave, like the heroine in my stories. Nancy Drew wasn't afraid of anything. All I could think about was the tall man in black.

"Please stay away, please stay away," I chanted in a frightened whisper. I felt like I'd walked into a trap. Whoever it was that had turned on the power switch, it wasn't Bobby.

Drawing a deep breath, I gripped the edge of the pool table with one hand while I reached down for the power switch with the other.

In that moment, the white car that was my favourite, roared to life, its tiny headlights illuminating the track in front of it. Screeching in fright, I backed away. I tried to make up some sort of explanation how it could be working, when the wired controller for it lay untouched on the other side of the set, but I was having no luck. Even dad's 'electrical anomaly' explanation wasn't going to work here. The tiny car picked up speed and zoomed along the track, through the twists and turns, fishtailing and finally derailing itself at it took a turn too fast. The little metal projectile left the track and launched itself straight at me, striking me hard in the chest. My frightened screams brought both my parents running.

"What's going on here?" My dad filled the doorway seconds later. I was sprawled backwards on the carpet, the white car in one hand and frightened tears glistening on my face.

Words tumbled out of my mouth, but they were disjointed and didn't make any sense.

"What's going on? Are you hurt?" Grasping my arm and turning me from side to side, he inspected me for damage. "Talk to me, are you okay?"

"I'm not hurt, dad."

"You were supposed to turn it off, not play with it," he admonished.

"I-I wasn't," I managed to say. "It just ... just did that."

Dad folded his arms. "Right, all by itself? I believe we've heard that tale before. It's time for bed. Better get going."

"But dad," I protested, sure they had to believe me now.

"But dad nothing," mom said, coming up behind him. "Scoot."

Still gripping the car in one hand I left the room. I heard the sharp click as dad shut down the power on the track. "Don't make me sorry I bought this," he cautioned.

No matter how my parents rationalized it, I knew what I saw. I just didn't know what to do about it.

Loss

22

A couple of days later, when I was once again back to my usual barn chores, I heard a deep, rumbling cough right behind me.

I whirled around, expecting to see nothing, but to my surprise, my pony stood there, his body trembling as though he were about to fall down. I threw my pitchfork to one side and glanced at the outside door, which was now partially open.

"I guess I didn't close the door right, huh? Poor thing, are you sick?" I said to him, running a hand gently down his velvet nose. Charlie's eyes drooped and another shudder ran through his short, stocky frame. I wasted no time throwing a horse blanket over his back and fastening the straps. "That should help, big guy," I told him.

The usually stalwart horse hesitated only a moment before lying down atop the hay I'd just given him to eat.

"Dad!" I screamed, already running at top speed for the house. If there was one thing I knew, it was that horses didn't usually lie down, especially not on top of their supper.

Later that day, the vet took my father aside and casting a worried glance in my direction. He spoke so softly I couldn't hear.

"It's a bad case of Pneumonia," was all my father would say, as the vet's green station wagon rumbled off down the driveway.

That night, my beloved pony, past the point of all help, had died.

"I'm sorry, Ginny, there was nothing anyone could do," dad said. "He was old and his body didn't respond to the treatment in time." I sank down onto my knees, the cold of the concrete floor seeped through my jeans, and my legs rapidly lost muscle control. The same crushing sadness that attacked me only days earlier, was now a stark reality.

"Oh my God!" mom rushed over to me and her face paled. "Not again!"

I looked up at her as she gently eased me up from the floor and our eyes locked. Realization seemed to dawn in hers; I only felt hot tears in my own. I don't remember much after that.

~~~~~

Grief is a funny thing. It seems to come in waves and it's never what you expect. It was a dark time for me, made even stranger by the realization that somehow I'd foretold this sad event. New Year's Eve came and went. Soon, it was time for me to go back to school and I attended on autopilot, not feeling much of anything. The feeling went on and on. It was the first time I'd lost anyone close to me.

One word finally brought me out of my emotional stupor.

Gift.

Julia often spoke this word casually when I visited her, but never explained it to my satisfaction. The more I thought about this, the more determined I became, and the depression finally faded, to be replaced by a deep sense of need.

I was frantic for answers, but they were in short supply. Who, in my circle of friends and family, were going to give me the kinds of answers I needed in order to move forward?

Julia's words always had double-meanings, and I had to be sharp if I was going to divine the meanings hidden behind her words.

Your gift, she'd said to me. What did she mean? Was that why I saw things my parents scoffed at? So far, it hadn't seemed like much of a gift. More like a curse.

But there wasn't any other explanation for what happened, was there? Coincidence was an annoying, untruthful word.

One of the research books at the Library had shown a drawing of a séance and given a short definition. It depicted a group of people, seated around a small wooden table with their hands clasped. The definition that I'd read said that it was a meeting to speak with the dead or a meeting at which a clairvoyant attempts to receive communications from the spirits of the dead. Whoah! Dutifully, I had written down this golden nugget and stuffed it in my pocket for later. Pulling that out from between my mattress and box spring, where I kept my treasures safe from prying eyes, I read it again. Questions sprang to my mind.

What was a Clairvoyant? How did it work? Did the person hear voices in their ear or in their head? Was the process different for everyone? How do people tell if they have this ability? Were there obvious signs, or did they simply know?

Was I one?

This last question was, of course, the most important and I couldn't stop thinking about it.

As I mulled over my research, it became obvious to me that there would be only one logical way to find out for sure. All the books pointed to it; it made perfect sense. If it was possible for me to be a Clairvoyant, then I assumed it was eminently practical to conduct a séance.

The following Saturday, I tagged along to the Library again, ostensibly to research Buddhism for a class project, but in reality, my covert operation was designed to net me more practical information from the Alternative Psychology section. I needed some hands-on details.

Once more, as soon as I pulled the first book, I was consumed. Hours went by, but I barely noticed their passing.

What I discovered was even more fuel for my ill-conceived plan. It seemed that people all over the world experienced paranormal events, and had been doing so for hundreds, maybe even thousands of years. The ancient Egyptians were so convinced that they spent half of their lives preparing for their own death, constructing intricate tombs large enough to house their own mummified remains and all their accumulated wealth.

I snickered to myself. Apparently those ancient Pharaohs thought Heaven was like a country club. Perhaps they thought they'd have to pay their way in with gold bars.

But even in ancient times, there were always people who held special knowledge in this area. The names differed, of course, but they were all Clairvoyants ... they all had *gifts* that made them special.

That night, I went to bed early, with mom's suspicious gaze following me.

"You're going to bed already?" she asked.

"Yeah, I'm pooped," I said, trying hard to curb my enthusiasm and look properly exhausted. I carefully closed my door with a barely audible click and wasted no time pulling out my crumpled notes. There, on the lined three-hole-punch paper was my childish scrawl, written out, plain as day. CLAIRVOYANT. The copied definition stared back at me: Somebody who is believed to transmit messages between living people and the spirits of the dead —PARANORMAL, see also psychic, mystic, spiritualist, medium, perceptive, telepathic, far-sighted.

I re-read the passage with increasing interest. People often referred to me as perceptive. Was this what they meant? It seemed like a stretch. But then, when my sister wanted to tease me, she'd often say I was telepathic, weird or far-fetched. Was that the same as *far-sighted*? I didn't think so, but I couldn't ignore what was going on in my house, even if the rest of my family wanted to.

Was I really like those people in the books? It was strange to think that other people couldn't see what I saw … the black shadows that moved on their own, the little boy that I knew I had seen, and played with for heaven's sake!

Why couldn't people see all this? Maybe, they simply didn't want to. That's what created the difference, I decided. Nevertheless, I rolled these mindboggling ideas around in my head while sitting cross-legged on my bed, waiting for inspiration. But instead of answers, all I had were more questions.

How was I going to do this? *Could* I do this? There weren't any listings in the various phone books I checked under Psychic Mediums and it was disappointing. I stared again at the photocopied picture in my hand. There were six people, hands clasped, seated at a small round table with their eyes closed. Surely if it was important enough to be listed in a reference book at the library, then there should be at least one person advertising in the phone book?

But even if I'd found one, what was I going to say? I shoved my hands deep into the pockets of my kangaroo jacket. Something small touched my fingertips and I pulled it free, suddenly remembering the two little balled up pieces of paper I'd shoved into my pockets while I ran to find my mother in the Library at closing time. I carefully smoothed out the wrinkles, and laid them flat.

"Medium, an intermediate state or condition halfway between two extremes," I whispered to myself, reading the childish scrawl. A tingling sensation washed over me.

On the second scrap of paper, I'd written another definition. It read: Purgatory—A place of suffering.

My eyebrows knit together as I read on. I remembered copying it from an old text, the worn leather cover and its embossed gold lettering lending it an air of ancient importance. The speaker-system at the Library had been announcing imminent closure and I'd hurriedly copied the words without really reading them too much.

A miserable situation. An extremely uncomfortable, painful or unpleasant situation or experience.

Was this correct? Surely, this had to be *old school* thinking.

I gulped and lay back on my bed. It was an inescapable fact that Bobby was dead. Maybe he knew about Purgatory being awful and that's why he was hanging around my house. Did everyone have to go there? If my Catechism classes were correct, then everyone did, but ... a place of suffering? No wonder he wasn't in a hurry to leave. My mind wandered, eventually piecing together a disjointed, far-fetched theory. I was now more determined than ever to go through with my experiment.

The séance was not going to be perfect, I knew. It would have to be done with dolls, and without the extra energy of the people sitting at the table, I would have to rely on myself, but I'd been doing that all along, hadn't I? Besides, involving live people was out of the question. None of my friends would ever cooperate without spilling the beans at the first sign of trouble.

My next big problem was how to ditch Diana. Whenever mom left her in charge, she got on a power trip and followed me everywhere, giving me chores until I feigned sleep to get away from her. What kind of opportunity was I going to get with her around?

One Saturday however, mom and dad said they were going out to do some grocery shopping. It sounded like a golden opportunity to me.

"Diana, we're leaving you in charge. No capital punishment please, and just for the record, T.V. watching is not a crime."

"But Mom, I'm supposed to go out with Rick!" Diana protested. "She's ten, can't she stay by herself?"

My heart leapt.

"Diana, we live in the middle of nowhere. Use your head," mom said.

Aw, man. Crushed again.

"But what about Rick? We have plans."

"Ask him to come here," she said.

"Oh joy," I commented sarcastically, leaning against the wall. Diana just glared at me, but she did that so regularly I hardly noticed. In the back of my mind a plan was beginning to form. I knew I could count on Rick's cooperation, whether he knew it or not. Diana got very distracted whenever he was around.

As I sat in my room, biding my time, I took special notice of the temperature. Since it hadn't plummeted to zero, I breathed a quick sigh of relief. According to the books I'd read, the temperature dropped when spirits were near. If he showed up early, before everything was ready, what then? Would everything still work out ok, or did I need those formulaic saying and special candlelight? I needed to believe that somehow, Bobby would communicate with me, even though I hadn't seen him since that day when I'd discovered his photo.

Was I completely bonkers conducting a séance? I hadn't needed one before, I reasoned.

But you didn't know you were talking to a ghost then, my conscience reminded me.

I thought again of the strange dreams I had where he appeared, excitedly waving his arms and chattering at me. What was he saying? Everything would be so much easier if I could hear those words. If I could, for instance, "transmit messages between living people and the spirits of the dead"?

Perhaps this séance wasn't such a lunatic idea after all, but would he understand the new words I'd managed to glean from those dusty old books?

Time would tell.

And so my plans began to take shape. I would wait for Diana to relax, and let down her guard. Once she and Rick were distracted, I'd sneak out to the cupboard and set up the scene in the living room of my dollhouse. There was a short hallway between Diana's room and mine where my Barbies were kept. My dad had built me a massive wooden doll house, complete with two bedrooms, a bathroom, kitchen and spacious living room, and it was there that I would conduct my experiment. Over the past year, I'd steadily lost interest in Barbies, but now, their tiny human forms seemed to fit the bill perfectly.

The rest would take care of itself, I figured. Would Bobby recognize a séance? Would he know that I was trying to talk to him and cooperate? The books were vague on the mechanics of the actual event, but they did seem to suggest that lit candles were important, because electricity interfered with spiritual energy. I wasn't entirely sure why, but it was too late to turn back.

Everything was ready. The dolls were arranged. Their expressions frozen into complacent smiles, their pose-able arms and legs arranged as though waiting for something amazing to happen. The Barbie's tiny plastic butts were balanced on chairs I'd made the previous summer out of clothes pins, and the effect was precarious at best. Barbies, it seemed, weren't meant to just sit there. Occasionally one would tumble from its perch, creating a domino effect and the whole scene would have to be set up again.

Diana and Rick were *occupied* in the family room, ostensibly watching T.V., but still Diana found time to check on me routinely.

"What do you want now? Can't you stop bugging me for five minutes?" I complained when her form once more threw a shadow over my shoulder.

"Don't be such a grump," she said. "It's good to see you playing with all that, I thought you'd outgrown it by now."

"Nearly," I answered truthfully. "It has been a long time." I continued to brush the hair of the doll I held in my hands, combing the matted snarls out of her synthetic curls was a mundane task, but if Diana thought I was absorbed, maybe she'd leave me alone for five minutes.

"Well, okay," she said, sounding reluctant—an act no doubt. "Rick and I are gonna watch a scary movie. You want to come watch with us?" She knew darn well that I wouldn't, and this confirmed my suspicions that they didn't want me around.

"Nah, I'm just gonna stay here and play awhile. You know I don't like scary movies."

"Oh yeah, right."

As soon as Diana had gone, I dug out my notes from the back pocket of my Levi's and smoothed out the wrinkles.

"Solemnly we gather," I intoned as I produced a small lighter that I'd found out in dad's workshop days earlier. "Respectfully we request," I continued.

The small Barbie living room began to glow with a soft reddish light as I lit the tiny red candles that I managed to filch from Mom's Christmas ornaments. The soft *snick* of the lighter filled me with trepidation. There was no turning back now. If Diana came in and caught me with all these candles, I was cooked.

The trouble with thinking that way is that when it actually happens, it seems totally unreal at first.

Even now, I don't know what would have happened if Rick and his exceptional sense of smell hadn't given me away.

I had just sat back, all the dolls sitting placidly around my makeshift table, the candlelight reflecting off of their shiny, plastic faces when an astonished gasp behind me nearly made my heart stop.

Rick and Diana moved in on me fast.

"What the hell!" My indignant sister was the first to drop to her knees and gape at my set-up. With a look on her face that would freeze rocks, she leaned forward and blew out my carefully arranged candles.

"Ginny are you mental?" she cried once they were out. "Are you trying to burn down the house?"

"That's two stupid questions and I refuse to answer either of them!" I shot back.

Rick was trying hard to stifle his laughter, and failing.

"Hmm, we'll see," Diana's voice was ominous. She grabbed a nearby laundry basket and started shoving all my careful preparations into it like she was collecting evidence. "GET OUT OF HERE AND GO TO BED!"

I wasn't sure whether it was my bad mannered response to my sister or the ill-advised séance that earned me a swift grounding when mom and dad got back, but either way, in the days that followed, I consoled myself with martyrdom. I was Rapunzal locked in a tower; I was Cinderella, doing endless chores for her evil step-sisters; I was a simple country girl cursed with a *gift*.

While the first two were pure fantasy, the last one was closer to the truth than I was ready to admit. Although my experiment was a total failure, I wasn't beaten yet. Eventually, my freedom would be granted. Thoughts of how to resurrect my séance competed with thoughts of how to ditch Diana long enough to do anything.

To this day, neither Rick nor Diana realizes the true significance of my Barbie candle-scene or why I was so upset at their untimely intervention. Rick still laughs about it and couples it with some bizarre Barbie hair-cutting thing—which I don't remember at all—but I'm just as happy to go along with his fuzzy recollections. It's simpler that way.

Nightmares are Real

23

"How much do you like this house?" my father asked us as we gathered at the table for our Saturday morning breakfast. We all just stared at him, forks hovering over plates full of syrup-laden pancakes, my mother's coffee cup rattling as she set it back onto the saucer.

"What do you mean, daddy?" I asked.

"I mean, how much do you like it? There are better places, you know. Maybe this country living doesn't suit us after all."

"What?" a clamor of voices, followed by rapid hand-waving and unfinished questions ensued.

"Are we selling?"

"Where will we go?"

"Will I have to change schools again?"

"No-o-o-o!!" My father held up his hands in mock surrender. "Okay, okay, settle down. I didn't say anything about moving ... yet. After all, do you see a 'for sale' sign on the front lawn? It was a hypothetical question, family: just an idea. That's all. Let's get back to our breakfasts. We've got lots to do today."

And with that, my father just went back to reading the paper and calmly cutting and chewing his pancakes as though nothing had happened at all. I could tell my sis and mom weren't buying his nonchalant attitude, but I didn't spend any time wondering why. All I knew was my heart was pounding. I really didn't want to move. Not now that I had a plan. Sure, there was something in the house that I didn't like, but I wasn't about to lose all the other things that I loved so much about this place: namely, my pool.

I gulped some air to slow my breathing and started back into my breakfast. Whew, that was close, was all I could think for awhile as I chewed. I figured in my childlike way that this was the last I would hear of such a terrible idea.

For days after that odd conversation at the breakfast table, Diana showed that dad's *terrible idea* was at the forefront of her mind. While my mind was wrestling with grade five math problems, she brought it up in brief comments, like "well, maybe I'll be married by then anyways" and "Mom never liked the idea of being a horse farmer you know."

When I think back now I realize she continued to watch our parents closely, like she was trying to see through their casual conversation, looking for hidden meaning in their words.

At the time, her behavior was just strange to me and I thought she was just being irritating. I told her this on many occasions, but instead of starting the usual fight, she would merely shrug and say, "you don't have a clue what's going on. Mom and dad are going to sell and you and I are going to do this all over again!" She made a sweeping gesture with her hand as she said it, and flounced out of the room.

As usual, I only understood the very edges of what she was talking about when she got like that and so I figured she meant the paranormal activity that was happening. Would this follow us? Is that what she meant?

As mom and dad patiently went on with their daily routines, I felt myself growing more confused and wished someone would take the time to explain it, but my parents steadfastly refused to open up on the subject again. That left Diana, who was more ticked off than secretive. When Diana got ticked off, she liked to talk, but only when mom and dad went out and left her in charge.

"So look, I don't think it's an accident that dad brought up that thing about moving. Mom never liked having horses around, and after I move out, they'll probably sell and move. You'll just have to accept it. You've been acting weirder than usual since we've lived here, and I'm not just saying that because you're my annoying little sister. I think this ghost business has affected you, with a capital 'A'. Maybe you need to talk to a professional about this."

"Now you're just being stupid!" I retorted hotly. "Who would I talk to anyways? It's not like any of you want to talk about it. I hate it when you do this! You act like this is my fault!"

Diana actually looked shocked, but instead of turning up the heat into a full-blown argument, she sighed, shook her head and walked off down the hallway to her bedroom.

"I'll be in my room. Don't go to the barn without me. Everything's frozen out there." She tossed the comment back over her shoulder as she passed down the hallway into her bedroom.

I glared at her back and felt really, really angry. She didn't have the right to talk to me like that, I thought. What, did she think I was four? She had no right to make comments about how I was acting!

"I've been acting like myself, not a weird-o! And I'm not possessed either!" I shot back at her. That should get her. I resented her words far more than the prospect of moving away.

I flopped down to watch T.V. for awhile, but the signal was screwing up again, with the heavy snow that continued to fall outside. The 'snow' on the screen seemed to match the weather. I thought of calling Diana for help, but decided I didn't want anything more to do with her and her negative comments.

I started pacing the otherwise empty house, turning her words over in my mind. I knew the temperature had dropped outside and the barn taps were all frozen, but since when would she worry about that? *Don't go in the barn without me*, she'd said. Why? Was there another reason she didn't think I should go alone? Why couldn't anyone in my house just say what was on their mind? It was so frustrating!

I found myself swinging open the back door and marching off purposefully, a carrot clenched in my gloved hand, to give Charlie a post-Christmas treat. I was determined to show Diana that her attempts at controlling me were gonna backfire.

The snow had covered the gravel path that ran alongside the pool, its winter wrappings lending a dreary cast to the back yard. Bundled up in my down-filled coat with a red toque squashed onto my head, I glanced down at the carrot and thought of Charlie's brown and white forelock bouncing up and down as he enjoyed the tasty treat.

Halfway to the barn, memory flooded back painfully. Charlie was gone.

I kept walking, like an automaton, not paying any attention to where I went. My tear-blinded eyes stared at the ground as I put one foot in front of the other, listening to the squeak of the new snow as it compressed under my boots. I didn't know where I was going, but I remember thinking that it didn't really matter anyways.

I'm not sure what made me stop, but as I stood outside the long low building that served as my father's workshop, a small bit of movement caught my eye and I looked up.

I shouldn't have.

When we moved in, dad had claimed the little building, immediately, saying it was perfect for housing his tools and projects. He'd spent a few days sweeping it out, cleaning up debris and actually washing the small panes of glass in the antique windows, before piling it high with stuff he'd collected over the years. My mother casually termed all of it as "junk" but dad proudly tinkered in there whenever he got the chance. Motorcycles in varying stages of disrepair accounted for the majority of dad's treasures.

These tiny panes of glass drew my attention now, their surface reflecting the sunlight back at me. A vague sense of movement behind the glass drew me even closer as I narrowed my eyes for a better look.

A scream gurgled up out of my throat as my mind registered the frightening scene behind that glass. A pale skinned face with eyes that seemed to glow red looked back at me with anger, the whole face pressed to fit within the confines of that one pane.

A mouth filled with yellowed teeth opened in a scream I could not hear.

I recognized him immediately. I'd seen this face before.

Backing up in a flurry of steps, my feet slipped on the loose rock under the snow. Confusion and fear made me whirl around in a 360, but I saw no one else in the yard. Breathlessly I checked for the impossible face that could not be there.

But it was there. The eyes still watched and the mouth was turned down in a furious scowl. Now I was the one screaming.

As I ran, over my shoulder I heard impossible sounds of pursuit.

Metal things crashed together, as though someone was making their way hurriedly through all that junk.

I couldn't seem to run fast enough.

It was my dream, become reality.

The door to the shed banged behind me. Whether it was open or closed I didn't know, but it didn't matter. All I knew was this impossibility was chasing me!

I closed and locked the back door after stumbling through it, then barricaded myself in my room pressing my back tight against the wall. If I'd had time to think about it, I would have realized that wooden doors and locks were no match for this type of threat, but I couldn't stop to think.

Far off, on the other side of the house, a door slammed. I screamed and covered my ears.

I heard Diana's voice call out, "Ginny? Quit slamming doors already. You're gonna get it!"

Of course, that statement made everything all right.

Weeping with relief that my sister was there to help me, I listened carefully, but heard nothing. That couldn't be right. Where was she? Had the apparition gotten into the house and hurt my sister? What was he? A ghost? Something worse?

"Ginny?" Diana called again. "Where are you?"

"In here," I managed weakly, relief washing over me at the sound of her voice. My back was pressed up against the wall where I huddled in a protective crouch. I was shaking and crying, not wanting to explain something that no one would believe, but needing to warn Diana so she would know to be careful. Something had chased me back to the house. Something dangerous. There was no use denying it.

She was at risk too.

After a few minutes, I grew brave enough to creep to my door and open it just a little. I felt cold all over. Like I'd been touched by something evil.

"Diana," I whispered into the deserted hallway. "Are you there?"

The silence in the house did nothing to assuage my fear and I quickly closed it. I didn't ever want to see that face again, but something told me I would.

Scenarios began to play out in my head.

If I ran full tilt and screaming out of my room and straight out the front door, it shouldn't have time to grab me.

Right. And go where exactly? And if there wasn't anything there, as my family maintained, then my sister would call the men with white coats and I'd be dragged off as a lunatic.

Okay, scratch that. Next?

If I crept down the hall like a spy, being careful not to make a sound, I could possibly sneak past whatever or whoever it was that chased me from dad's shop. Perhaps they even had Diana prisoner and she couldn't call out to me.

Hang on a sec. While the plan seemed sound, I wasn't sure I could pull it off. After all, there were two spots in that hallway that would give me away as soon as I stepped on them. One lay only a few feet in front of my door. There was no way to go around it, unless I could fly, and the only information I had to go on was an unearthly silence.

I was so tired, physically and mentally but I didn't dare close my eyes.

I jumped back suddenly as a heavy pounding on my door ensued. The handle turned as someone put their weight against the door, crashing into all the debris I'd piled up against it repeatedly, forcing it open bit by bit.

Someone screamed. I think it was me.

My sister's frantic voice called to me.

"Ginny, are you ok? What's blocking the door?"

"Oh! It's you!" The door was open a crack, and her pale worried face looked back at me.

I'd never been so grateful to see my big sister. I flung my door open and almost fell into her.

"Whoah. What's going on here?" She said, looking around and then at me. "Look," Diana said. "You don't have to overreact. I'm not interested in fighting … hey, are you okay? Why are you looking at me like that?"

I squinted at her for a moment in confusion. What was she talking about?

"You know," she said. "When I called you a weirdo, and said you were affected, I didn't mean it. I mean, sometimes you act really strange and I guess I didn't realize you'd take my comments to heart like this."

Oh.

I frowned at her, realizing she had no idea what had just happened. For a moment, I considered telling her everything, unburdening myself in a way I longed for. But as much as I wanted to, I had to face the fact that I was the only one who'd seen the entity.

It was clear to me then. I was the one he wanted, and he was getting inside my head to do it.

And my sister? She was the one who thought I should see a shrink.

"I'm sorry." Diana smiled at me and opened her arms. "This place has us all on edge. I don't understand it any better than you do. But I know we gotta stick together … truce?"

"Sure. Truce," I said and hugged her with relief. She was still my sister and she wanted to understand. "Diana?" I asked hesitantly, my arms still wrapped around her middle.

"Yeah?"

"Do you feel different somehow, living here? I mean we ..."

Her strong hands wrapped themselves around my shoulders and pulled me free so she could look into my face. "We're still the same people Gin. No matter what anyone tells you, we didn't ask for this."

Her serious tone caught me off guard for a moment. Gone was the teasing and sarcasm that usually greeted my questions. It occurred to me later that Diana's serious response was likely brought about by her own fear. It was a sobering thought.

Later as I lay in my bed, feeling grateful that my body was too exhausted to react, I wondered how Diana did it. Night after night, she just closed her eyes and drifted into a peaceful sleep, while I fought hard just to keep my eyes closed. In an effort to relax, I often repeated the mantra my mother taught me in the hopes that this night would be different.

"There's nothing in the darkness that isn't there in the light," she'd said, kissing my forehead tenderly and tucking the covers in around my shoulders. "Relax, you're alright. Ssh. Go to sleep."

Sometimes the mantra worked.

Inside My Head

24

My parents called it "withdrawn" and their friends often commented that I was "moody", but I'd already learned that being honest with them about the real reasons would get me nowhere.

No one wanted to talk about things like that.

My days were spent waiting for things to happen. I felt it, all the time, the way you would feel a change in the weather. It was like a pressure that sometimes thrummed in my ears, it was so strong. I went about the details of my life with a watchful eye.

What would it do next? The constant stress began to take its toll. Each night, I would fall asleep exhausted, only to get up feeling just as tired and worn out as when I'd gone to bed.

It was hard trying to act normal when everything around me was so far from it.

~~~~~

Days later, I sat in a comfortable arm chair with my cat Timothy, absently stroking his fur and reading, while Christmas music played softly on the large, old stereo on the far side of our spacious living room. I love Christmas music, and even though the holidays had passed, I couldn't get enough of the old classics. Suddenly, my curious tabby rose up and snarled; this was so at odds with his usual demeanor that I knew instantly something was very wrong. The fur on his back stood away from his body as though a surge of electricity had hit him.

Then the music I'd been listening to fell silent and the tell-tale click of the power button was audible even from where I sat, heart thumping with that familiar, sick feeling spreading through my body.

Timothy, his eyes wide with terror, jumped from my arms, and ran full tilt for the kitchen only to screech to a stop about a foot from the entrance, as though something big barred his way. Circling back in a different direction, dodging an invisible opponent, he raced back to where I now stood, in astonishment. I lunged to grab him, but missed. The small tabby cat hissed and snarled, backing up in a low crouch, the fur on his back raised in a long line along his back. Although I couldn't see the threat, I knew it was there all the same. And I had a good idea who or what was causing all this.

"Leave him be!" I shouted, tears streaming down my face. "Leave him alone! He's just a baby!" My voice came out as a screech, so desperate was I to stop this insanity.

Immediately, something cold and damp slid over my head and shoulders like a used beach towel, and I shivered uncontrollably, wind-milling my arms to wave it away. A feeling like gossamer cobwebs dragged across my face and I spluttered and whirled, trying to focus. What was going on?

Shaking my head to clear the sensory overload, I tried to calm my frantic heartbeat, even as my eyes continued to dart everywhere. Timothy was long gone, but a patch of coloured fur still clung to the carpet where he'd been crouched. Was he okay? My poor little cat. This was something I'd never seen before and it scared like nothing else.

Looking around, I noticed that the room had grown dark. Moments before, as I read my book in peace and quiet, our living room had been flooded with sunshine, but now it was shadowed, and it wasn't even past noon yet. Coincidence? *Ha!* There was no such thing in that house.

My hand reached for the lamp beside me and stretching for the switch, I became aware for the first time of a searing heat in my palm. A second later, I was staring in disbelief at a deep gouge between the thumb and forefinger of my left hand.

"Where did this come from?" I wondered aloud, clutching at my wrist as the pain intensified. Obviously, Timothy, in his blind terror, had left his mark. But why hadn't I felt it until just now?

The blood, a deep maroon, was pooling in my cupped hand and would soon stain my mother's light-coloured carpet if I didn't get to the bathroom quickly, but I couldn't seem to get my bearings. I felt like the world had been tipped on edge.

Why was it so hard to focus? Everything seemed wrong.

The blood from my hand had begun to drip down my forearm, and my legs didn't want to work properly. Unsteadily, I made my way down the carpeted hallway to the bathroom. Somehow I managed to get my bleeding hand wrapped in toilet paper, before I sat down heavily on the toilet lid, light-headed and frightened.

What was happening to me?

I turned to regard my face in the bathroom mirror. The whites of my eyes gleamed in the semi-darkness. In my haste, I hadn't put on the light, but there was still enough daylight to see by.

Out of the corner of my eye a flash of movement darted past the open doorway, disappearing quicker than thought.

I stared back at my reflection, my mouth hanging open in surprise. What now?

Carefully, I unwrapped the layers of toilet paper from my damaged hand, inspecting the jagged cut. I was going to have to apply some first aid there, I could see. It might even need stitches, I thought with a shudder. A quick, one-handed search yielded a box of band-aids stuck in the back of the lower cabinet. My hand throbbed insistently as I worked to open the frustrating wrapper.

"Ahem"

The unexpected noise made me glance up at the mirror in surprise.

My surprise quickly turned into a scream.

That face I'd tried so hard to forget stared back at me, his face only inches from my right shoulder.

"No, No!" I shouted, whirling around to regard the empty space behind me.

Mercifully, when I faced the mirror again, the old specter's image was gone. But in its place, two large hand-prints were visible on the glass, as though he'd pressed his big hands against the mirror's surface and rested a while. They were spaced about two feet apart, and were already beginning to fade. They seemed to frame my startled reflection.

The darting movement past the doorway and my cat's erratic behavior started to make sense. Somehow, the dark spirit that infested the barn and other outbuildings had found its way into my family home.

But how?

Moments later, with my heart still beating fiercely against my ribcage, I stood on the front lawn, out of ideas. He was inside now. What did this mean? More importantly, what was I going to do about it?

~~~~

This was real. Despite what my family said about my fanciful ideas and grand imagination, there was no other way to explain this. I decided right then that I was finished denying it.

It took a long time for my hand to heal. Although it hadn't required stitches, it remained bandaged for several weeks. Mom and dad only knew that my cat had inexplicably attacked my hand. "Strange", mom had commented. "Timothy loves you. It's not like him to be so vicious."

"Cats are like that," was my father's comment. I remember that I smiled and agreed with them. They didn't need to know the rest. I knew they wouldn't believe it anyways, so to my way of thinking, it was simpler that way.

The deep gouge eventually turned into an angry red scar that would serve as a sober reminder for months to come. Even now, as I type this, the scar has faded to a thin, silver line, but the memories of that day are as clear as ever.

~~~~

"What the hell? Where'd you –? Where are you? Oh my God! No, no, no; not on the road! No! Don't!! No! No! Bobby!" The words that were not mine screamed through my brain in a rush. I felt a surge of raw adrenaline, and my limbs twitched spasmodically.

"Come back! Oh no, no, no! Oh my God, no! Baby, come back! Bobby! Listen to Mommy!" The screaming was louder now, and I sat bolt upright in my bed, gasping for air while my body shook uncontrollably.

My heart was beating so hard I felt like throwing up.

"Ginny?" My mother's voice was alarmed as she rushed into the room, the ties of her hastily donned robe trailing on the floor. "What's going on? I heard you screaming, baby. Were you, swearing?"

"I—I was screaming?" I was truly puzzled. "That was *me*? What's happening to me?" As I sat there, trying to figure it out, I came to a very shocking conclusion. My dreams were no longer my own.

"Mom?"

"Ssh," she whispered, as she held me close. "It's alright." Pressed against her chest, with my face resting in the crook of her neck, I could tell she was crying too.

I knew with sudden, inexplicable clarity that the words I'd screamed in my sleep were the last ones Bobby had ever heard.

I didn't understand how I could know that, but I didn't question it. I simply knew. For reasons I couldn't understand, I'd just been handed a snapshot of that fateful day.

The idea scared me so much that my trembling increased and my soft tears became sobs.

"Oh, my baby," mom said, gathering me into her arms and rocking me. We sat on the floor together, with my mother holding me tight. "I'm here. It's alright, it's just a nightmare; it will pass. I'm here." The deep pressure felt good and I let myself melt into her embrace. It was a long time before I let go, and even longer before I let myself fall asleep.

~~~~~

"William, we have to talk," mom said to dad later that evening, as he sat watching the six o'clock news. I saw my mother swallow with effort and I knew she was going to talk to him about my behaviour earlier that day. She obviously didn't see me, as I was hidden from her view, still on the other side of the kitchen doorway.

"Mm-hmm," he said, still eying the T.V. "Can it wait? They're going to announce the winning lottery numbers here. Can't we talk about this later?"

"No we can't," mom said, her voice rising. "It's Ginny. I'm not sure what's happening, but we need to …."

Dad leapt up from the couch, suddenly his eyes wide and excited. "Did you hear that? I can't believe it! Would you look at that! I won!"

"What?" mom said, the irritation on her face was unmistakable. "What did you win?"

"It finally happened, hon, the Lottery! I, I uh—I won … er, we won! At last!" dad spluttered.

"What? Are you kidding me?" mom seemed to forget everything and rushed to embrace her husband, turning him to face her. "Look at me … you're not joking, are you? You're serious?"

"Of course, I'm dead serious. Course, it's not all six numbers, so it's not the grand prize, but I have five honey! FIVE!"

"Oh my," mom said, her tone a mix of excitement and wonder. "Let me see the ticket!"

"The ticket ... yeah, I gotta just grab it and check it again."

"What? You mean you don't have it? How can you be sure it's a winner?"

"Oh no, I'm sure alright, I always play the same numbers, have since Ginny was two years old." He leaped up and headed straight for the doorway. "Hey kiddo," he said, passing me. "We're rich! I'll be right back. Ticket's in the bedroom."

Dad always kept his things strictly organized, so no one thought it would be an issue finding one of his prized lottery tickets. That is, until dad walked down the hallway minutes later, his face devoid of colour to announce that the ticket was gone ... missing without a trace.

"It has to be in the house somewhere!" dad said his voice nearly frantic. "I can't believe that I've spent all this time and money, faithfully buying tickets, only to have a winning ticket go inexplicably missing."

Dad began rummaging through the junk drawer in the kitchen. "Go look in your room, Ginny, check everywhere; it's got to be here!"

"Oh honey," mom said. "It'll turn up. Did you check your wallet?"

"Sure. First place I looked."

"Oh, okay, well maybe..."

"The fridge!" roared dad, leaping to the refrigerator and hauling open the door.

"The fridge?" mom asked.

"Yeah, don't ask." But as we watched dad, with worried frowns on our faces, his frantic search yielded nothing.

"Oh well, we have time, right? You don't have to claim your prize right away, do you?" mom suggested.

Dad's withering look silenced any further attempts to make him feel better.

~~~~

In the wake of the missing ticket, my "nightmare" was forgotten, as every spare minute was spent looking for dad's ticket.

Faintly in the other room, I heard Diana. It sounded like she was talking on the phone, again. Picking up my trusty notepad and a pencil, I crept along the hallway that separated our bedrooms. Once mom and dad heard what she was saying, she was gonna get it. Last time I listened in, I'd

213

heard her complaining about me to her friends. 'My sister is so weird, I can't have anybody over. She acts like she's possessed.'

Her words made me so mad.

Diana had a phone extension in her room, another perk of being older. I paused just outside her closed bedroom door and listened.

"I love you too," she was saying.

Ooh! This was better than I thought. Flipping open my notebook I prepared to write it all down. You never knew when this could come in handy, right?

The pencil fell from my grasp unexpectedly, landing without a sound on the carpeted hallway.

Bending to pick it up, I felt my muscles give-way and I slid to the floor with a gasp. A tall black shadow, like a piece of night, hovered across the end of the hallway. It obscured the wall, the carpet beneath it and my way back into the kitchen.

"What is that thing?" I whispered. A shadow for sure, but what could be casting it? It was night and the only light was the single bulb encased in the crystal, beaded fixture that hung in the centre of the hallway. In front of ... whatever this was. It should have been illuminated by that light.

It hovered, like some monstrous sentinel at the end of a brightly lit ordinary household hallway. I tried to smile, tried to convince my racing heart that this was nothing: just a trick of the light, of my eyes, of anything. Transfixed, I watched and waited for it to fade. I'd almost convinced myself that it must be something natural when it did something that shadows aren't supposed to do by themselves.

It moved.

Closer.

I did the only thing I could think of in that moment. I screamed and threw my notebook at the shape, scrambling away on my hands and knees, back pressed against the wall as I yanked open my sister's door and fell backwards into her room.

"What the hell are you doing in here, you little spy?" My sister yelled, wrenching the door back open and pointing back out into the hall. With an imperious finger, she pointed through the opening. "You can leave the way you came," she said, but in an instant, her tone changed and she turned to look out into the hallway with a puzzled frown. "What's the matter? What's going on out there?"

I shook my head and continued to back away across the room.

With another glance at me, and one for the hallway, Diana pushed the door closed, leaning into it with the weight of her body. After a moment, she locked it and backed away herself. She turned to me then, a worried frown deepening on her face. "Why are you so frightened? What's wrong with you? What happened?"

"Nothing you'll believe," I shot back, finding my voice and my courage at last. "I can't, I don't want to—can I stay here a little while?"

"Yeah, okay," she said, looking nervously back over her shoulder at the closed bedroom door. Her confusion was evident. "For a while."

A Child's Game?

25

"Okay, so here's your weekly allowance," mom said when I got up for breakfast that Saturday. "It's a beautiful morning and it's not even cold outside: a rare thing for February really. Did you want to go for a bike ride? Perhaps you can call Jessie?"

Instantly suspicious, I narrowed my eyes to think. Mom was trying to get rid of me. But why? Sure, dad had been impossible since the lottery ticket had gone missing, but I was confident it would surface again, just like everything did. It would appear when the ghost wanted it to. It was a child's game, so it made sense that the only one who knew the rules was me. As soon as dad stopped looking, there it would be.

As I sat eating my cheerios, the only sound in the room was the rhythmic clanging of my spoon against the ceramic dish in front of me. Dad remained hidden behind his weekend newspaper, his coffee growing cold on the table-top. Mom busied herself spreading jam on a piece of toast.

A normal morning.

I sat up straighter, listening to the sound of my sister's footsteps as she came down the hallway behind me. What sarcastic comments would she have for me today?

The floor creaked and the muted footsteps continued. As I chased the last few Cheerios around my bowl, I thought about asking Diana if we could double on Koko. She only hated me when Diana wasn't there. It'd been a long time since the two of us had gone riding like that, and with everything that was happening, I would feel good to have that closeness again.

Content with my plan, I returned happily to my Cheerios.

There were two spots in that hallway that squeaked when someone walked on them, so as we enjoyed our breakfasts, it was only natural that we expected to see Diana emerge into the kitchen. But when the footsteps ceased and still no one appeared, mom got up to investigate. I followed her with my eyes, watching as the colour drained from her face.

"Will," she said, her voice shaky. "There's no one there."

"What the—"

Dad's blistering comment was interrupted a moment later when the large picture frame behind me crashed to the floor.

Naturally, I screamed.

"Oh," I heard my mom whimper. "Not again. On top of everything else?"

"What the hell is going on around here?" My father, his face red with anger slammed down his paper.

The room had a bad feeling to it, like the void after a small explosion. I looked across the table at my mother, who pushed some money across the shiny surface towards me with a tight smile.

I kissed her cheek hurriedly and took her hand, trying to lead her away too. "Mom, you should come outside with me. It's nice."

Mom patted my hand and turned to dad, who was already inspecting the wall and floor.

"Hmm, the picture hook is fine. I don't understand it," he muttered.

Mom threw a glance at me and practically shoved me outdoors through the patio door.

Why can't I have a normal family? I thought, as I trudged heavily across the patio to get my bike.

I couldn't help casting a longing look out into the pasture, still feeling the sharpness of loss for my beloved Charlie. As my gaze slid over the familiar landscape, I noticed another horse standing tall and proud in our field. It wasn't Koko—she grazed with her back to this new horse, seeming to ignore it. It was a big black horse, and its ears pricked forward as it watched me approach.

"Who's that?" I wondered aloud. "A new horse we're boarding? Why am I always the last to know? I thought you weren't coming 'til next Saturday?" My steps took me all the way to the paddock. In wonder, I watched as the big black horse moved gracefully over to meet me, eagerly presenting a soft, velvet nose to be stroked.

"Ooh, you're a beauty, aren't you?" I muttered as I ran my hands down her face and neck. "And so trusting, too, what a gentle girl."

The horse seemed to enjoy the attention, moving as close to the fence, and subsequently my hands, as she could. After my scare of the night before, I was eager for something as soothing as the presence of this mare.

She and I became fast friends on the spot. "I'll bring you a treat when I get back, I promise," I told her, thinking of the small produce section at the corner store a few blocks away.

I met Jessie at the pre-arranged halfway point between our two properties. It was a run-down shop; the wooden siding used to be white, but it was in bad need of a new coat of paint. A large green sign hung over the door, proclaiming the need for 7-Up to all who drew near. A pair of cheesy Christmas bells hung over the door year-round, set to jangle whenever someone walked in, so the owner could yell, "be there in a second!"

Jess held the door wide for me as I leaned my bike against the hitching post that was located out front. This was horse country, after all.

I followed her inside, trying not to look at the big chestnut already tied up outside. He was beautiful and his owner was already untying the reins and swinging up into the saddle as my friend and I disappeared into the store.

Charlie. How I missed him.

"Ugh," Jess commented. "Are you ever getting in here? I'm getting old waiting for you."

"I'm here, I'm here, quit naggin' me," I said. "What's wrong with you today? Why so cranky? Your parents again?" This was a favourite complaint of Jessie's and secretly, it made me laugh to hear it. Her problems were so normal.

Jess let out a big, dramatic sigh. "Yeah, it feels like I'm trapped in a box. Too many rules."

"Yeah."

"Hey, quit staring at that guy's horse," Jessie poked me hard enough to leave a red mark on my arm. "I know you miss Charlie, but people are gonna think you're a weirdo."

"You're right." I turned away from the picture window where I'd been watching the big chestnut canter off down the road. It was my turn to heave a big sigh. "This calls for an overdose of sugar," I said. Forcing out laughter that I didn't feel, I led the way into the candy aisle to load up.

When I returned home, my allowance spent, I was super-charged on sugar and the exhilaration that comes from laughing hard while riding uphill.

As I approached the barn, however, the smile slid from my face. I dismounted in a hurry, tripping over my own feet.

"Hold her! Hold her!"

Dad was shouting from inside the barn.

I arrived just in time to see the black horse I'd met earlier, backing awkwardly into an open stall while trying to kick anyone who drew near. She reared, stamped and pawed the air, snorting and tossing her head. The whites of her eyes glowed in the darkened barn, as she threw her head back and screamed. The sound was something I'll never forget. It sounded almost human. Her body twisted around in a wide arc as she kicked out at the hands holding her. As I watched, transfixed, she reared again, the lead rope stretched taut as the horse fought to get away. I stared in disbelief. What happened to the calm, gentle mare I'd met only an hour earlier? The terrified-looking girl holding on to her was familiar to me: my sister's best friend. This had to be the horse she'd convinced her father to buy for her.

My big sister was, of course, right in the middle of this mess. No doubt she'd arranged the whole thing, knowing that mom and dad needed to make a go of the horse-boarding business.

Diana held tightly to the second lead rope, and as I watched, she was somehow able to maneuver the frightened black horse safely into her stall. Dad moved quickly to secure the half-door, darting in and out with surprising agility. Safe at last, all three humans moved back, watching the mare as she continued to rage, kicking at the walls of the stall in apparent panic.

"If she keeps that up, we'll have the vet here," dad said to the young woman as he rubbed nervously at his forehead. "You said she was gentle."

"She is, I don't know what's wrong with her," she said.

"Well, talk to her Nancy, do something!" My sister stood there with her hands in the air.

"Star, Star! Calm down girl! It's okay. Ssh!" The teenager clucked her tongue at the huge animal, a tried-and-true method for horse-people everywhere, but the big mare was beyond caring. "Hush now! Star!"

Nancy turned to Diana, a desperate plea in the eyes that now glistened with tears.

Diana stepped up to the horse and brought her open palm up to its mouth with speed and confidence. I was just fast enough to notice the sugar cube that rested on her palm before Star gobble it down in spite of her agitation.

She turned back to Nancy. "The sugar may calm her for a minute; give her something else to focus on, because it won't last long. Let's get her out of that stall and back into the pasture. She was fine before we brought her in here."

Uh-oh, I thought. The barn again.

Nancy nodded slowly, but to her credit, she moved quickly, and grabbed the lead shank in her shaking hands.

"Th-there's my girl," she said, her soft voice quavering a little. She continued to speak softly and soon, her words were lost to us. Little by little, taking small, hesitating steps, the big horse's hooves stopped their incessant stamping and the nostrils no longer flared and snorted. Finally, the exhausted horse allowed itself to be led out into the sunlight spilling through the open barn door.

"That was weird," she said, as she watched her friend go. "I honestly do *not* know what that was."

"Don't you?" I muttered.

Diana swung around and gave me a hard look before following her friend through the sliding door to the pasture beyond.

Little did we know that our new horse-boarding venture would turn out to be a short-lived, but wild ride.

For three days in a row, Star was a pleasant, well-adjusted horse that seemed compliant in every way. But when darkness fell, that same horse took on a different personality. Diana was often seen running to the barn. She worried, cajoled and comforted, while dad cursed and paced the kitchen, muttering to himself about half-baked ideas. Each night after dinner, when the sun started to go down Star's protests would begin anew. The sounds of her distress were so loud that we could hear them clearly, even inside the house. Each time Diana or dad would rush down to the barn to find nothing amiss; but the after-effects of Star's temper-tantrum were obvious. The horse herself was lathered and breathing hard in the center of her stall, the whites of her eyes still showing, while convex hoof marks and freshly splintered wood bore the evidence of her fear.

No one seemed to understand what was going on.

Eventually, Nancy and Star went looking for another barn.

"You know, I've been thinking a lot about Star's behaviour," Diana said one evening at the supper table. "She seemed afraid, didn't she?"

"Of what?" dad grumbled. "Being locked in a stall? Koko's not bothered. That horse is just stupid."

"Well, it's possible that Star was reacting to something we couldn't see."

I paused in the act of bringing a fork to my lips and looked up at her carefully.

"Like what?" dad asked, gripping his fork and knife as he cut through the pork chop on his plate. "What do you think she sees?" he asked her.

"I don't know," she said thoughtfully, twirling her fork in the mound of mashed potatoes on her plate. "Maybe Koko's used to it? Maybe she knows something we don't." She looked at me meaningfully. "Maybe you should have a chat with her. The two of you could figure it out I bet."

I slid a startled glance at our silent parents, and was about to speak up in protest, but dad beat me to it.

"I should have known where you were going with that," he said. "That's enough."

I clenched my teeth in anger, as Diana blushed and went back to her meal.

Later, as my sister and I cleaned up the supper dishes, I broached the subject again. "So you know there's something in the barn, too." I couldn't quite keep the accusation out of my voice.

Diana glanced around nervously. "Oh what are you *on*? Ooh, scary, things that go bump in the night." Her tone was heavily sarcastic, but her eyes said she was scared too. As she spoke the next phrase however, it was hard to keep my gaze on the dishes, and my hands stopped of their own accord.

"It doesn't matter what I believe anyways, 'cause mom and dad are gonna sell the house and move us all outa here." There was no-doubt she saw the look of shock on my face, and she smiled triumphantly. "Your pals Bob and John will just have to find someone else to haunt. Dad said that if they can't make money boarding horses then they'll sell the house, so we'll be getting out of here and away from all this ... mess quite soon."

"Bob and John?" I squeaked. "Sell the house?"

"Haven't you been listening to dad when he says: this place is costing me an arm and a leg?"

"Uh-huh."

"You're still such a baby," she said, flicking a handful of soap suds at me. "Time to open your ears and listen. You might learn something useful."

Sundance

26

Several nervous days passed, and no one talked about the things that I most wanted to discuss.

Like, who the heck was this "John" my sister referred to, and how come she thought he was my 'pal'? And where did she get off saying mom and dad were going to sell the house?

Irritatingly, life just went on. Mom and dad made sure we became a family consumed with a single idea. Find the ticket, find the ticket, find the ticket … Nothing else mattered.

Laundry was duly searched before washing, in case the offending ticket was in a back pocket or just lost in a jumble of dirty clothes. Jacket pockets were searched in the front closet, purses were emptied, and cars were searched and vacuumed. Bit by bit, every inch of the house was searched, cleaned and tidied. It had now been five days since the lottery draw, and other people were busy claiming their prizes. Dad was growing surlier by the day.

I immersed myself in make-believe, finding solace in the company of my Barbies, despite the memories surrounding my failed séance attempt. When I wasn't at school, I was at my desk writing in my orange duo-tang or playing Barbies. Diana called it predictable and childish, but I called it safe. When my mind was occupied, I found that I could keep the other thoughts out. And that was the only thing that mattered to me.

It was a beautiful spring morning and the sunshine was already warming up the earth and drying the wet grass outside my bedroom window when I awoke to the sound of a low rumble. Rubbing the sleep from my eyes, I padded down the creaking hallway—it creaked in exactly two spots—to find my dad pacing the kitchen with the telephone to his ear.

"Look, I don't care what she said; she doesn't pay the bills around here. This whole thing is just ridiculous."

Dad's face was already red, and it didn't look like the conversation was making things any better. I grabbed a banana off the counter and retreated to the family room for Saturday morning cartoons. It wasn't until later that I learned the significance of the phone call.

~~~~~

"Daddy, I couldn't bear it, that's all," I heard my sister whimper as I went past the feed stall, the handles of the wheelbarrow heavy in my palms.

Hmm, I thought. The sound of manipulation at work. Diana could get dad to agree to anything. She's always had a way of plucking just the right heart-string when it comes to our dad. I still marvel at its effectiveness.

"Well you should have talked with me first," dad said. His tone said clearly that he was annoyed, but knowing Diana, his temper would be cooling within minutes.

"There wasn't time, dad. They were gonna kill him." Diana pleaded.

"But you've already got a horse, Diana. And we've only just gotten rid of Star, she kicked the crap out of my barn! I'm still fixing it!"

"Da-ad," she whined. "We've got room. It's a six stall barn!" She grabbed for his hand. "C'mon dad, the slaughter house? How could anyone send their horse to a slaughter house? We can't allow it. He's beautiful! It's criminal!"

"Look, people do stupid things; it doesn't mean you have to get in the middle of it."

"You and mom always teach us to do the right thing. Well *this* is the right thing dad!"

Uh-oh, I thought. The you've-raised-me-this-way speech. Dad was doomed.

"I see," dad replied.

"Daddy...please? Can't you at least look at him?"

I heard my father groan with defeat. "Alright, since you've practically arranged it already, we'll go take a look."

"Excellent!" she chirped. "Can we go now?"

"Now? I haven't even had my coffee yet. Simmer down."

"But..."

"Look, go and phone them. Tell them we'll leave in about half an hour."

"Okay," Diana sounded sullen. I suppressed a giggle. She was working this very well.

"And ... then you can go get the trailer ready."

Planting a noisy kiss on dad's forehead that I could hear from two stalls over, Diana practically sprinted from the barn. I just caught sight of her red hair streaming out behind her as she disappeared through the door. She'd won again. I sighed and went back to my chores. So what was with Diana's weird about-face? Now she wanted to stay? What was that going to mean for the future of our farm?

~~~~~

The horse Diana had saved from the slaughter-house was gorgeous. I had to agree with my sister that it would have been criminal for this animal to be killed. He stood eighteen hands, and was the colour of fire. Eighteen hands is tall for a horse and looking up at his back, I couldn't fathom how anyone could ride it, especially my vertically-challenged sister, but somehow, she vaulted up onto his back with only a "leg up" from Dad. She rode him bareback around the riding ring, his head tossing and his body weaving first one way and then the other, entirely under her control, as she laid the reins gently against his neck.

Diana made it look easy. He was headstrong, spirited and slightly dim-witted, but the beautiful Arabian was putty in my sister's hands. Day after day, she exercised and trained with him, teaching him to jump, lunge and pose. I dimly recall that he had some lessons, but they didn't stick too well. Still, he loved my sister and that was all that mattered. They were clearly enjoying each other and I found myself often leaning at the fence watching the two of them.

Little did I know what kind of trouble he was destined to become.

For starters, he had the weirdest name: Sundance.

"Are you serious?" I asked my sister, holding my sides. I was laughing so hard it hurt.

"Oh shut up," she said. "It's because he's registered. All registered horses have names like that. There's a whole list of names that goes with that."

"Whatever you say," I said, still smiling. "That'll strike fear into their hearts at the shows!"

Diana was good at pretending she didn't hear me.

~~~~

"Look, we've got an injured horse here. I've done what I can but we need the vet now!" I watched with wide eyes as dad waited for the person on the other end to finish speaking.

"Yes ... uh-huh ... sure, that was the first thing I tried. He's still losing a lot of blood ... yeah, no, he won't let me get close enough. He's going to need a sedative ... yes; okay I'll go down to the barn and wait there. Hurry!" He banged down the phone and hurried out the back door, not even noticing me in the kitchen behind him.

"What's going on?" I asked Diana as I entered the barn a few minutes later. I'd rushed to throw on some clothes and ran out after dad as soon as I could. Diana was standing just outside the barn door, her forehead cupped in the palm of her hand. I could see she'd been crying.

"It's Sundance, he's cut himself, he-he might have broken his leg!" She said, her voice tight. "Just look at his stall!"

I looked where she pointed and gasped. I could see daylight where the wood was splintered and torn through. Even in the shadowy light, I could see the dark smears of blood surrounding the jagged edges of the hole.

Sundance lay on his side, his chest heaving, trying unsuccessfully to raise his head, unable to do anything but thrash about painfully. His amber-coloured coat was a testament to his name and it showed the wound all too well. Tears sprang to my eyes. I'd seen enough old westerns to know what people did to horses with broken legs.

A large green station-wagon pulled up to the barn just then; a man with a felt cap, gum boots and a black doctor's bag jumped out of the driver's seat. Our vet was a colourful character, but the sight of him conjured up memories of Charlie and brought a lump to my throat. I stood back into the shadows and tried not to cry.

He wasted no time on pleasantries, but ran straight into the barn and yanked open his bag.

Diana followed him inside to where Sundance lay in his stall, my dad holding his head steady with a lead rope attached to his halter.

"Is that the sedative?" dad asked, eying the large hypodermic syringe in the vet's right hand.

"You bet; never leave home without it." His light-hearted answer seemed out of place, but we knew that this vet was quick and precise. I peered at the bag, looking for a firearm but found none. Even so, it wasn't until a half-hour had gone by, and the horse was neatly stitched and casted that I let the tension drain out of my body.

As the vet pulled away down the driveway, doffing his cap out the window, dad walked up and put an arm around each of us, exhaustion making his face haggard.

"We're going to have lots to do when he wakes up," dad said. "Let's go back to the house for awhile."

The concern in dad's eyes as we walked back to the house made me think of Diana's dire prediction.

"Dad?" I ventured.

"What is it?" he replied wearily.

"What's gonna happen now?"

"Lots of things," my father said. "Be specific."

"To us. To the house?"

"Oh. Well, we'll see. We'll see."

~~~~

I wasn't surprised when, in the days that followed, my parents' conversations turned to the value of real estate once again.

"I don't know if we can afford to move," Mom said.

"Well we can't afford to stay. That vet visit wasn't cheap."

"Oh, Will."

"The market's come up some, but we still owe too much on this house to make any really good money. We'll be taking a risk for sure, but if we downsize, we might be able to pull it off. I just hope we get the amount we need."

"Well, we can't board any more horses. Whatever it is about that barn, I don't know, but Diana's friend has been talking. Word's already gotten around in the horse community."

"That was fast," dad said.

"Too fast," mom agreed. "How are we supposed to make ends meet now?"

"We'll think of something," dad replied.

I gulped. I already knew what dad meant by 'something' and unfortunately it involved realtors.

~~~~~

Dad was still frantic about his missing lottery ticket and it was all he could talk about. It had been weeks since he'd seen the winning numbers announced on the television, and although he and mom still searched, it was nowhere to be found.

"It defies logic," my father said one morning.

"So do a lot of things around here," mom agreed.

Diana and I glanced at each other and then back at her. Where was this going?

"Oh, your father's here!" mom said to dad a moment later. Someone was tapping on the glass door at the back of the house. "Come on in dad!" she called.

My grandfather had arrived to start work on a project he and dad had planned for weeks: our new garage.

"Grandpa!" I squealed, as he strode into the kitchen, back straight, toolbox in hand.

"There's my little girl!" Grandpa exclaimed, stooping to wrap me in a big bear hug. My grandfather was a powerfully muscled man who'd worked all his life as a bricklayer. It was tough, heavy work, giving him a strong work ethic and thick calluses on both hands. His faded green work pants hid athletic legs; his flannel work shirt was rolled up at the arms, and neatly tucked in at the waist. Although he was now retired, he was still fit and strong.

My dad's faded jeans and cotton t-shirt made him look like an unkempt teenager beside his father. The two men wore identical work boots, each pair scuffed and comfortable.

"Hello dad," my father greeted him. "Did you have any trouble on the drive in?"

"No more than usual; traffic was light," he said, clapping a big hand on my dad's back in greeting.

They set to work almost immediately, and I chose a spot out in the grass, not that far away, where I could watch the process.

"So Will, why the hang-dog expression?" My grandfather asked with a gentle twitch of a smile forming on his lips.

"Oh, you know," dad replied, rolling his eyes and looking over at me. "Lots of things."

"Daddy," I called. "Does Grandpa know you won the lottery?"

Dad frowned at me and I pressed my lips together hard. Oops.

"What's this?" Grandpa turned to his son.

"Ah, yeah ... well you know that I buy lottery tickets each week, right?"

Grandpa nodded. "Waste of money, that."

"Well, that may be, since I can't find the one I bought last Friday," he said. "It's a winner, dad. Five out of six numbers."

"Be serious." His quiet voice offered no hint of emotion.

Dad stood straighter. "It's true. Scout's honour."

"Well." My grandpa could pack a lot into one word. He paused to cinch up his tool belt, settling it on his hips like a favourite pair of jeans.

"I figure you've already looked in the obvious places," he said as he began to fill the pouches with the various tools he would need for the job.

Dad nodded, his face glum.

"Well then, what you ought to do now is forget about it."

My father was incredulous. "Dad! That's thousands of dollars! How can I forget about that? Especially now."

"Phah! That's not what I mean ... just do something else," he said gruffly. "Once you're busy with something else, it'll turn up. Always worked for me ... here, hand me that level, let's get started."

Dad looked dubious, but he did as he was told. "We're not talking about misplacing the car keys, dad," he said.

"Works for that, too," Grandpa told him, grabbing his carpenter's pencil from the pouch at his waist. No hint of a smile played on his lips, but I knew from his tone of voice he was teasing his son. Moments later, as I watched the two men sawing and hammering, I realized that dad knew it too. His expression had changed as he worked shoulder to shoulder with his father, their muscles straining as the concrete spread into the square form they'd created for it.

"But seriously dad, no one will admit they took it."

"William," Grandpa barked at him, holding one side of a framed-in wall. "If you worry like an old woman, we're never gonna finish this.

There's no time for talk, son. Pick up your hammer! I need that side braced."

Grandpa was a hard man to distract, and so my dad was forced to commit himself, body and soul, to the task.

It seemed that the skeleton of a garage grew out of frustration that day.

Dad hardly talked to anyone that evening. I knew he was still brooding over the ticket, but wisely, we avoided the topic at the dinner table and afterwards, as he sat down to watch some T.V., with a bottle of beer clutched in one hand. Mom was the only one who dared join him.

The next morning, I was jolted awake by a strange noise. As the fog cleared from my sleep-addled brain, I realized that the noise was a woman, screaming at the top of her lungs!

I rushed to the glass door in the rec room and peered outside, when the most outlandish sight met my eyes. Out on the grass, giggling and whooping like children who've eaten too much Easter candy, dad was twirling mom around in her nightgown and fuzzy pink slippers!

"What's goin' on?" I said, poking my head outside.

"This is it! I found it! It's here! I don't know why it's here, but I don't care! The winning ticket! Just look at it!" Dad's face was wreathed in smiles, his feet doing a quick two-step as he held out a small piece of paper in one hand. "You'll never guess where it was!" He danced around again, oblivious to the fact that he was now dancing by himself.

Mom broke away from my father with a fond smile and took up the narrative. "When your dad came out to set up the tools this morning, there it was, balanced right across the sawhorse! It's the strangest thing! They were just working there last night!" She frowned and seemed to mentally shift gears. "Anyways, finding the ticket is the important thing. Dad and I are going to the lottery office to claim the money today! Isn't it exciting?"

"Wow!" I said, my excitement brimming over, now, too. "Really? Is it a lot of money, dad?"

His answering grin was all the reply I needed. Maybe now, we'd be able to 'make ends meet' and we wouldn't have to sell the house. Maybe.

The Blessing

27

"So what will you do?" I asked Pastor Smith as he entered through the front door.

"Ask the Father to watch over your family," he answered.

"Doesn't He watch over us already?" I asked.

"Of course, Ginny," replied our Pastor in the gentle tone he always reserved for teaching. "He watches over us wherever we go, but sometimes it's nice to have a little more. Something a little bit specific, you know?" He grinned and his dark beard, minus a moustache, stuck out just a bit. He had a very kind face.

"It's a traditional house blessing dear," mom said. "I can't think why we didn't do it when we moved in, but since we've finally found that crazy ticket, we can all get back on track again. Your father and I felt this was a nice way to get a fresh start, so to speak. Maybe we'll all sleep a bit more soundly."

"You have to admit things have been a bit off around here lately," dad grumbled. "Bad luck or something."

Pastor Smith grinned and reached into the pocket of his suit jacket, extracting a worn, brown leather bible. Always curious, I sidled up to him as he began flipping through the pages.

"Will this make them go away?" I whispered. I expected him to say, "make who go away?" But thankfully, his answer was quite different.

"It may," he whispered back.

Shocked at his openness, I took a step back and we exchanged tentative smiles.

On the table, three white, tapered candles sat in plain glass holders. I hadn't seen these before. Had mom placed them there?

Carefully, Pastor Smith struck a match and lit one of the candles. He seemed to be murmuring to himself as he did so.

With a gentleness that was characteristic of the man, he reached into his other suit pocket and brought forth an item wrapped in a plain white cloth. He laid it in his hand and unfolded the edges of the cloth to expose a beautiful golden crucifix, about six inches long. Thrusting the cloth into his pocket again, he grinned at my obvious delight.

"Beautiful isn't it?" he asked.

"Yes," I breathed, spellbound. I'd only ever seen this during church service. I never realized he took it with him for house blessings.

I don't know what I expected to see, but I followed Pastor from our living room to the kitchen, through to the family room and watched him as he peeked into the adjoining laundry room. He might have been a prospective buyer for all the care he took, looking over the house. I watched as he came to stand in the center of our kitchen. My eyes focused on the intricate crucifix that dangled from a single red ribbon connected to the worn Bible Pastor held in one hand. The length of ribbon was looped lazily around his fingers, and the crucifix at the end, a heavy bit of metal, swung and twirled as he turned the pages.

I stood at a discrete distance, watching him reading from the Bible and holding up the golden crucifix. His words were pitched low and I couldn't hear, but it wasn't long before I could see beads of perspiration standing out on his forehead.

Wow. He was working up a sweat.

Pastor turned and walked the few feet into the family room, stopping suddenly and looking around him as though something had caught his attention. I glanced around too to see if it was Mom, but both she and dad had stayed back at the kitchen table, talking in low tones. Dad was absently stroking the fur on my cats back as it lay on a chair by his side.

The clergyman stood straighter, and drew back his shoulders. Coming around to his side, I saw his brow crease in thought and, glancing at me quickly, he held up his hand to still my words. The crucifix continued to sway in the silence. It was hypnotic. Pastor looked around the room and, lifting his hands in supplication, he began the formulaic prayer that he'd spoken in the kitchen.

"… amen," he finished, bringing his arms down by his sides once more. He paused to drag his handkerchief across his sweaty forehead and tugged at the white collar around his neck as though it was suddenly too tight.

He grinned at me a moment later. "It's alright, don't look so worried."

"Okay," I said, but he looked far from all right. His face had grown red, as though he'd just had a long run.

"Okay, this feels like a good place to conclude. Ginny," he turned to me. "Let's open that door," he said, indicating the door to the laundry room, "Get some air circulating."

The door swung open at his touch, a little too quickly for the gentleness of his feather-light touch. I sucked in a sharp breath. The atmosphere had changed. The room we stood in felt electric.

I saw him frown, and this time the words he spoke gained volume. "Most Merciful Lord," he intoned. "You took flesh through the Blessed Virgin Mary, when you sent your son to dwell among us. We now pray that you will enter this home and bless it with your presence. May you always be here among us; may you nurture our love for each other, share in our joys, and comfort us in our sorrows. Inspire us with your teachings and lead us to follow your example."

My eyes had grown wide as I listened and I felt light-headed, as a mixture of sensations warred with each other. I was vaguely aware that my parents had gotten to their feet and were standing just behind me.

"Peace be with this house and with all who live here. Blessed be the name of the Lord. Bless this house and protect those who live here. Protect them, Lord, from all possible harm," Pastor Smith said, walking forward.

All possible harm?

The phrase resounded in my head.

If only it were that simple, I thought.

Pastor Smith reached the middle of the kitchen and he raised his voice once more as he lifted the golden crucifix he'd brought, and making the sign of the cross with it in the space before his body, he said: "In nomine Patris, et Filii, et Spiritu Sancti."

"Sorry," I muttered, feeling a firm pressure on my shoulder. I moved to one side, assuming mom or dad needed to get by.

But when no one did, I turned and realized that although my parents still stood there, they hung back a few feet, and neither one looked like they were going anywhere. Mom looked back at me with a question in her eyes.

"What's wrong kid?" dad said.

"Um, nothing," I responded, my shoulders slumping in defeat. Come on Pastor Smith, I thought. Make them go away.

The presence of another person standing at my back had been so real. I could literally feel someone pushing on my shoulder. That physical touch was a new and unwelcome sensation.

As though he'd sensed it too, Pastor Smith turned to me, his kindly face aglow with perspiration now. "Yes," he said simply. "It's alright."

I stared at him. Could he really be saying what I thought he was saying?

"Would you hold this please Ginny? I'm rather warm," he said, handing his Bible to me and digging in his coat pocket for the spare handkerchief he kept there.

As I took hold of the small Bible, our fingers touched and the kindly smile slid from his face. He stopped in the act of wiping his forehead to stand very still, squinting at a point over my right shoulder. I didn't need to look, but I did anyways. I saw what I expected to see. Nothing but the unremarkable room we'd just left.

When I looked back a second later, Pastor's face was no longer red and flushed. Instead, his skin looked ashen, as though he were suddenly ill. He turned confused, frightened eyes towards me, then back again to the same spot. As I watched him control his breathing and make an effort to steady his shaking hands, my heart pounded faster too. *Someone* was there, but this was no child. This energy felt sinister.

Pastor Smith's eyebrows knit together in a worried expression. He seemed at a loss for words.

"Pastor?" I said, my voice coming out as a squeak. "I ...." Suddenly the edges of my vision darkened and my head shook and swirled. Abruptly my knees let go and the floor tilted at an odd angle.

I don't remember hitting the floor.

Later, I awoke in my own bed, mom sitting on a chair beside me. She was humming quietly. The song was an old one I remembered from when I was a baby.

"Mom?" I said, my voice sounded funny.

"Oh! Honey," mom said, the relief in the voice was evident. "It's good to see you awake."

"What happened?" I asked, pushing the long wisps of hair out of my face as I sat up.

"Oh not much, you just fainted," she replied sarcastically.

"I did what?"

"Fainted. You know, passed out? Well, you're up now and that's what matters." Mom breathed a sigh and helped me up. "When was the last time you ate?"

I shrugged, still trying to remember what happened. My memory was elusive.

"Well then, let's go to the kitchen and I'll get you a snack."

Mom disappeared quickly out the door and I followed shortly afterward, my legs heavy. Mom was humming to herself again while putting together a grilled cheese sandwich at the kitchen counter. I couldn't help wondering if she hummed out of happiness or discomfort? Was she aware that the tune she hummed was a children's lullaby?

"Where's Pastor?" I asked, the memories coming back as I stood there.

"Gone," she said. "After you fainted, daddy carried you in here. Pastor said a special prayer over you, and he must've asked a hundred times whether you were okay before he finally left. I suspect you didn't eat anything today after breakfast? Am I right?"

"Well," I said. "Not nothing, but I don't exactly remember lunch." I cast wary glances to my right and left, looking for any sign of the presence I'd felt just before my collapse, but the house looked normal.

"Oh Ginny!" Mom's tone expressed her annoyance. "You know better. You must have terrified the poor man, fainting right in front of him that way. He was very distraught, poor Pastor."

He was distraught? Oh boy.

"I'm sure he was fine, Mom." I said, trying not to talk through my food as I chewed. With the first bite, I suddenly realized I was ravenous. While it was true I had missed my lunch, I'd never been prone to fainting over a missed meal before.

Ghost Charade

28

"What are we supposed to do with her?" Dad was pacing back and forth in the kitchen. Mom sat at the oval kitchen table, her hands folded. I sulked in the rec room, trying to pretend I couldn't hear them. I knew they were talking about me.

"I don't know, why are you asking me?" mom replied. Her voice was sounded like she was on the verge of tears. "I can't very well make the child go into the barn when she's terrified."

"Well we also can't keep doing all her chores and ours too," dad said. "It's gotten ridiculous around here with all these ghostly sightings of hers."

"Will, that's not entirely fair," mom warned. "She's been through a lot."

I wanted to die. I was terrified and now it was clear that my parents didn't believe a word I said. I couldn't seem to do anything right.

"Mom? Dad?" I said, my fingertips creeping around the doorframe as I carefully edged into the room with them.

"Yes honey, it's alright, come on in," mom said. I caught the meaningful look she directed at her husband.

"I know what this seems like to you guys," I said.

"Oh do you?" dad said. "And what is that?"

"A bid for attention," I said. "At least that's what your friends are telling you, isn't it?"

"What makes you think that we're talking about any of this nonsense with our friends?" mom said, rising from her chair.

"Mom, why do you always say, this is nonsense, whenever I try and talk to you?"

"Why must you always do this Ginny? It's one drama after another," mom said, her voice escalating. "Let me see if I have this right: you can't do your chores because there are ghosts in our brand new barn; you can't sleep at night, because the house is spooky; yet you spend all your time writing ghost stories in that orange book of yours. So why do you think you see ghosts everywhere? They're in your head to begin with! Oh and don't forget about that imaginary friend of yours. The one you're too old to have in the first place! I suppose you see him lurking about playing havoc with the lights, too? Have I got it all correct or is there another chapter you'd like to add?"

"Mom!" I wailed, feeling miserable and blinking back tears.

"Alright dear, you've made your point," dad interrupted. "I think Ginny knows we're concerned about this." Dad turned to me and his voice softened a little, "you mentioned 'attention', I believe?"

I nodded, wiping tears from my cheeks with the back of my hand.

"Attention? So that's all it is?" mom said, looking at me with narrowed eyes. "Hmm. Well I highly doubt that's all there is to it."

I stared at my shoes for a long time without saying anything. The awkwardness of the moment intensified, but still I had nothing to say and obviously neither did they.

Eventually, mom cleared her throat. "Well, I have things to do, excuse me."

Left alone with me, dad cleared his throat and sat forward on the edge of his chair. "Ginny, I don't know who's been filling your head with these ideas, but you have to start considering that maybe that's all they are: ideas. There are more things going on here than you know," he continued. "Do you understand what might happen if you continue to believe in this?"

I shook my head.

"You're fast becoming an adult, and it's time you realized that adults have very different ideas of what is real and what isn't. For example, did you ever think what would happen if these things were true and we did talk to people about it?"

"They are true," I muttered, then, catching his sharpened look and raised eyebrows, I shrugged. "No, not really."

"I didn't think you had," he replied. "Let me just say it wouldn't go well." He sat back and took a deep breath, maintaining eye contact as he did. "Look, we'll work something out with your chores, okay? Mom and I aren't unreasonable, but she's frustrated and so am I. So let's drop this ghost charade and get back to work, alright?"

My head snapped up at that and I felt my mouth fall open in protest. Charade?

"Just do us a favor and think about what we've said," he interjected before I could protest. "You might be surprised how things will work out."

Dad stopped talking and rose from his chair, but all of a sudden, he turned abruptly and sat back down. "And let's have an end to this ghost nonsense, huh?"

"Yes sir," I managed to mumble, still outraged on the inside. I sat there on the wooden kitchen chair for a long time after he left the room.

It was all so unfair.

~~~~

Parent-teacher interviews were always complicated when I lived in that house.

The year had started out with such promise: new school, new house, a whole new me.

Now, this new me was in trouble.

It was March and that meant Spring Break was near. In my school, that also meant interim report cards. All the kids got one last opportunity to bring up their grades, which meant that the teachers and the parents would be talking. I suppose it made sense to know just how bad things were before the end of the year came and the report cards were handed out.

Enough time to do something about it, I guess.

I tried to think of other things as I waited for mom to get home from the interview that night, but try as I might, I couldn't erase the worry from my mind: my grades weren't good. In fact, they'd begun falling dramatically as I found out my homework was going missing. A couple of days of frantic searching never yielded results, but as soon as the due date passed, there it would be, almost artfully arranged in the middle of my tiny bedroom desk.

238

Or worse, outside, tucked in the crook of a tree branch, or stuck in behind the couch cushions, where my father would discover it, when he settled down to watch the news.

That never went well.

I rubbed my arms briskly, trying to erase the goose bumps that stood out on my flesh. I could just imagine my teacher, Mrs. Hudson telling mom about my "inability to focus" during class time. But what was I supposed to do about that? It wasn't like I could confide in her. I could imagine how that would go: so yeah, my house is haunted, I'm dreaming about ghosts pursuing me and sometimes, I think the ghost takes my homework and hides it. Yeah, right. Seriously, I'm not crazy or anything.

As if.

I rubbed my arms again. Why was I always so cold?

"I don't think so," dad warned, staying my hand as I reached for the thermostat. "It's plenty warm enough, young lady."

The minutes dragged by slowly. Desperate to keep busy, I put away all my clean laundry, folding until my fingers cramped.

At last, as I was in the middle of changing the sheets on my bed, the sound of crunching gravel announced the arrival of the car.

"I hope you appreciate what I go through for you," mom said sternly as she entered the house and began to remove her coat. My heart sank. Although her words were sharp, her tone remained calm. "I was so embarrassed in there. To think that you've let your grades slip so much. Not handing things in and not paying attention ... well, enough of that. Your teacher is sending home a list of missed assignments and you'd better see that I get it. I told her I would personally guarantee they got done, and I won't be made a fool of, especially in front of that woman." She took a deep, steadying breath and turned to hang up her coat. "I just won't let that happen."

Her words left no doubt that I was seriously on the hook. Just as obviously, the wonderful Mrs. Hudson had made an impression on my mother too. I took a small amount of comfort in that.

Sensitive

29

It was Thursday afternoon and dad was at home. That fact was strange in itself, since he went to work before I was even awake each day and returned just in time for supper and the six o'clock news.

I looked out the window, expecting to see something that would give me a clue as to why dad was home so early, but I saw only what I'd seen when I got home from school: nothing.

A knock on our front door started my heart thudding. Who could be coming to visit at this time of day? It was just past three.

"Ah, Eva, won't you come in?" My mother greeted a woman at our front door. "I must admit I was surprised to get your call, but it's lovely to see you."

This was getting interesting. What was Eva Geiry doing here? I knew her daughter from church, but why would she be visiting us? Besides, mom and dad weren't religious enough to be asking the church for help with a problem they didn't even acknowledge. So what was going on? First Mrs. Hudson and now this?

As the adults settled down to talk at the kitchen table, I began fixing a snack at the counter, but mom was having none of it.

"Ginny, have you taken care of your horse yet today?" Mom regarded me with a serious stare.

"Uh, mostly," I lied.

"Uh-huh, sure. I know that look," she said. "Off with you, I'll make you a snack later. Right now, you have work to do and this is an adult conversation."

"Fine," I said. "Can I have a bathroom break first?"

"Make it fast," dad said. And with that, I was banished. Not to be thwarted, of course, I made a show of walking off down the hall and closing the bathroom door so they could hear it plainly. After waiting a few minutes with my ear pressed to the door, I carefully opened it a crack and sank down onto the floor to listen. I wasn't about to miss this. I had a lot of questions.

"Well, as I said on the phone, this concerns your daughter," she took a breath like she was going to say something, then another sound intruded.

The unmistakable sound of the laundry room door, swinging open and banging hard against the opposite wall seemed to halt all discussion. I didn't have to be in the room to know what had happened.

I heard mom's nervous giggle, and dad jumped in with, "crazy house is always settling." He cleared his throat several times.

I inched forward as far as I could without risking detection, straining to hear every word.

Once again, Eva Geiry took a deep breath, and plunged on. "I came today because...well, I'm concerned. We all are. I ... I'd like to help you," she said.

"With wh-what?" mom said. "You said this concerns Ginny? How?"

"It's evident that you've been under a terrible strain. Everyone at the church is concerned about you."

"So we're the talk of the church now," dad asked. He sounded irritated.

"Your family is under terrible stress," she said. "I've seen it for weeks now, only I wasn't sure I should say anything. I know it's something ... complicated and difficult to talk about."

"I beg your pardon?" he asked. "What can you possibly think ...?"

"We have to be straight with each other," she interrupted him. Suddenly, she stopped and through my sliver of view, I saw her turn completely around and look pointedly at my slightly open door. I felt my face flush and backed away, losing my vantage point, but fully expecting that any moment she would give me away. I waited in silence to be found out, and crept to the toilet to flush it for added effect, although doing so muted all conversation.

Damn. I was too smart for my own good.

As the gurgling water noises subsided, I heard voices again and realized Eva was still speaking.

"… you realize your youngest is a Sensitive."

I lost my footing and banged against the bathroom door as the air whooshed out of my lungs.

"Ginny!" dad called out, his voice booming. "I thought I told you to see to those horses! Now get out of that bathroom and get going!"

I was through the room in seconds, ducking my head to avoid any startled glances, my face hot with shame. The back door banged closed behind me. In moments, I was at the barn, my thoughts tumbling over each other, as I stroked my new pony's soft black and white nose and tried to calm down.

I was in trouble and I knew it, but I couldn't help feeling just a little bit vindicated.

I backtracked in my mind, sorting through the conversations Heidi and I had shared after catechism classes while we waited for our parents. Was it something I said or could she tell just by looking at me? What did she tell her mother to make her come here and talk to my family?

Right. If only I could concentrate, but those words still echoed in my brain.

A Sensitive.

I already knew what it meant. If only I knew what to do about it.

~~~~~

"Now let me see if I have this straight," Elise said a few minutes later when we were seated inside. "You're saying that Eva actually called you a Sensitive?"

"Yes. She came over especially just to tell my parents about it."

"Yes, that sounds like Eva. She's very direct. What did she say?" Elise asked, her eyes bright.

"Nothing that I could hear. Dad caught me for eavesdropping." I looked down at my feet and waited for the lecture I was sure would come.

"Oh!" She answered instead. "That's a shame."

My head snapped up in surprise. "Um, oh. I guess so, yeah, but what am I supposed to do now?"

"Do?" They chimed in together, looking at me strangely. "What do you mean?"

Elise looked out the window at my home across the street and in a very low tone of voice, she asked, "Did you talk with your parents yet?"

242

I was startled at her frankness and I suppressed the urge to laugh at the absurdity of it. "Uh, no. They don't really want to hear it. They're convinced it's all in my head." I paused thoughtfully for a minute or two. "Elise, what if it is? All in my head, I mean?"

"Well in a way, it is," Elise replied, suddenly laughing at my expression. "Now don't take it like that." She darted a look at her sister. "If Eva says a thing, she usually means it, doesn't she Penny?"

"I've never known her to lie," Penny said, her expression serious.

"Do you know her well then?"

Both women nodded. "For quite a few years, actually. If she said that, then she meant it. Penny and I have been thinking about this for awhile."

Silence stretched between us and I stared at them in wonder. My eyebrows climbed high on my forehead.

"Have I told you about the house where Penny and I grew up?" Elise said at last.

I shook my head.

Elise turned to her sister "Penny, quit wandering, you're making me tired just watching. I was just going to tell Ginny about our house on Fraser Street."

"Oh!" Penny looked startled at fist, and then something unspoken seemed to pass between them. "Of course, that's a good idea," she said. "Fraser Street."

"It isn't there anymore, of course. Too bad, but it was an old home when we lived there. Like so many old homes, our Fraser Street house had a past."

"Yes," Penny picked up the narrative. "Our big brother George saw things there. Now, you need to understand, George was a 'strapping man': all full of muscles and about six foot two. It took a lot to scare him, but ooh, he didn't like going to do the milking."

"The milking?" I asked.

"Cows," Penny replied. "There was something about that time of the day, I guess. Cows are up early and so George had to be as well. But you see, when George brought each cow in to be milked, he'd look around that barn and darned if he didn't see shadows, moving to and fro, looking for all the world like people! Farm hands, carrying shadowy hay bales and cleaning tack that wasn't there. You see, they came to work, right alongside our brother. It gave George quite a turn! He never did get used to it."

"How many were there?" I asked breathlessly.

"George said there were usually three or four. They wouldn't all appear at once, of course, but the funny thing was they acted very casual. They were dressed in coveralls, carrying pitchforks and shovels that were as insubstantial as they were. One man was busy for a long while shoeing a horse that looked as if it were made out of mist. They never once acknowledged him."

"If they had, I don't think even George could have stood that," her sister added.

I was fascinated. "What did he do about it?" I asked.

"Do?" Both women seemed genuinely surprised by my question.

"I don't remember him doing anything," Elise said quietly. "That's just the point. They didn't interact with him. Spirits come and go for reasons of their own, I think," Penny said.

I let out a deep sigh. "That's not very helpful. Did he tell your mom and dad?"

"Oh my, yes."

"Mother, of course, was a very practical woman but even she saw things on more than one occasion."

"What things?" I asked excitedly.

"She never said," Penny replied. "But we knew."

Elise nodded at her sister. "Yes."

"And your dad?" I asked breathlessly.

"Father? Well, he was a very practical soul, but he loved us children with all his heart. He viewed it as childish pranks, I think."

Penny nodded her agreement. "Father was like that. If he didn't acknowledge it, it wasn't happening."

"So what happened then?" I asked.

"Happened? Oh, well nothing really. Mother just shook her finger at us both, cautioning us not to speak of it to anyone. In those days, if you saw things that others didn't, that meant you had to be crazy." Elise shook her head. "Your mother's response is a timeless reaction, I'm afraid."

"So no one did anything about these ghosts? Didn't it scare you?"

"Well I suppose it did at first. We ended up just thinking that our home was such a nice place, that they really didn't want to leave. And so … they just stayed. In time, they seemed almost … familiar. Like part of the family."

"Wow," I said.

"I did say almost. Time went on as it always does and one day we just stopped seeing them. Or at least I did," Penny turned to her sister for confirmation and received a short nod. "Ghosts are like that. As I said, they seem to come and go on their own terms."

Suddenly, the back door of the cottage burst open and Fred pounded into the room.

"Ho!" shouted Penny, her voice like a thunderclap in the relative stillness of the room.

Surprisingly, the huge dog skidded to a stop, inches from the table where we sat.

"Freddy, you feisty pup, you've gone and pushed open the door again!" She shook her finger at him as she spoke. Fred, his tongue lolling out sideways, did not look very apologetic.

"Believe it or not, this is an improvement over the way he used to be," Elise said. "When he was younger, there was no containing him."

"Yes, but he's a very good dog," I commented, reaching out to pet him.

"Oh yes," she agreed, ruffling up his ears. "Pretty good for still being a pup."Fred sat on his haunches and accepted the attention with a big doggy grin.

"He's still a puppy?"

"Oh I know he doesn't look it, but that's just his breed. We love our Freddy, don't we?" She rubbed the dog's ears vigorously. "Penny and I haven't regretted taking him in even once."

"Taking him in?"

"Oh, my daughter and son-in-law couldn't keep him. It was just impossible."

"They wanted to," she hastened to explain. "But … well, you can't blame a puppy … the circumstances …" Elise faltered, looking away.

"Let *me* explain dear," Penny interrupted. "After the funeral and all that, they put the house up for sale. Of course, I'm sure you know *that* part. So when the house sold, they wanted a clean start. Didn't even want to take the pup, there were too many painful memories. But we just couldn't see him going to the pound. Painful memories or no, we ended up taking him in. And it's been a good arrangement. He's learning to be a very good guard dog." She stroked Fred's back affectionately. "Having Bobby's pup here feels a little bit like he isn't gone after all."

"Fred is *Bobby's* puppy?" I asked, realization dawning at last. For some reason, that made perfect sense. "But why couldn't they keep him?"

"It was too much, sweetie. You see, Bobby was chasing Fred at the time …"

Penny's eyes dropped to her lap and she took a several deep breaths before continuing. "He's grown quickly, hasn't he?" The old woman smiled sadly as she stroked the silky head. Wiping away a stray tear from her cheek, she muttered, "Such a good dog." Her voice was husky with emotion.

Not sure what to say, I sat quietly, waiting as the two women quietly grieved. Their hands stroked the fur of the puppy that'd caused such tragedy in their family. I almost heard the clunk as another piece of the puzzle dropped into place.

"Oh Fred," I said to him, as I stroked his silky head. "If only you could talk."

Cats

30

"Chores don't do themselves," dad said the next morning, his lips pressed tightly together. "Besides, that paddock has turned into a mucky mess with all this rain. I've got to dump more shavings in there, just so it's still usable. I can't do your chores too."

I knew there was no way I could get out of it, but I was so tired of being afraid and confused by everything. It felt like the inside of my head was filled with fireflies pinging off my brain. I'd awakened that morning feeling as though I'd never slept. Sandy-eyed and physically tired, I worked on autopilot. Half of my chores were done before my tired brain remembered to be afraid, and I roused myself enough to jog quickly to the barn radio and turn it on. This was my defense against the noises that shouldn't be there, as I bent to fill up the food dish for the barn cats.

The cats were another defense. Tiger's litter had grown, as cats tend to do, and my parents didn't have the heart to give them away.

"They'll be good mousers, like their mother," dad had said.

I was grateful. Random noises can always be blamed on a cat. A group of cats was even better.

My fingertips were just inches from the dial when a scraping sound, like a boot scuffing across the floor, came from the empty loft. As I stood frozen, the sound repeated.

Cats, I thought instantly.

But when the banging continued, growing louder, more insistent, I knew it was too loud to be feline.

"Oh no, not again", I groaned aloud. "Who's up there?" I called. Exhaustion had made me careless. "Look, I don't know what you want from me," I stated, my voice starting to shake as I went on. "But I know someone's up there, so either show yourself or get lost!"

As though in answer something heavy banged overhead, sending down a shower of dust and debris onto my trembling shoulders. Eyes wide, I tried to swallow the lump in my throat. Heavy, dragging footsteps sounded again, running across the loft, toward the stairs and me.

This was no cat.

Show yourself. Oh Good call, Ginny you idiot!

Unnerved to the roots of my hair, I didn't wait. I took off, running hard for the house. I was already outside and down the path before I heard the metallic clang of my hastily abandoned shovel hit the floor.

~~~~~

Mom and dad were arguing. There seemed to be a lot of that going on.

I stood motionless.

"This is very poor timing, Will."

"I'm aware of that Elizabeth, but dodging her chores is only the first step. Now she's taken to inventing these crazy stories. It's getting worse."

"Well what are we supposed to do?"

"I don't know," dad answered. "Look, I don't want to seem heartless." I heard him sigh. "Maybe we should think about listing the house again."

A long pause followed. I started to back up slowly. Did they know I was listening?

"If only she showed us that she was making friends. I know she's the new girl at school, but surely she's got to have some friends by now?"

"Maybe ... maybe we should take a holiday?" dad replied. "Just get away from here for awhile. That would do all of us some good."

"Well ...." mom seemed to consider it. "I would like to think that a distraction like that would be enough, but I'm not that naive. We're talking about her state of mind. Don't you think it's creepy how she knows things sometimes?"

"We've been over this," dad sighed. "She makes assumptions and pronouncements all the time. She always has. We should be thinking rationally here."

"I don't know, if it were one or two coincidences I might agree, but Will, our daughter knows things. She always has."

Dad's heavy sigh was loaded with unspoken objection.

"Will, would you just listen to me? I don't know what to do," mom said.

"Nor do I," he replied. "But if I don't do anything, I'll go crazy."

~~~~

"We're going to the cabin for Easter," dad announced when he got home from work one Friday in early April. "We all need to get away."

Diana's moaned complaint could be heard from the far side of the room. "Aw, dad!"

"I don't want to hear any of that young lady," he told her. "You can be without your boyfriend for one weekend. Besides, what's he doing for Easter? I'm sure his family has plans too."

Preparation for a trip to our beloved cottage always started at least three days in advance. Sort of like a game of dominoes. One thing led to another and so on.

And so it was that mom packed boxes, shopping bags, stuffed blankets and sheets into garbage bags and did mountains of laundry, all in preparation for our weekend away, which resulted in a surly and short-tempered mother.

"Is anyone going to help me with all this?" she complained.

Anyone was usually me, as it was pretty much guaranteed that, at the tender age of ten, I was the only one without any pressing social plans or work obligations.

I now realize that every trip we took was a lot of work. But, as mom is fond of saying, it was always a labour of love. After the constant strain our family had been under since moving into the unpredictable farmhouse, I was looking forward to a break. Although I knew my parents would be cranky before-hand, at the first sight of that A-frame cabin in the woods, they would sigh happily and say, "we're home guys." And as our old truck meandered up the twisting, dirt driveway, not much more than two tire tracks surrounded by tall grasses, we felt the excitement too. We truly were home. I've always felt that.

That Easter saw my sister and I, baskets in hand, avidly hunting through the forest for chocolates … you're never too old. Really.

Dad dutifully chopped wood like a real lumberjack, swinging the heavy axe with ease so my mother could feed the two wood stoves inside the house.

The beautiful little stream that runs through the property has always been a source of comfort for me. I've spent many hours there, staring into the crystal waters, trying not to think of home.

The day our much-needed vacation came to a close, a sense of fear gripped me. I realized that I was actually afraid to return to our house, and the thought sickened me. On the ride back to civilization, as mom always termed it, my stomach churned.

"Car sickness," mom said with a slight shake of her head. "I wonder if you'll ever outgrow that."

Despite my heaving stomach, I must have managed to doze off. The big wheels of our pick up crunched loudly on the gravel driveway and my head came up with a start. Wiping the sleep from my eyes I wondered for what had to be the thousandth time how everything could look so normal on the outside. It was a pretty little farmhouse, the huge windows in front made it look like a show home, and the freshly painted siding announced to all who drew near that we cared about this place.

If only that was enough.

As dad opened the front door, with his usual sigh of resignation, thoughts of home and school were interrupted by more unanswered questions.

"Aw, Ginny, I thought I told you to clean up in here before we left?" Mom's voice reached me from somewhere inside the house as I grabbed my bag out of the truck.

"What Mom?" I called, following the sound of her voice back inside the house.

"The rec room," she called back. "It's a disaster!"

"Can't be," I said, walking into the room. But sure enough, a mess of board games, their contents spilled out in a heap, rested on the carpet at the foot of the open storage closet. The closet was a large one, with two bi-fold doors that swung away from each other: plenty of room to store board games, books, decks of cards and other household clutter. Most of this now lay in an untidy pile on the floor. In all honesty, it looked like a group of naughty children who couldn't quite reach the shelf had pulled it all down in their haste to play.

"What the heck?" I wondered aloud. It looked as though I'd never cleaned it at all.

But I did.

"Virginia," mom fumed. "If you pack things carefully into that cupboard, they won't fall out again," she explained, one hand on her hip.

"But I did, Mom."

"And I suppose you closed the doors too?"

"Yes ... I can't explain it." I repeated, daring her to say more.

"I don't want you to explain it. I want you to clean it," she said. "Now."

There was no point in arguing. Running to drop the armload of cabin stuff on my bed, I quickly returned to the scene of the crime and started tidying up the mess.

"Bobby, sometimes you can be such a jerk," I said under my breath as I re-stacked decks of cards, put away dice and stored playing pieces, making it all as neat as possible, casting anxious looks over my shoulder. "If you can't reach something, just leave it alone. Maybe you're laughing your ass off," I spoke to the thin air around me, "but it's not funny to me." When the last board game was stashed away again on the shelf, I slammed the cupboard door as hard as I dared and stalked out of the room. "I know you did it, you bugger. Thanks a lot."

In the kitchen I could hear mom muttering too.

"At least she didn't leave the fridge open this time. That girl. Honestly! I don't know what gets into her sometimes."

Over the next couple of weeks, the only sound that helped me to know the invisible trouble-maker was still there, was a tell-tale hum, that was always followed by the unmistakable swish of my electric racing set.

Often I would go to play with my new toy only to find that, inexplicably, the pieces were disassembled and scattered. The little plastic tabs had been broken off the individual sections of track, where they attached to each other, rendering them useless. In time, my fabulous race track was relegated to the back of the closet with the rest of the junk.

Predictably, mom and dad blamed the cats.

The Car

31

Diana had grown increasingly insistent about the fact that she had to have a car. It was necessary, she said, since we lived so far from civilization and she had a job to get to.

The litany went on from there.

Of course, talking like that was counter-productive with my father, whose only answer was to move out of earshot.

Dad bobbed and wove through rooms, trying not to catch her eye as he went. Her conversations always seemed to begin with "Oh dad, by the way...."

Finally, as spring turned slowly into summer, he agreed to let her look at cars if only she'd be quiet, bringing the points balance to Diana 1: Dad 0.

"What kind of car are you getting?" I asked her.

"I don't know yet. Dad and I are going on the weekend to the used car lots. I can't wait!" She clapped her hands excitedly.

"You're going with dad?" I asked, making a face.

Diana stopped mid-clap and stared. "Yeah, why?"

"Oh nothing," I said, pretending nonchalance. "It'll be interesting, that's all."

"What do you mean?"

"Don't you live here?" I said. "It's been 'who left this on' and 'where did that go' and 'you're driving me to the poorhouse' and 'this is costing me a fortune' for as long as I can remember!" I waved my hands for emphasis and looked back at her. "Ring any bells?"

"Well, it's not like I have a choice. He's paying for it."

"Oh," I said. "Well now I know what kind of car you'll be getting ... cheap."

Diana made a face at me and closed her bedroom door with a resounding bang.

~~~~~

The rain came down in gusty sheets on the day Diana went to look at cars with our dad.

"It figures," he said as he sipped his morning coffee and stared out at the stormy weather.

"I don't suppose you'd consider going another day," mom asked.

"No need," dad said. "A car is a car. This way we won't buy something that leaks."

Surprisingly, just as it was getting dark, well after the supper dishes had been cleared away, Diana pulled into the drive in her used car, the little round headlights announcing her arrival. Dad turned in a few seconds later, bringing his sleek sports car up beside the house and cutting the engine.

He looked tired, but Diana bounced past him in a state of extreme excitement.

Diana's pride and joy turned out to be a 1973 Toyota Corolla. I remember thinking the name was fancy, but when I looked at the faded orange compact parked in the driveway, I found myself at a loss for words. It was *well* used. It was also a sickly sort of orange; Diana assured mom and I that the colour would shine right up with the proper amount of something called cut-polish.

"It's mechanically sound," dad said. "That's the main thing. Everything else is cosmetic."

"I will reserve judgment for the unveiling," I told her pompously.

For days afterward, only the lower half of Diana could be seen sticking out of her car. She scrubbed, vacuumed and cut-polished. She made several trips into town for supplies, behind the wheel of the orange dynamo, buying annoyingly cheerful seat covers with big white daisies on them. She trotted various tools out into the driveway to 'adjust' this and 'tweak' that. Soon her new-used car looked a whole lot better.

"Doesn't look too bad," I commented, causing my sister to beam.

"Yeah," she said, running a hand lovingly over the fender. "Turned out good, didn't she?"

"Uh-huh," I replied. "Does this mean you can drive me to the mall now?"

Good thing all Diana had in her hands was the rag she'd been using to polish the car. Rags don't hurt when they hit you in the head.

Ouija

32

Five ten year-old girls giggled as they unrolled their sleeping bags on my living room carpet. All of them, including me, waiting for a ghost. It was all due to a harmless bit of bragging, and I had only myself to blame.

Over the course of a relaxed, summer day, five friends lounged in the tall grass in the empty lot beside the corner store on Fraser Street.

"Oh sure, the house is really active," I'd said, trying to sound casual, while my friends stared at me, their attention rapt. "It's the spirit of a little boy," I'd said. "He's about five, I think. At least, he looked five. Maybe six, but he talked so grown up, it was hard to tell."

"You mean you've actually seen him?" Meridee asked.

"And talked with him?" Judy chimed in.

"Uh-huh," I replied proudly. "Lots of times."

"Are there any other ghosts?" Meridee asked excitedly.

"Um," I hedged. Admitting to the ghost of a small child was one thing. But talking about *him* was another matter entirely.

"We should hold a séance at your house," Jennifer interrupted, rubbing her hands together in delight.

"I don't think that would be a good idea," I said, remembering my failed attempt. "Candles are a definite give-away, and we'd have to keep this quiet."

"Oh!" Jennifer cried out. "Oh, oh, oh! I have just the thing. But we have to do it at your house, Ginny. Can we? It'll be fun. We can do it like a sleepover. No one will ever know."

And that was all it took. By the end of the day, I was arranging it with my parents. Of course, I strategically left out the part about my friends wanting to look for ghosts, almost as neatly as I'd dodged their questions about the creepy, dark apparition, who seemed to appear in window reflections and scare the crap out of me. No matter what they said, they weren't ready for that. My fondest hope was that he'd stay away and leave my friends as innocent as they were now.

"You want a what?" mom practically squealed, a large smile on her face.

"Just a few girls, Meridee, Judy, Denise and Jennifer."

"What about Jessica?"

"Jess doesn't know these girls. They're from school."

"I thought you didn't like Jennifer?" she asked.

"Oh she's okay, as long as she thinks she's in charge. She's a lot more relaxed when we're not in school."

Mom laughed and gave me a warm hug. "Oh honey, you bet! Would the girls like to go for a swim in the pool? It's all ready."

"Oh yeah! Just try to keep them out," I said.

~~~~

"So how long will we have to wait for this thing to put in an appearance, anyways," Judy asked, tossing her slightly damp red curls for effect. Judy lived for effect.

"Yeah, like we don't have all day," Denise added. Denise's big brown eyes gave her the appearance of being perpetually shocked. She had freckles sprinkled across her cheeks, but coupled with her dark hair and trim figure; she had all the boys at school thoroughly confused.

Meridee turned her round face towards me and rolled her always-exotic eyes, "You mean all night!" She giggled, tucking her short legs under herself and rubbing her hands together in delight. We faced each other in the dim glow of my mother's living room lamps. Clad in our pajamas, muscles loose and relaxed from our afternoon in the pool, we were munching happily on popcorn while Jennifer tried to set the mood.

"It's about the right kind of dark," she whispered. "The witching hour approaches."

"It's 9:30," I replied drily.

"Shut-up, I'm on a roll," she quipped.

Meridee giggled and Jennifer shot her a dark look as she walked away.

"Hey," Jennifer called to us in a loud whisper from the doorway where she stood, her slender arm inside her overnight bag as she struggled to pull something from the bottom. "Are your parents asleep yet? Get a look at this. I snuck it out of my brother's room."

From the depths of the voluminous bag, she brought forth a board, approximately two feet square. At first glance, it looked harmless enough. In truth, I didn't even know what it was, until somebody squealed, "a Ouija Board!"

That snapped everyone else's head around and they all stared at Jennifer. She stood proudly, holding up the wooden board for all to see. She tossed her head, sending her long blonde hair sailing back over her shoulder in a gesture of triumph. Her blue eyes were sparkling.

"How does it work?" I asked. Hadn't I heard somewhere before that these things were evil?

"Wait and see," she answered mysteriously.

"Oh relax," Judy commented. "What's the harm? We'll ask some questions and that thing on the board will spell out the answers. It'll tell us what's truth and what's not. We all want to know if you're making up these ghost stories. Right girls?"

Four heads nodded up and down, as they looked at me. They wanted to know all right.

I stared at them, speechless. What's the harm? I'd heard some vague stories about these things. None of them were good.

Finding my voice at last, I turned to Jennifer "So it does ... what? Truth or dare?" I asked hopefully. Maybe it wouldn't be so bad after all. We were just silly girls, asking silly questions of some silly board. It probably had batteries in it somewhere. It was made by Parker Brothers, for goodness sake. Maybe the stories were exaggerated.

"Mmm, sort of," Jennifer answered. "It allows us to communicate with the dead."

I must have blinked at her in shock.

"Ginny?" she said, reaching out to shake my shoulder. "What's the matter with you? It'll be fun, just wait and see."

All I could think was: *Oh crap! I'm gonna regret this.*

I sighed in defeat. There was no way out of it now. This was my fault and I had to see it through. Not knowing a thing as to whether there were rules to this, I believed that our innocence would protect us somehow.

"I'll go check on my parents," I said, sidling off down the hall.

"Please be awake, please be awake," I thought, tiptoeing down the hall. "Get me outa this."

I heard dad's snores before I got even halfway down the dimly lit hall. Mom was lying on her left side, her face hidden from me. My shoulders sagged and I licked my lips nervously, heart pounding.

Damn.

My heartbeat was so loud as I returned to the living room, that I felt sure they'd all be able to hear it as I moved closer, but they were so intent on the board in front of them that they barely noticed my approach. The girls sat cross-legged in a loose circle on the deep plush carpet. All the lamps had been extinguished but one. The small amber globe nearest to them remained on, the circle of light from its cylindrical shade casting sinister shadows into the corners of the room.

"That one won't go off," Jennifer said, pointing to the lamp. "I pulled the chain over and over, but it just stays lit. We're supposed to have dark."

"Yeah, that one is a bit weird," I said, silently cheering. If the lamp was doing that already, maybe my friends would see something after all and I wouldn't be branded a liar. "Do you want me to unplug it?"

"Nah, leave it alone," Judy said. "We need some light, so we can see what we're doing after all."

Meridee patted the empty space on the carpet beside her. "Waiting for you," she said, in the sing-song voice she used when she felt nervous or excited.

"So how do you start this thing?" Judy said to me as I sat down. Judy was the only one in the group that I thought had an ounce of sense, and here she was, impatience and curiosity making her reckless and bold.

"How should I know?" I said irritably. "It's not mine." I sank down beside Meridee with another reluctant sigh. Mentally, I was imploring Bobby to save me from this. "Anytime now," I thought. "Make the lights go off, make a noise … anything. Distract them." The errant thoughts in my head skittered around like dandelion seeds on a summer breeze. My eyes must have been rolling around like marbles, because Meridee pointed at me and cried out.

"Look, she's going into a trance!"

"What?" I said, giving her a flat stare.

"Oops," she replied. "False alarm."

"Okay," Jennifer said to all of us. "Let's get serious. My brother showed me how to work this. Everybody reach forward and with the tips of your fingers, rest them very carefully on this thing, there." She pointed at a framed glass disc that looked like half of a pair of glasses. "No pushing. As long as we all agree to let the, um, spirits move the pointer, it will spell out the answers to our questions."

I could see that the board was filled with letters, numbers and strange symbols.

"Who's gonna ask the questions?" Judy said.

"I will," Jennifer said with an air of superiority.

Denise sniffed with derision. "I think Ginny should do it," she said. "It's her house."

"Oh!" I said, my heart suddenly beating staccato on my ribcage.

Jennifer, not easily thwarted, pretended to acquiesce. "Well, that makes sense, I suppose, but she doesn't really know anything about it, does she?"

We all agreed that this was so.

"Well there you go," she said. "We can't ask her to do something she doesn't know how to do!" She looked around at the other girls, seeking friendly cooperation. "After all, my brother taught me all about it."

No one said anything, but my earlier eye rolling seemed to be contagious.

"Okay," she said, stretching forth her fingers so she was just touching the strange-looking disc. "Let's start. Eyes closed once you've made contact with the disc."

Taking slow, steadying breaths, I reached out and touched the disc, my fingers encountering the smooth surface, noting its cool temperature against my super-heated skin. It looked and felt like some weird kind of paperweight. I closed my eyes and waited.

Rustling movements told me the others were doing the same. Soon, Jennifer resumed her instruction.

"Nobody pushes, because it's not fair that way," she said. "If a spirit wants to talk to us, then we have to be ready."

Something like an electrical impulse went up my backbone and my eyes snapped open. I looked around, eager to see if any of my friends had felt the same thing.

Four heads were slightly bowed, eyes closed as though they were praying. I felt a deep sense of guilt for what we were about to do, but as a follower in this game, I wasn't sure how to stop it, or even if I could.

Jennifer opened one eye and focused it on me. "Close your eyes, Ginny, no cheating!" she snapped.

"Oh, yeah, yeah, whatever," I said, shutting my eyes tight.

"We humbly ask for a strong spirit to guide us tonight." Jennifer's voice sounded funny, and kind of theatrical. "If there are any spirits here who would like to communicate, please come forward to speak with us." To us girls she said, "If you feel the disc begin to slide, don't try to hold it back, just go with it."

A tugging sensation began twitching at my fingers, and although I'd seen more deliberate things than this happening in my home, my eyes flew open as the disc began to slide across the surface of the board.

As one, all of us cried out and withdrew our hands, the combined momentum sending the disc skidding across the polished surface.

"Did you feel that?" Meridee said, her eyes wide as she rubbed at her fingertips. "Like an electric shock."

"That was creepy," Judy exclaimed. "Like my fingertips were on fire!"

"I didn't think it was gonna work," Denise commented dreamily, her big, brown eyes staring straight at me.

"Oh my God! Look at that!" Jennifer interrupted the flow of our chatter. "It's still moving!"

In truth, what I thought had been the momentum of everyone withdrawing their hands, was clearly not the case now. The disc was still moving. It stuttered along, as though it didn't have enough energy, stopping when it framed a letter on the board. I felt my breath catch in my throat. The absurd little monocle rested over the word: YES.

Meridee squealed, the high-pitched noise causing everyone to chatter at once.

Jennifer wasted no time commanding us all to silence.

"We've got to focus, you can't just freak out like that. Honestly!" With another hair flip to show how much better than us she was, she leaned forward and placed her fingertips back on the marker. "Okay, let's go," She said. "Remember, you've got to focus."

With nervous glances at each other, my friends followed her lead.

"Is anyone from the spirit world here with us?" Jennifer intoned.

The silence stretched on, punctuated only by the insistent ticking of the kitchen clock in the next room.

One by one, accusing glares developed on their young faces. I felt my own face redden with embarrassment. All eyes were on me.

Trying to relieve the ache in my arms and break away from the accusing looks, I sat forward to stretch my back, being careful to keep my fingers on the marker, lest Jennifer call me out.

I looked around the room, ostensibly to stretch my neck, but in reality I was looking for those tell-tale shadows. I knew they were there. Why were they hiding *now*? As soon as my eyes came back to rest on the board in front me, I saw the marker twitch.

"Did I imagine that?" Although the thought was also mine, the voice belonged to Meridee. She'd seen it too?

"You saw that?" I asked.

She nodded, narrowing her eyes and staring at the marker with intense concentration.

With the uncertain motion of a butterfly, the marker stuttered to life once more.

I open astonishment, we cooperated with the movement, until it came to rest on a letter: B.

I gritted my teeth, but said nothing. It was probably just one of those errant flukes, everyone trying to freak each other out after all that silence. I couldn't help thinking this was still just a stupid child's game. There was no *real* way this little board game could communicate with the dead ... could it?

A sound, like a metallic tinkling could be heard from the kitchen to our right. Silverware in the sink? Breaking glass? Someone squeaked in fright. The lights were off everywhere else. I knew my parents were asleep and Diana was still out with Rick.

"Don't worry," I said with a bravery I didn't feel. "That's probably just my sister and her boyfriend. They must've come back already." Doubt was clearly etched into my friend's expressions.

"I didn't hear anybody coming in." Meridee's voice was small and hesitant.

"Why didn't they come in through the front door?" Jennifer, obviously just as shaken as the rest of us, seemed determined to regain her composure.

I shrugged. "Maybe they didn't want to bug us. Maybe they thought we were asleep?"

Great. Can I be more pathetic?

"Sure, I guess," Denise agreed. "Maybe we should put this away. Do you think they'd stop us from playing this?"

"Don't be such a baby," Judy commented before I could answer.

In truth, I shouldn't have bothered to hide this from them. Wasn't this what they all wanted: evidence of a haunting? So why had I blamed that noise on my sister? I knew it wasn't her.

The answer eluded me.

"So which one of you pushed?" Jennifer said suddenly.

"Ginny?" Denise asked. "Was it you?"

"No!" I said heatedly. "I wouldn't."

"No, I agree that would be too low," Judy commented. "Even for her."

"Thanks," I answered drily.

"Jennifer?" Meridee asked.

Jennifer was looking off to her left, her eyes squinting as she leaned forward, trying to see something in the semi-darkness.

"Jen!" Meridee said louder.

"What?" Jennifer said, obviously startled.

"Did you move it?"

"The marker? Of course not! I wouldn't do that." She seemed unsettled, and I cocked my head to one side as I watched her, suspicion slowly mounting.

I recognized the look she wore. Jennifer had seen something, and like so many others before her, she was keeping silent, but I couldn't figure out why. Shouldn't she be crowing about it by now? Maybe the mighty Jennifer had met her match.

I was surprised at the feeling of triumph that roared to life in my chest.

"Hey!" Meridee said. "Anybody want to try again?"

All of us moved back into the circle, giggling nervously, glancing at each other as we settled back onto the carpet.

This time, I felt more sure of myself as I took my place beside them.

"Fingertips only just touching it, remember," Jennifer cautioned. "Let's see what happens. Eyes closed and no cheating this time!"

At first, nothing seemed to happen, and my tense body began to unwind, backbone curving, muscles softening.

It was a shock when the indicator moved again, the hard plastic scraped across the wooden board and hovered briefly over the letter 'O', then it was on the move again. Our eyes flew open, but this time, no one withdrew their hands. We looked nervously at each other, secretly still harboring the suspicion that someone was pushing.

"I don't know that we can play this," I said, sitting back and taking my fingertips from the marker. "We don't trust each other, and isn't trust kind of important in this game?" One by one, my friends nodded and moved away from the marker, until only Jennifer and Meridee were left touching it.

Suddenly, another scraping sound caught our attention. Had it moved again? We all froze, watching Jennifer and Meridee for a sign that they'd moved it for pure fun, but Denise spoke up before we could frame the question.

"Look there, the letter B," she said, pointing.

"B-O-B?" Jennifer said, smiling, her tone made it clear she was unimpressed. "Is that all you could come up with, Meridee?"

Meridee shot her a look filled with venom. "It wasn't me, cheater," she said, sticking out her tongue. "Watch! It's still moving! Hold on!"

"Bobby!" I whispered, watching as the marker spelled out his name. The word escaped my lips like a gust of wind. "But which of you knew his name?" Tears stood in my eyes and I forgot to feel self-conscious. A hushed silence followed my exclamation. "I never told anyone his name."

Denise turned her penetrating gaze on me. "Who are you talking about? Is that the ghosts' name? You never told us that ... did she?" She turned to the other girls, who shook their heads, their eyes still large and fearful.

"Okay, okay, someone's having a joke. Bob's a very common name. That's the only explanation."

Her about-face was understandable, but the others weren't buying it.

"Jennifer," Judy said matter-of-factly. "It was you that dragged this thing out here and got us all going. Let's finish this."

"I *am* finished," she said. I couldn't help but notice that she shuddered as she stood there, arms folded defiantly. "I think Ginny's right. We can't trust each other not to move it just for fun. Let's do something else." Her hand gestures had grown impatient. I knew she was desperate to change the subject and frankly, so was I.

"What? Another fun board game?" Meridee's sarcasm was evident. "I don't think so."

"How about some music," I said, wiping tears from my eyes and trying to smile. "I got some new records for Christmas. We can play them on there," I indicated the large wooden cabinet on the far side of the room that housed our stereo system. I hesitated and looked around at them, noting their frightened faces and suddenly feeling a surge of guilt. "My sister and Rick should be home any minute. It'll be okay."

"Oh yeah, that's … great. Good idea. I brought some records too," Jennifer heartily agreed. Meridee and Denise both nodded. Judy grabbed her overnight bag and began to rummage through it. "Hang on a sec," she said, stopping abruptly. "Didn't you say your sister was already home?"

"Oh," I said, my face going hot with shame. "I guess I was wrong."

Judy's eyebrows shot up and stayed there.

"Don't just stand there, let's go," Meridee said, coming up beside her and grabbing her arm. "I don't want to talk about this stuff anymore." Arm in arm, they disappeared down the hall to my room.

As the rest of the girls drifted out of the room, the Ouija board lay forgotten on the floor. The last two people out of the living room were Jennifer and I. She turned to face me, wearing an expression I'd never seen on her face before.

"I'm sorry," she said. "It was just supposed to be fun, but maybe it was stupid, after all."

"So you did move it?" I asked.

"No."

"Well I didn't," I said.

"Yeah, I know."

I blinked at her in surprise. "What? You know? How?"

CLICK

Behind us, the lamp in the corner went out.

"Tell me the light bulb just burned out," she said, raising her eyebrows, smiling and nodding.

"Probably," I lied.

Jennifer looked startled and afraid as she fled down the hall.

Frowning to gather my courage, I realized that I couldn't follow her yet. I knew I had to put that thing away. It would never do to have any of my family see this *game*.

As I bent to pick it up, I noticed that the marker was now in a different position. I swallowed hard. Two words were framed under the pointer.

"Good Bye".

Nearly tearing the fabric of the bag, I shoved the offending board and its marker back into Jennifer's overnight kit, pulling the drawstring closed with finality.

Putting the game away made me feel a little better as I stood staring at the bag, hoping that nothing else would happen. I wanted my friends to see, but not like this.

Be careful what you wish for. The statement filled my head and the irony of it made me want to laugh out loud.

I literally leaped a moment later when the front door opened. Diana and Rick were home.

"Whah!" I shouted.

"Whah to you too," Diana quipped good-naturedly. "What's going on? A sleepover?" She looked around, noting the sleeping bags and overnight kits strewn around the room.

"Yeah," I muttered, my heart still beating double-time. "Something like that."

Sleep would not come easily to any of us that night, and as the four girls left my home the following morning, I couldn't help envying them.

I still had to stay.

~~~~

"I think it's time to call Tom," mom said as she faced dad over their morning coffee. I had just returned from the chicken coop with an ice-cream bucket of unwashed eggs in my hand.

"Are you sure you want to involve him in this? I thought we agreed that when the time came, we'd keep friends and acquaintances out of it?" Dad cast a sidelong glance in my direction. I squinted at one and then the other. What were they talking about? Whatever it was, I certainly didn't have a clue as to who this Tom person was. Friend, acquaintance or whoever he was, my parents weren't about to enlighten me, so I passed on through the room, deposited the eggs on the counter and breezed out before I could be called back to wash the yucky things. Washing eggs was worse than mucking stalls in my opinion. At least when I shoveled out the horse manure, I didn't have to touch it with my bare hands.

Down in my room, I took a long look at myself in the oval mirror of my dresser. As I sat on the edge of my bed, the hot pink of my comforter clashing with my red shirt, I admired the stone at my neck. I'd fastened it in place that morning, deciding it had languished in my drawer long enough. The crystal caught and held whatever light it was subjected to, refracting it and making it dance. It seemed to glow with all the colours of the rainbow and it felt nice. I thought it was odd that colours could evoke feelings, but these sure did. It was like I was floating, my feet brushing the tops of clouds as I soared through the bright blue sky...

"Ginny, what are you doing?" my sister called, unexpectedly.

"Nothing," I called back, through the closed door. She had interrupted my concentration on the crystal, though I continued to admire it in the mirror.

"Then get out here and help me with dinner."

"Not on your life," I answered. "Besides it's too early for dinner."

"What are you talking about?" she said, yanking open the door and staring at me like I'd gone mad. "Mom and dad went out. They left instructions."

"What?" I said. "They couldn't have. When did this happen?"

"Hours ago," she said. "Didn't you hear them? They yelled good-bye loud enough for the neighbours to hear."

What a liar, I thought. How gullible did she think I was? I glanced at the alarm clock by my bed and blinked in surprise. What had felt like only a couple of moments was actually much longer. Two hours had passed since I'd sat down on the edge of my bed to admire the crystal.

It was obvious to me that the dancing colours had hypnotized me somehow. I wasn't sure whether I should yank it from my neck in disgust or never take it off again.

Dream Visitor

33

Washing dishes was never my favourite, but Diana and Rick had gone out, so there wasn't anyone else to help. Mom's rule was: I cook, you clean.

To make things more interesting, I made faces at the dirty breakfast dishes and sorted through pretend scenarios where I was magically released from my chores by my own personal fairy godmother. Dad was seated at the kitchen table with an adding machine. His face was serious as he added up totals from the scraps of paper he had strewn across its surface.

He was adding up bills.

I hardly noticed when my mother wandered into the room, until she began a conversation with dad that took an interesting, if curious, turn.

"Will, maybe we ought to do something else," mom said.

"What?" dad answered irritably. "Whatever it is we can't afford it."

"Oh, be serious," she scoffed. "Look I know it sounded crazy before, but now, I really think we ought to look at it again."

"Okay, you're either talking about real estate or that other thing," dad said with emphasis. "Maybe both."

I looked over at them, but mom was still just standing by the table with her arms crossed. No help there.

"Doesn't make sense to rake things up," he said. "We've already had him here once. Do you really want to start people talking again?"

"They're already talking," she said. "At least we'll be doing something. Pastor Smith is well respected in this community."

"I don't know if I'm comfortable with this idea."

"We could just ask," mom assured him.

I frowned. Pastor? What did Pastor have to do with their plans?

"Geez honey," dad objected. "This has gotten ridiculous. What more can he do anyways?"

"Oh be serious,a' she said. "I thought you said you didn't want to move again?" I perked up immediately, trying even harder to look nonchalant. "Didn't you say you'd try? There's no harm in asking."

I saw dad shrug out of the corner of my eye.

"Pastor Smith is very sensible," mom continued. "I'll give Julia a quick call, she'll know the number of the rectory," mom said, ignoring dad's glare, as she crossed to the drawer where she kept her phonebook. "I know I wrote it down on the notepad, but I can't seem to find it now. I hope Julia's home."

"Don't say anything weird," dad cautioned as mom went to the phone.

My heart was hammering in my chest, but I kept washing dishes, being careful not to fling soap suds everywhere or drop a dish. As long as I didn't call attention to myself, maybe they'd keep talking.

As mom reached for the phone, a scant three feet from me, I mechanically circled the soapy dishcloth over the dinner plate I held in my hand. My mind was reeling.

"Ginny," mom said suddenly, breaking the spell. "Go and get my purse from the car, would you? I think my reading glasses are in there."

By the time the purse was delivered, the phone was back in its place and a satisfied smile was on my mother's lips.

~~~~

"So now you're saying that a house blessing wasn't enough?"

Dad's voice was incredulous and I stopped forking hay into the stall in front of me. "And did Pastor actually come right out and say that?" he asked.

Aha, I thought. *So that's it.*

A low murmuring was all I could hear as the answer, and I wished I could get closer to hear more.

"What's that supposed to mean?" dad's deep baritone cut through the solid wood walls, even though he was two stalls away from me.

Trying to appear nonchalant, I picked up the handles of the wheelbarrow I'd just emptied and drove it out into the centre of the barn.

"Oh, hi Mom," I said, wheeling past her.

"Hi sweetie, helping daddy?" I nodded and I could feel her eyes on me as I forked more sweet-smelling hay into the scarred metal wheelbarrow. This one had to go out into the paddock but I was dawdling as much as possible, pretending to become engrossed in the twine that held the bale together, even muttering to myself about it in the hopes she would once again pick up her end of the conversation while I was still within listening distance.

"Get going big ears," dad prompted. To his wife he added: "Well?"

"Uh, the mmm …" mom flicked a gaze at me before continuing. "… unusual nature of the request did bring in some helpful information. Julia was quite forthcoming with details. She knows everyone around here." I continued to work on Koko's breakfast just a few feet away, but my ears were straining to hear every word.

"Marnie and her husband Bill had a very real, er, success," mom said, obviously trying to win dad over with statistics while still talking in code. "No more, uh, disturbances."

I ducked my head and smiled. It was obvious what they were talking about, but their efforts to hide it had become painful.

"Well," dad said. "I wonder how disturbed they were once word got around?" He leaned one arm casually on the handle of the pitchfork he held, the tines pointing down into the scattered hay. "So, I can see from the expression on your face that you're determined to do this. I suppose you have it all laid out?"

"Yes, we've talked."

My heart raced but I kept my head down. Now was the time to practice patience and quiet. Maybe they'd forget I was there.

"But?" dad asked.

"He won't do anything without hearing from both of us," she answered, obviously irritated at the idea.

"Well I don't know. What we really need is a way to make people a little more productive around here, right Ginny?" dad tossed off the comment with emphasis on my name. With a start, I jumped and wheeled the hay off towards the far door.

Dad chuckled as he watched me. "Just hold up a second, young lady," he said.

Uh-oh. Busted.

"When you're done with that, I have a surprise you." I peered at dad carefully and he laughed. "Not a bad surprise. You're gonna like this. I guarantee it."

The wheelbarrow and I flew over the concrete and through the side door. Koko tossed her head and nickered at me as I threw the hay into a soft mound and retreated.

"What is it dad?" I asked warily. Mom's eyebrows were raised as she faced him squarely, hands planted on her hips.

Dad grinned mischievously and walked briskly to the last stall on the left. "And you two call yourselves observant," he chided. "Didn't you notice there's one too many stalls prepared today?"

His grin was wide as he slid open the stall door and reached through it, clucking his tongue as he did so.

I could barely believe it.

A black and white pony walked in on the end of a lead rope, his black mane even more unruly than Charlie's had ever been. He tossed his head and snorted softly.

"Oh daddy!" I squealed, forcing myself to calm down before walking forward to stroke his velvet nose. "He's adorable! What's his name?"

Dad smirked. "You're never gonna guess."

"Oh for heaven's sake!" mom said with a sigh.

"Nope," dad said, still smirking as he caught her eye.

"Uh, Rumplestiltskin?" I said, with a smile of my own as I ran my hand over the pony's smooth neck.

Dad laughed. "Close, but no. His name's Chuck!"

"Chuck?" I asked, hardly believing my ears. "Are you serious? Chuck as in short for Charles or … Charlie?"

"Yup. I got him from one of my friends down at the Co-op. He's still young, and not nearly as polite as Charlie was, in fact he's a bit of a brat, but I know you'll teach him some manners."

"Wow dad, this is great," I said, reaching out to clasp my father in a fierce hug and plant a noisy kiss on his high forehead. "I love him already." I was reluctant to let go of my father's neck, since tears were now openly streaming down my face, but dad was already handing me the lead rope.

"Hey now," he admonished, disengaging my arms. "There's no crying in horsemanship. Just remember that he's your responsibility. You two better get to know each other."

~~~~

270

I knew in my heart that Bobby wasn't gone. How could he be? We'd been through so much.

He probably knew I couldn't see him anymore. Not like I used to. My heart was no longer as innocent as it had been and that innocence had been his doorway, but he couldn't just be gone.

As I went through my day, lugging water for the horses in their outside paddock, collecting eggs, taking out the trash, grooming and exercising my new pony Chuck —who really was a huge brat— my thoughts were only of him.

Bobby.

I missed his funny laugh, his easy sense of humour and the way he just let me talk about anything, without interrupting. He was a good little friend, even if he had made trouble for me when he left messes around the house. I wished for the thousandth time that things didn't have to be like this. I wished that he was alive. We could have been such awesome friends. Thinking back over our times together, I had to believe that he wished for the same thing.

I detoured slightly on my way back to the house, looking longingly up and down the long country road, remembering the carefree conversations we'd had, before I'd known.

Before. So much was tied up in that one word.

Later, emptying the dishwasher, I glanced up at every sound. As I brought my laundry to the washing machine, I paused, so strong was the feeling of being watched.

Bobby?" I whispered.

That tell-tale feeling told me someone was there. Was it my friend, or the more sinister dark entity? I couldn't be sure. Apparently, it was free to wander wherever it chose. The thought made me shiver and I pulled my sweater around my shoulders more tightly.

The sense of familiarity I'd always shared with Bobby was gone now. He was probably mad at me for calling him a jerk, I thought.

As I set the table for dinner, I kept one eye on the doorway. The last thing that I wanted now, was for someone to sneak up on me.

Mom placed a steaming dish of barbecued chicken on the table. "Looks good, huh? Your dad's been barbecuing!"

I jumped slightly at the sound of her voice.

"Honestly, you're so jumpy today," she said. "Are you alright?"

"Oh, no, I'm fine." I tried to sound casual, but I wasn't fooling anyone.

271

"All day you've been acting so suspicious."

Dad untied his black and white striped barbecue apron and draped it across the back of his chair before sitting down. "Smell that," he said. "Smells like summer!"

"It's great," I said.

"Why so glum?" he asked.

"She's been nervy all day," mom said. "Almost like she's expecting someone to come along and surprise her."

"Are you expecting a guest?" dad joked.

If they only knew, I thought. So close too; just a couple of letters off.

Bobby was nowhere to be found, of course, but I stubbornly refused to accept that he could really be gone from my life.

As I lay down in my bed that night, the tears came easily, sliding from the corners of my eyes to dampen my pillow.

Just breathe, I told myself. Breathe and try to rest. I was just starting to drift into sleep when I noticed the fog. It seemed to come all of a sudden and I felt its clammy touch on my skin. The grass was cold and I shivered as I stood there in my nightgown, confusion rolled over me like a wave.

Wait a second. *Grass*?

What was I doing outside? Where was I? I didn't know this place.

Everything moved in slow motion. Vague shapes of trees and bushes loomed just beyond my scope of vision. Where was my house? Who was out there?

The fog lifted slightly and I saw my friend.

Happy tears slid down my cheeks and I smiled, tasting my tears at the corners of my mouth. Bobby! I almost ran to him, but something in his face made me pause.

His expression was serious and his lips were moving, but I couldn't understand the words he spoke. Noise assailed my ears. It might be voices—insistent, demanding—I could hear the tone but couldn't decipher the words.

Concentrate!

The noise grew louder and I held up my hands for silence, but still it kept on. The noises—were they voices, layered on top of each other? There was no discernible pattern, like a portable fan turned to 'high'; they confused my senses. Soon the noise changed and sounded like buzzing.

Bobby reached out to me, and he was right there. The cuff of his shirt brushed my arm. At the feather-light touch, the noise diminished. His face was a mask of concern. "Be careful." He stepped closer and placed ice cold hands on my shoulders.

I awoke gasping, with a pounding heart and head. Another nightmare. I glanced at my bedside clock, hoping that morning was imminent: I didn't want to sleep anymore.

No such luck. The clock read quarter to three.

"*Ginny.*"

"Wha—?" I said, slipping one elbow up behind me as I tried to sit up in bed.

Was that the wind outside or had someone just whispered my name?

Was I still asleep?

I turned at another sound and rubbed my eyes, trying to focus. A dark shadow seemed to loom up from the foot of my bed.

I sat up straighter, a squeak in the back of my throat threatening to become a scream. Scrambling backwards and clutching at my covers, I managed a harsh, frightened whisper. "Go away!" There was no question that I was awake now.

The vague, human-shaped shadow stood motionless. In the continuing silence, fear gave way to curiosity, and as my eyes adjusted, I grinned sheepishly at my own paranoia. The high back of a wooden chair, pushed up against the foot of my bed was draped with discarded clothing. In the gloom and the augmenting shadows, it had resembled a man.

A man in a long, black coat.

In relief, I looked at the rumpled blankets clutched to my chest, their floral pattern distorted in the dark. Something had awakened me, or had I imagined that too?

"Bobby," I whispered in remembrance.

Turning around, another figure confronted me.

"No!"

I fell out of bed and landed painfully on the carpet, arms and legs flailing. I scrambled upright in an instant, my heart racing before I realized that the 'figure' was my own reflection. I had seen my own tired, rueful face in the framed mirror.

Shivering, I pulled the quilt up around my shoulders. Why was it always so impossibly cold in my room? Even in my new room, the temperature was always colder than the rest of the house—I stopped short and sighed. There I went again, I chided myself. Dad was right. I was a superstitious ninny, scaring myself with wild imaginings.

Idiot! Lots to be scared of, you don't have to make things up!

Absently I watched the warm glow of the portable heater just a few feet away, thankful I hadn't fallen on that. It was cranked up to 'high'. So much for the heat of summer.

How I could still be so cold?

Heavy eyelids slid closed of their own volition. A jaw-cracking yawn took over my face and I settled back into bed. Within moments, I was drifting off, unable to resist.

"Stay away from John. He's dangerous. He's not your friend."

The whispered phrase echoed in my sleepy head.

"Who?" I mumbled, yawning again. "John?" The name seemed vaguely familiar but I was too tired to wonder about it. "Bobby? Is that you? What did you say?"

Unable to raise my head from the pillow, I fell completely asleep wondering why I expected an answer.

Secrets

34

I awoke with the memory of the strange dream stuck firmly in my mind.

Who was John? There was only one logical answer and it make me very nervous to think that Bobby had come to me in my dreams, only to warn me about the man with the long dark coat. The one I referred to as the dark entity had to be 'John'.

As soon as I made the connection, I understood that my sister had been warning me about him for months, without even realizing it.

"Your pals Bob and John" she'd said.

It all made sense now, but the fact that I had no recollection of talking about John, or even knowing his name made me wonder what else I'd forgotten.

The memory of her conversation with my mother about my strange sleep-talking episodes made my skin go cold.

Something very wrong was happening here, and I didn't know how to stop it.

Stumbling out into the sunshine, I felt better as the sun heated my skin. Sitting by the pool, the sparkling waters reminded me of the crystal that hung around my neck. The water seemed to call to me. In truth, swimming was the only way I had to block out everything else. When I was swimming, nothing else mattered. I could pretend I was an Olympic diver, winning the Gold for Canada and I practiced relentlessly as often as I could, counting down the days until Summer vacation when I could practically *live* in that swimming pool.

I wasted no time getting my suit on and I swam on and off for most of that day. It was a glorious Saturday, and even with my chores, the bright sunlight added an element of safety that helped me feel more secure as I raced through the gloomy barn, throwing hay and filling water buckets for our horses. I saddled Chuck and rode him briefly in the safety of the riding ring, where he did his best to be an idiot, jumping around and stepping sideways when he should have gone forward. I was frustrated and tired by the end of day, and that night I slept soundly. Thankfully, no memories of strange dreams lingered when I awoke.

Packing my days full of activity was an awesome coping skill, and one I intended to repeat, so when Sunday morning began with a blanket of fog covering everything, my mood darkened significantly. The weatherman promised sun later in the afternoon, and I focused on it as though it was a lifeline. I realized when I heard the forecast, just how single-minded I'd become. I imagined basking in the warmth of the sun, floating on my back in the clear waters of our pool ... and how it felt to have the wind whipping through my long hair as Chuck and I ate up the miles, his sturdy little legs blazing along, attentive to my commands. A slow smile spread across my face. The images were powerful and the emotions that were tied up with them even more so. But with thoughts of Chuck came images of the trails I would ride him through that wound along through the back of our property. Brightly coloured flowers, tall waving grasses, and the crystalline stream trickling past with its musical sounds made me think of Bobby.

He was so alone. I wondered again why he wasn't able to go and visit the sisters anymore. I realized with a start that it had been a long time since I'd seen them myself.

I didn't know if I would see Bobby again, outside of my dreams, but at least the sisters were easier to find. Before too long, I was traversing the long driveway, with the now customary egg carton in my hand. I knocked at the tiny front door of the cottage across the street.

"Good morning," I called through the screen door, knocking on the wooden door-jamb.

"Ah, Ginny, how nice to see you." Penny waved to me from the kitchen where she stood, holding the phone to her ear, a gardening trowel on the counter in front of her.

"Hi," I ventured, wandering inside.

"Do come in," Penny said, lowering the telephone back into its cradle. She was stripping gardening gloves from her strong hands. "It's been some time since we've seen you. Your mother said you'd come by. I see you've brought our eggs, what a sweet girl you are."

"You're welcome." I stood looking around the small cottage for a moment. "Uh, where's Elise?"

"Oh, don't worry. Sometimes, Elise doesn't sleep too well at night. She's taken her pill and gone for a lie down. She has a heart condition, you know. Once she's had a nap, she'll be right as rain. Why don't we have some tea?" Penny said. "I happen to have some of those cookies you like too. Do you have time for a chat?"

"Yes please," I said.

Penny busied herself at the sink washing her hands and then arranging the tea and cookies on a tray before bringing them all over to join me at their small table. She leaned forward and cocked her head to one side as she smiled at me with gentleness.

"You're troubled, little one. And I don't think it's for worry about Elise. What's the matter?"

"It's nothing," I lied.

"Oh, it's like that, is it?" she asked, a gentle smile still playing at her lips, but she leaned away and folded her arms for emphasis.

"No..." I heard myself saying. "It's just so ... complicated." The sigh that escaped then was a heavy one. "You're gonna think I'm crazy too."

"Me?" she responded, pointing at her own chest. "Me think that of you? Somehow, I don't think so. You're the most sensible girl I've ever met."

"I don't feel very sensible right now Penny."

"Hmm. Whatever this thing is, it's bothering you tremendously. I can see that. Why don't you just come right out with it? You might be surprised how talking about a problem can take the power out of it."

I sat straighter and took a deep breath. I did want to confide in someone, but I was worried that whoever I told would run straight to my mother.

"Do you swear not to tell?" I asked. It felt ridiculous to be asking this of a woman with white hair, but I leaned forward, intent on the answer.

If Penny thought it was ridiculous too, she didn't show it.

"I swear," she answered solemnly.

"Okay, here goes," I began uncertainly.

"Do you have dreams?" I asked her.

"Sure, I think most people do."

"Not like mine." I looked away out the front window and sighed again. The sun was just beginning to come out, chasing away the last of the dreariness.

"Let's go out on the porch for a bit," Penny said, obviously catching sight of my wistful expression. "It's nicer out there, and we won't wake Elise that way."

We'd barely settled onto the thick cushions of her wicker porch chairs when she turned to me and the look she gave, full of understanding and sympathy, seemed to break something loose inside me. Suddenly I found that I couldn't hold back.

"Penny, it's all just wrong. So wrong! I just can't ... I don't know." I felt miserable. "They already think I'm crazy, and, well, maybe I am. Dad says I'm creative—like that explains it."

"Well, it seems to me that there's a lot pent up in there," she pointed to my chest. "Now, I'm no miracle worker, but I am a good listener," she said. "And I also know that you are creative and you aren't crazy. So go on, start at the beginning."

As if by magic, her words and her simple offer to *listen* released an inner storm. I spilled my tears, my story and very nearly, a glass of milk as my gestures became more and more animated. As the story wore on, Penny only nodded her head seriously. Her eyes were kind. She interjected an "oh my!" where it was required, but mostly she just let me talk.

Eventually there was nothing left to tell and I fell silent, panting slightly as I realized for the first time how tired I was.

"How have you kept all that inside? No wonder you feel so terrible."

"But what should I do about it?" I asked her. "I know our house is haunted ... don't you think so?"

"Well, I should think that's obvious. But is that really the only question you have?"

I frowned at her, surprised at her casual agreement, and yet lost by the obscure meaning behind her question. "What? I don't know what to believe anymore."

"Then start with what you know," Penny responded. "I've always found that to be a good place."

"Well, I know that I don't have an imaginary friend!" The words came out with such force I surprised myself and felt my cheeks redden.

"Of course. Go on," she urged.

Pausing for a moment to think, I saw him in my mind's eye. A normal little boy, standing very still, but he seemed so sad. Eventually I continued, my voice small and subdued. "I swear I saw him as clearly as I see you right now. If he was imaginary, wouldn't he be see-through or something?"

"I don't know, would he?"

"I don't know, I think he would. That's how it is in the movies anyways."

"Movies can make things seem very real, can't they?" She agreed. "It's often like that with things you can see. Sometimes you may wish that you couldn't see them at all."

"I keep wondering if I could've made the whole thing up."

"You think that's it?"

"What else could it be?" my shoulders slumped.

"Well … I think it could be lots of things. Some people think it's imagination, while others believe that confused spirits really do appear to children. Children are innocent you see, and more open to such things. Either way, it's wonderful to contemplate."

"Confused spirits? I've never heard of that before."

"I don't imagine you have," she said.

"Well, anyways I don't think it's very wonderful. Mom and dad saying things like 'you're so creative'." The sarcasm in my tone was heavy. "What they really mean is they think I'm nuts."

"Oh you don't truly believe that, do you?"

"If I don't, I'll bet Diana does."

Penny chuckled at my negative attitude. "Hmm, your big sister, right?" I nodded. "Have you considered …" she paused and shook her head thoughtfully before continuing. "Sometimes when I feel alone and scared, I take comfort in this and what it stands for." She reached for the neck of her shirt and withdrew a beautiful golden crucifix, dangling from a gleaming gold chain. "My dear, sweet husband bought it for me so many years ago. It helps me feel safe. I know you're a Christian girl, you must have something like this?"

I frowned and shook my head. "Not until Confirmation. I'm not old enough yet."

"Oh! Penny seemed shocked and confused. "Not old enough … for the Lord's protection? What a strange concept."

"Well," I said, "putting it like that I guess it does seem strange, but I've never thought about it. I still believe in God, I'm not a heathen or anything."

Penny laughed good-naturedly. "Oh for goodness sake, you're a funny girl." She touched her chin with the fingers of one hand while absently reaching for a cookie. "Still, it is odd."

My eyes narrowed slightly.

Penny turned to me and all mention of protection and crucifixes was over as quickly as it'd begun. "Do you have a favourite flower Ginny?"

"Excuse me?"

"A favourite flower?"

"Um … no. They all look so much the same to me. I can't tell. If it smells nice I like it." I wondered at her swift topic change and where this was going.

"I'm going to do some gardening tomorrow. Would you like to come by?"

"Uh, sure," I agreed. "I have school tomorrow, but I can come agfter." Seeing her sudden, bright smile I wondered why I felt so suspicious.

As I crossed back into my own yard, I turned my head automatically to scan the neighbour's corn field. My feet halted, and I squinted into the sunshine. Had I really caught sight of a small figure there, at the near edge of the muddy field? I blinked fast but the image was gone. Maybe I just wanted to see it.

Oblivious

35

I couldn't help it. I hated Grade six. My teacher, Miss Jones, hadn't helped. Even though we owned horses, and she was very much a horse person, we didn't have the right *kind* of horses. It was obvious to me within the first week of school that she wasn't just a horse person, she was a horse snob.

Koko, or 'barrel guts' as my father called her, simply would not impress. And my little black and white pony, Chuck, was still just as bad-tempered as the day I'd gotten him. Despite my efforts to sweeten his disposition, he still tended to nip me on the back as I tried to tighten up the girth strap on my saddle. Again, not the kind of horse that garnered the approval of my teacher, so no luck there.

The only time I saw Miss Jones in a different, more generous light was when our class took a field trip to her farm. In those days it wasn't weird for a teacher to bring her class to her own house. I'm sure the school districts looked on it as *cost effective*. Liability be damned.

When the bus arrived at its destination, it was obvious that our Miss Jones owned a racetrack.

Well, it looked like a racetrack to me, but in truth it was an exercise yard. She explained, quite patiently which wasn't her usual mode of address, that this was where jockeys could come and exercise the race horses, away from the crowds and other distractions. We were able to pet some of the sleek-coated thoroughbreds that she had there, and two lucky students actually got to sit on one. When a dappled grey came to the fence and nuzzled against her looking for treats, I saw a special gleam

281

in her eyes, the kind that she would never have for any of us. I understood Miss Jones better after that day, but even though I understood her, I still didn't like her. It seems the feeling was mutual.

October was when the first Interim report card arrived.

"I often catch Ginny staring into space and day-dreaming when the rest of the class is working," the personalized report began. "Ginny often rushes through projects and should pay better attention to the quality of her school work." I couldn't help wincing as I read that. No doubt my ghostly paranoia was still having an effect on my schoolwork. "Her attention often wanders during class instruction."

Oh wonderful, I thought drily, handing the paper back to my mother. I could tell that this wasn't going to end well.

"Explain yourself young lady," mom said.

"She hates me," I replied, as truthfully and respectfully as I could.

"I doubt that," mom answered. "Perhaps I'd better go have a visit, and let's hope this doesn't go as badly as the last time."

Yeah I hoped that too.

Unfortunately, that was only the start of the trouble.

I suppose, looking back on it now, it was only inevitable that I'd get into trouble sooner or later with all that anxiety building up inside me.

"But mom," I whined, later on that month. "He called me big nose. Nobody gets to call me that!" I was hugely sensitive about the fact that my most prominent feature was rapidly turning out to be my aquiline nose.

"You didn't have to hit him!" My mother admonished. "What were you thinking?"

Well, I guess that's the point: I wasn't thinking.

Incidents like these peppered my grade six year and although I should have been suspended, I always managed to get out of trouble as quickly as I got into it. Somehow. To this day my parents won't say what they told the Principal behind closed doors. I have to admit, perhaps it's better that I not know.

Grandpa

36

I remember feeling really conflicted in the days that led up to my sister's wedding. I grudgingly endured shopping with my family for the endless wedding details, but something kept nagging at me. It felt like something was badly wrong, but I couldn't figure it out.

Several days later, I received a shock that helped me put all of that out of my mind.

"Morning," I greeted Mom, rubbing sleep from my eyes. "Where is everybody?"

"Uh … well hello sweetie. How about sitting down and I'll help you with your breakfast?"

"Mom," I said, instantly suspicious. "What's wrong?"

Mom stood straighter and thrust her chin up bravely. "Okay, I see we're going to have that kind of morning are we? Fine." Mom sighed. "Daddy's gone to the hospital. Your Grandpa's very sick."

My stomach lurched and the knot that had been growing inside of me suddenly crashed to the bottom. "What's wrong with grandpa? Is he going to be okay?" My grandfather hated doctors and more so, hospitals. The fact that he was in the hospital, meant that he must be very sick.

"I don't honestly know. Grandpa had terrible stomach pains last night. The doctors are doing tests."

I was floored. My grandfather never went to the doctor, he never complained about anything. He was stoic and calm, the one I adored, the one who always made time for me. It felt wrong that this was happening and all I could do was cry.

"Daddy will call when they know anything."

"Where's Diana?" I asked, blinking back my tears.

"She had to go for a final fitting at the bridal boutique. Her bridesmaids came to pick her up an hour ago." Mom busied herself wiping down the table and placing breakfast dishes before me, giving me a meaningful look. "I'll tell her when she returns, so don't say anything."

Mom squared her shoulders. "You and I need to just carry on. Grandpa wouldn't have it any other way. You know he doesn't like a lot of fuss."

"You're talking like he's dying mom," I squinted at her suspiciously.

"No I'm not!" She replied heatedly, spilling her coffee on the tabletop. "But he is very sick. What we need to do is go about our business, wait for word from daddy and pray that Grandpa will be okay."

And so we waited and prayed, keeping ourselves busy but still feeling distracted for the rest of that awful day. At lunchtime, dad called to say that he was heading home.

"But what else did he say?" I quizzed my mother as she hung up the phone.

"Nothing else. He just said we'd talk when he got home. He was calling from a pay phone."

Mom must have wiped every surface over three times, going through the house banging cupboards closed, and then straightening things that had shifted from the force. She chucked things into piles and then turned to straighten them again.

I made myself scarce, choosing to spend my time outside in the last bit of summer weather that seemed to hang on well into autumn.

When dad got home, mom and I tried not to crowd him, but we were anxious for news. Mom's long-fingered hands twirled the dishcloth she held into a tight spiral and she paced back and forth in the kitchen. I knew she was marking time, waiting for the right moment to ask dad how Grandpa was. It was strange that he had been home for a full twenty minutes but all he'd managed to say was "hello family."

Finally, I couldn't stand it anymore. "Daddy! How is grandpa?"

"Not good," he said, looking over at mom.

Mom looked up sharply from the far end of the kitchen. I could see tears glistening in her green eyes. She gave a short nod. "She knows. I told Ginny this morning."

"I see," dad said. "Well, alright, sit down you two," he said, lowering himself into a kitchen chair. "Where's Diana? I don't want to have to say this twice."

"She's out with her bridesmaids," mom said. "I can tell her later if you want."

Dad grunted his approval. "Okay, it's like this. The doctors say he is suffering from the advanced stages of liver cancer."

Mom gasped and the unshed tears spilled down her cheeks as she pressed her lips tightly together. Her response started my own tears. Cancer was a killer and it had already taken my other Grandfather and an uncle.

"But daddy, can't they do anything? They can make him well again, can't they?" In my naiveté, I didn't want to hear that this could be the end of my grandfather.

"No honey, I'm afraid not. Grandpa can't walk away from this."

Dad stopped speaking, drew a handkerchief from his pocket and blew his nose loudly.

Incongruously, the thought went through my head that it sounded like the honk of a goose.

"What's a liver?" I asked, my voice barely above a whisper.

Dad turned to me and an unexpected smile danced across his face. "So full of questions," he said, a quiet, tired smile twitched at the corners of his mouth.

"The liver is an organ inside our bodies. It cleans our blood," mom explained patiently. "And the cancer is like a poison." She stopped and drew a long, slow breath. She was being overly technical, but I guessed this was her way of shutting out the pain. "When an organ becomes poisoned it stops working." Mom turned her tear-streaked face to me and waited to see if I understood. Her lips quivered as she tried to keep from crying.

My tears came again quickly, and I wanted to scream, but instead I just nodded at Mom, and quietly stood up. Almost without thinking, I fell into my father's arms, buried my face in his shoulder and wept. The unfairness of it made me feel empty. Even with all my intuition and strange talent, my grandpa was dying and I couldn't stop it.

As the wedding drew nearer, my grandfather grew steadily weaker. Diana had been hoping he would rally, even if it was only temporarily, so he could see her get married, but eventually she realized, as all of us did, that his time was done. He was asleep nearly all the time. Twelve days before the ceremony, at 2:45 in the morning, grandpa's hand slipped from his wife's grasp, and his eyes closed for the last time.

It was a crushing sadness and my entire body was numbed with the sheer weight of it.

My grandmother, the tiny little redhead that I loved so dearly was doing her best to keep going. She had never let anyone see her cry, and she wasn't about to start now.

"I'm a Swede," she told me. "We're tough as nails. You've got Swede in you too, you know."

Only a couple of things really stood out for me on the day of grandpa's funeral. One was my own astonishment when I saw how many people crowded into the church for the service.

"He was loved by so many," my mom whispered. "He touched many lives, your grandpa did."

The second thing I recall from that day was the item my parents presented me with just before we left the house for the church.

"Good, you're ready," dad said as he straightened his tie. Dad was wearing a black suit and his shoes were so shiny I could almost see my reflection. I wore a high-necked white blouse, with frills at the neck and cuffs. The dark part of my outfit was the black velvet vest and matching skirt. It was not my style, but I remember that, at the time, I didn't care.

Mom stood in front of me and inspected my outfit, tucking in my blouse a little tighter and plucking a few stray cat hairs from the black velvet.

"Oh and I almost forgot," she said, pulling something from her handbag. "You need this."

I took the small white box from her and opened it. Inside, sandwiched between two pieces of flat cotton batting was a beautiful silver cross, suspended on a gleaming silver chain.

Mom bent to un-do the crystal, and fasten the new necklace around my neck as soon as I'd plucked it from the box. She deposited the crystal back into the small white box and handed it to me. "Can you put this away? I think the cross is more appropriate, what do you think?" I turned to regard my reflection in the small mirror that hung in our foyer.

"It's pretty," I said. "Grandpa would like it."

"I thought so too," she said. "We were going to wait for your Confirmation, but it seemed more appropriate to do it now."

As we walked into the church, hand in hand, I was conscious of it hanging about my neck, gleaming almost as though it was lit from within by a special power. I cried endless tears all the way through the funeral, while grandma patted my hand with characteristic selflessness. I don't remember the graveside ceremony or the reception that followed. I focused on the feeling that grandpa wasn't really gone. The little silver cross reminded me that he was supposed to be in Heaven with God now and that meant he was happy. I tried my best to be happy for him, but I found it very difficult.

It wasn't fair! I wanted him back so badly. My new knowledge only made me more worried. Was he going to become a wandering spirit too? I hoped not. I wanted him to go happily into Heaven, with all the love and acceptance he'd had on earth. I didn't want him to get stuck in Purgatory or anywhere else.

I tried to talk to my grandmother about it, desperate for some sort of closure. "Grandma, do you think grandpa's in Heaven?"

"Of course he is," she replied firmly. "Where else would he be? I can see him, you know. He's smiling and joking with Saint Peter." She looked at me with a tight smile and smoothed my hair back with one arthritic hand, her knuckles bulged and distorted. "He doesn't have any more pain."

"Can you really see him? Are you certain?" I replied. The weight of my sadness had exhausted me and in my innocence, I didn't realize she was speaking figuratively. "Is that where I get it from?"

I remember grandma looked at me curiously for a moment, but then she continued as though the last part of my question hadn't been spoken.

"I'm certain because it makes sense to be certain, Ginny. Upset and tears don't do any good, do they?" she said. "Mac and I loved each other. It was timeless; an *old world* type of thing. Do you know what I mean?" I shook my head.

"It's the kind of love that is not given to public displays. It was always private and it shall remain so. I owe him that. He was a good man and I will miss him."

And so grandma tried to be happy too, though I'm sure her heart was as broken as ours. She cleaned her house, looked after their dog and claimed that her eyes were "weak" when a lone tear would trace its way down her cheek.

Soon, our somber moods and black clothing were forced to give way to bright coloured flowers, yards of frothy white tulle and wedding decorations. The night of my sister's wedding rehearsal the whole family was gathered, sitting quietly in the church pews as we waited to be organized. I sat with my grandma, hands clasped together tightly, taking comfort in each other. Neither one of us could forget the last time we were together in that church.

The rehearsal was boring, but I tried to sit still, thinking of the dinner that we would go to afterwards. I always loved going out to dinner.

Pastor Smith talked endlessly about where people would stand and what they would say. He almost never looked at me, and I was okay with that. I had only a minor role to play as the junior bridesmaid, and besides, he was probably still thinking I was a weirdo. The last time he'd seen me, I'd fallen over in a faint.

That night, as I lay in bed, I thought of all the times I'd smiled and laughed that day and was instantly filled with guilt. How could I be so happy when my grandpa had just died? It felt so wrong, somehow, even though I'd heard mom and dad and even pastor say, "life goes on" I just couldn't bring myself to admit it. With thoughts and images of my grandfather's smiling face filling my head, I settled my head onto my pillow and waited to fall asleep. Inexplicably, I smelled warm, freshly-turned earth, a scent that held specific meaning for me. Delighting in the scent, I relaxed and let my mind wander back in time. I'd spent a week with my grandparents last summer and the smell reminded me of the beautiful gardens in their yard where we'd spend the majority of our time. The bedroom where I'd slept had pale green walls and faced those gardens. That room would often fill with the scent of freshly turned earth, wafting in through the big window at the foot of my bed. My grandparents loved their gardens.

As my eyes had opened one morning, over a year ago, there he'd been, standing firmly in my doorway, both hands on his hips.

"What's wrong grandpa?" I'd asked him.

"Something terrible," he'd answered, but his smile told me that he was pulling my leg.

"Oh?"

"Yeah. It's breakfast time and we're out of Corn Flakes! Can you believe such a thing could happen? You gotta get up! We've gotta go for an emergency Corn Flake run!"

Laughing at his dead-pan humour, I'd gotten dressed quickly and, hand in hand, off we'd gone for our emergency Corn Flake run to the corner store down the road.

The scent of freshly turned earth would always hold that memory for me.

I felt my body relax into the mattress, my head sinking deeper into the soft pillow. Soon, my breathing was slow and even, a sure sign that sleep was imminent.

It shocked me slightly when I saw him.

He stood straight and tall at my bedside, a bemused smile playing about his lips. As is the way with dreams, I suddenly wasn't in bed anymore, but seated comfortably on the couch in our living room. I could feel the threads of the green and gold brocade pattern under my fingertips. I faced my grandfather calmly, and we carefully balanced china cups full of hot tea on our knees. He spoke to me earnestly, his soothing voice reassuring and confident.

"How are you?" he asked.

"I'm fine," I replied automatically.

"I see," he said. "I'm fine too. It's good to see you."

"It's good to see you too grandpa," I agreed. I knew I was dreaming, but unlike my dreams of late, there was no urgency or panic. I was just having tea with my grandpa. What could be more natural?

He chuckled warmly. "That's my girl," he said, smiling. "Your grandma is a strong woman," he said. "You know that, but you should tell your parents. You tell them Mother is strong. She'll be okay."

"Okay grandpa. I will."

He grunted in response. A sound I knew well. "You know what? It's nice here."

"That's good grandpa," I answered. I wondered vaguely where 'here' was, but wasn't overly concerned.

"Your father's stubborn, thinks he's got it all figured out. There are still things he has yet to understand. You tell him I said that, okay?" Grandpa reached out and placed his hand atop my head. I could feel the warmth and pressure of his touch. "There's a good girl."

A moment later I was alone again, lying quietly in my own bed, and tears were leaking into my ears.

I knew it had been a dream, but perhaps it was something more too? The warmth of his touch still lingered atop my head. I blinked several times, trying to will him back from the shadows. I realized then that I was fully awake. I sat up quietly and perched on the edge of my bed, reliving the memory of my dream. Was this grandpa's way of letting me know he was alright? And what about the message for my father? How would I ever be able to say all that? And even if I did, who would believe me?

Gale-Force Wedding

37

The night before my sister's wedding, everything turned stormy, both inside and out. After supper, dad and I had gone into the family room to watch some T.V., but my thoughts were tripping over themselves. I was still trying to figure out whether my grandpa really had visited me, or if I just missed him so much that I'd invented it. Worse still was the dilemma over that message.

Mom and Diana were running from room to room, picking things up and putting them down. I knew why my sister was nervous; in a matter of hours, it would be her wedding day.

Later that evening, our brave German Shepherd refused to go into her dog house. She whined and cried at the back door, scratching desperately at the wood in terror. The uncharacteristic behaviour seemed to rattle my father, and I watched as his face got pinker by the minute, his blood pressure rising with each new situation.

"What's going on with Rookie?" mom commented. "Nothing ever bothers that dog."

"How should I know?" dad grumbled. "She's a dog."

Whatever the problem, she kept it up until dad let her into the laundry room and closed the connecting door firmly.

"Silly dog," he said.

"Maybe she knows something we don't," mom added.

Later as I got ready for bed, I watched in amazement as a strange mist developed in the corners of my dresser mirror, the same kind of mist you get on the bathroom mirror when you've been in the shower too long. I watched in wonder as it spread across the reflective surface, gradually whiting out my image.

Feeling confused and afraid, I ran to get my parents, but when I returned moments later with mom in tow the mirror had returned to normal.

"No more games, Ginny. Get ready for bed. You're tired and so am I. I've still got lots to do for tomorrow. I don't have any time to spare for this foolishness."

"But Mom, I swear ..."

"I know, I know, but it's late and we all have a big day tomorrow."

In the small hours of the morning, a sound like pebbles being thrown against glass awoke me from a fitful sleep. Expecting to see hailstones falling from the sky and bouncing off my window, I crawled from my bed and twitched open the curtains. But apart from an early morning mist, there was nothing going on with the weather. I shrugged checked the clock. 3 A.M.

"Ugh, too early," I mumbled, crawling back into bed, curious but not curious enough to stay awake to investigate.

Sometime later, I awoke to the sound of a loud roar, as of hundreds of little hailstones hitting the house. Bleary-eyed but fearful of retribution if I stayed in bed, I stumbled down the hall to the kitchen.

Outside, it was a scene like no other. A full-scale storm, made complete by dark clouds, hailstones, howling winds and blowing debris. Ten seconds later, there was a loud buzzing sound and a white flash seemed to ricochet off of the windows, knocking out the power.

"Morning sweetheart," mom greeted me. "Sleep well?"

Her good humour seemed ironic in the face of that storm. The look I directed at my mother, out of one eye, seemed to say it all. Her eyebrows climbed up her forehead and she said no more.

Diana didn't sit. She rushed and ran, flitted and charged from one room to another, as the minutes ticked by.

"I can't believe it!" She said as she rushed by. "I can't believe it, on my wedding day of all days."

Getting ready would be that much more difficult without power, but somehow we still managed, and soon, all too soon, it was time to leave for the hairdresser.

By the light of several candles, and with a noisy generator for the dryers and curling irons whirring in the background, our hair stylist worked her magic. Long extension cords snaked through the central corridor of the hair salon, plugged into the massive generator out back of the shop. Somehow, Linda, our trusted stylist and family friend, managed cascading ringlets, gentle waves, bouncing curls and sleek, smooth up-do's while managing to weave silk flowers into the intricate hairstyles. Make-up was liberally applied as we munched on a bag of day-old croissants mom had snagged on our way out the door that morning.

"We look amazing!" I said, my eyes wide with wonder. "I look goo-ood!"

My sister laughed and grabbed me around the waist, hugging me close. "Come on sis, let's get going." She looked funny in her wedding veil and faded jeans but it was about to get worse. Mom had brought some horrible, loud-patterned scarves that looked like they came directly from a bargain-store in Hawaii. Wincing slightly at the gaudy patterns, we dutifully tied each gauzy scarf over our heads to protect our new hair-dos. Not another soul braved the elements at the mall that day, which suited me just fine: I didn't want to be seen anywhere with this crazy orange scarf on my head.

It's funny how these details stand out in my mind now. Later that day, the wind continued to hammer at us as we stood the massive oak doors of the picturesque church. A flustered reverend, whom we'd never met, hauled open the heavy double doors at our fierce knock. Our regular Pastor was ill and couldn't perform the ceremony, so Diana and Rick had quickly chosen another Reverend to marry them.

I felt bad that he didn't have any warning, but when he began stammering at my mother's cheerful greeting, I knew he was headed for trouble.

"Wedding?" he said, scratching his head with a puzzled look on his face. "We can't have a wedding today," he turned around to indicate the darkened interior of the church. "We've got no power!"

Mom only hesitated about two seconds, before she went into action. "Listen, my daughter is getting married today, power or no power. We have guests that will begin arriving shortly. Now let's see what we can do with a little candle light," she said firmly. "Why look at how many candles you have right here! There's more than enough."

Mom nodded her head at him firmly and sent me and the other bridesmaids in our beautiful gowns scurrying through the building, rounding up every candle we could lay our hands on. Within the space of a half hour, mom had transformed that church into a celestial, peaceful place of soft candlelight, in the midst of the dark, chaotic weather that raged outside.

My cousin, already an accomplished musician at the age of 20, coaxed ethereal, hauntingly beautiful music from the aged piano in one corner, as the wedding guests started filling up the church. His strong fingers sent the cascading notes all the way to the rear of the church effortlessly.

At the appointed time, the wedding guests twisted around in their seats to witness the first person who would stride down the isle of the candle-lit church. I was me, and what they didn't know was that my legs were trembling uncontrollably under the layered skirts. I walked faster and hoped no one would notice.

One by one, my sister's bridesmaids joined me at the front where we waited, our faces shining in the glow of candlelight. When Diana entered, she was beautifully framed by the white lace and tulle of her ornate dress. Her smile was soft and shy, but her eyes were riveted on Rick. I realized with a start that the girl I'd grown up with had become a different person and I hardly knew her. The though took my breath away.

Power or no power, mom had said, and she was right.

Diana and her soul mate were united in marriage that day under raging skies amidst howling winds and against all odds. But the church had never looked more beautiful.

And there is no denying that the most magical moment of the day wasn't choreographed by any of us.

As the Pastor pronounced Rick and Diana husband and wife, the power in the church was unexpectedly restored and all the fixtures came to life in a joyous, though unexpected celebration of light. The congregation gasped. No doubt capitalizing on the dramatic effect, the pastor lifted his hands in the final Benediction, and our cousin, a talented and versatile musician, hurried to the church's pipe organ. He played the recessional hymn at full volume as bride and groom swept down the aisle, arm in arm, their smiles brighter than any light.

They paused in the vestibule, their beaming faces turned to each other for a final, excited "photo-op" embrace before braving the storm outside.

But instead of howling winds and driving rain, as if by magic, my sister had her perfect wedding day moment. The angry black clouds had swept aside, letting golden shafts of sunlight pour down. One by one, we all emerged into the sunshine and turned our astonished faces to bask in its sudden warmth. Diana and Rick stepped into the waiting limousine and the rest of the party followed in similar fashion for the customary wedding tour around the city.

I'm told that the skies opened again only moments later, but all I remember is how much fun it was to help the driver honk the horn of our fancy car as we trailed behind the happy couple through the streets of our small home town.

I'm also told that many of the guests that day were certain that mom, a talented organizer with a flair for the dramatic, had somehow planned the entire thing.

~~~~

"I've got to run Ginny back over to the church for the rest of the photos, I'll be back in ten minutes," dad said later, as he watched my mother frowning at the caterer. "Relax, everything's beautiful!" He waved his arm at the neatly set tables placed strategically throughout the hall. "Your parties are always fantastic and this one's no exception." Gently, he kissed Mom's cheek and led me away.

"Just tilt your head up this way towards your new husband, that's right. Now look dreamily into his eyes, perfect, perfect, hold it there. This'll be a great shot." The photographer stood on a chair in front of the wedding party, as we posed for photos back at the church. The moment, still and reserved and beautiful, was suddenly broken as both sets of the church's rear double doors inexplicably flew open. As one, we turned to stare in open amazement as the wide open doors.

We'd all assumed it was the storm that had blown them open, but no icy blast of air or any significant wind whistled through. In fact, there was no sign of the storm at all, and certainly no one stood near enough to those heavy doors to have pushed them open. Weak sunlight filtered in peacefully through the stained glass windows on either side of the church. A dead calm settled over the stunned wedding party, as the silence gave way to nervous low toned chatter. Two ushers, elbowed by the Pastor, hurried to close both sets of doors once again, and our attention turned back to our bewildered photographer.

"Um, okay that was weird ... well I guess we can carry on. Unless there's anyone else who wants to make their presence known?" He was smirking, but I could see that Diana had developed a tight look around her eyes.

I closed my own eyes and inhaled deeply for the strength to endure this crazy day. A moment later, my eyes flew open.

It was unmistakable. That smell. It shouldn't be here!

Pipe tobacco.

Trying not to appear as puzzled as I felt, I looked around casually. Stands of white Freesia and Sonya Roses flanked us, as we stood in a group. Girls clustered on one side, and Rick and his groomsmen, on the other. Even though this seemed to be taking forever, no one was smoking.

To this day that special smell makes me think only of him. I can still see him sitting in that black leather chair, drawing deeply on his pipe as he watched his grandchildren playing board games on the floor.

Drawing in the scent like a heady perfume, I closed my eyes and remembered. Could he really be there? Had he come to Diana's wedding after all?

I could feel the waves of calm washing over me, and while it might have been my imagination, I could have sworn I felt the touch of soft fabric against my cheek. Instantly, I was back there, in my grandparent's home, burying my face in his shoulder, the warmth and strength of his arms wrapping me in an embrace that fixed everything.

The emotion was powerful and I opened my eyes wide to fight back the tears. Taking a deep breath, I found my sister. She was across the room, surrounded by her bridesmaids, but her eyes were on me. I saw her smile, and her lips formed the word, "Grandpa."

For Sale

38

I remembered Tom as soon as I saw him again. He was one of mom and dad's casual friends from the social club they belonged to. He was nice enough, although his English accent made him sound very serious. He had medium brown hair that he wore cropped short, and his teeth, although gleaming white, were uneven, giving his smile a lop-sided look. He always wore an expensive-looking suit and dress shoes, even on the warmest of days and I marveled at his ability to endure the heat without sweating. Mom and dad said he had a solid reputation as a talented realtor. I guessed that meant he was rich. He certainly looked rich. All I knew for sure was that he was a friend of their friend, and that meant he was 'okay'.

"Hi Ginny," he greeted me, as he walked through our open front door, clipboard in hand, smoothing some faint wrinkles from his neatly pressed pants.

"Hi," I said, giving him a small smile. Dad followed in his wake and mom immediately after. She looked worried, the small lines between her brows deeper and more shadowed.

"Watcha doin'?" I asked her.

"Tom is assessing the house," she said, her eyes on the two men as they moved off down the hallway. "Did you clean your room like I asked you?"

"Define clean," I answered.

Mom groaned, shot a dark look at me and took off down the hall after them. A moment later, I could hear her making excuses for my untidy bedroom.

The truth was, I didn't want to sell. I had unfinished business here, and besides, this was my home! I decided right then and there, that I wasn't going to leave without a fight.

The day the sign went up on the front lawn, I felt sick all day. I watched from the living room as the workmen pounded a long white 'L' shaped post into the ground at the front edge of my yard, eventually hanging a swinging wooden sign from the hooks at the top. I stayed in my room while mom and dad talked outside with Tom. The house was eerily quiet.

All too soon, our first showing was scheduled.

The phone rang shrilly. "Hello?" Dad held the receiver to his ear. "You're on your way? Great! How long do you figure? … oh yeah, that'll be fine … okay, do you have the key I gave you? I'm gonna lock up … okay great. Yeah, talk to you later, Tom, goodbye."

We'd left the house just as Tom's car pulled up with the prospective buyers inside. Dad drove us into town at a leisurely pace for some ice cream, a forced smile on his face. But when we returned, a hastily-written note greeted us on the kitchen table.

It was part of Tom's routine to leave notes after a showing, and he wasn't shy about being bold with his clients.

"I don't mince words," he'd said.

And indeed, he hadn't.

His notes were short and to the point, printed in blocky-looking letters on the back of his business card.

"Problems showing tonight," the note said. "Strange odour in the office, but I didn't smell it. House overly cold. Oil furnace? No accounting for it, people don't like oil. We cut the visit short. Didn't make it to the barn. Don't expect an offer. Sorry."

Once they'd read the note and tossed it back to the table, Mom's eyes welled up with tears and dad grew even more somber. I thought they were over-reacting and said as much to my sister when she came to pick up some more of her belongings. The significance of the realtor's note missed me by a mile.

"Oh come on, you can't be that dumb," she said, rolling her eyes.

"What are you talking about?" I said.

"Oh really," she said. "Odours? Freezing cold? Puh-lease … ask your pals Bob and John," she said, shaking her head and walking away.

So. She thought Bobby was trying to stop this move? And what did she know about John? Bobby's cryptic popped into my head: *He's not your friend.*

The next couple that came to see the house met me outside as I returned from the mailbox at the end of the driveway.

"Oh! Hi, I'm Harriet? This is my husband Frank? We're here to view the house?" Her tone was apologetic, and the phrases she spoke ended in a questioning lilt.

"Oh, well, you're early," I told her. My tone was flat and unfriendly. "The realtor said you wouldn't be here until 4 and it's just 3:30 now. He's not here yet. You can wait in your car."

The woman looked shocked, but she backed away from me with another apologetic phrase. "I'm sure he won't be long? We'll just wait out here then?"

I'll admit my approach wasn't the nicest, and I could look forward to a lecture about it later, but I didn't see why I should make an effort.

The notes from our realtor were entertaining, at least to me. I'd decided to be a passive objector. I would do what I was told, but I wouldn't volunteer anything, I wouldn't give opinions and I would *not* be friendly to anyone who wanted to take my home away from me.

Mom, dad and Tom seemed to figure this out quickly.

"They're nice folks," Tom told my parents later, as they stood at our front door. "But apparently, Ginny met them outside and wasn't overly nice. I countered with the familiar 'kids will be kids' thing, and I did let it slip how she's upset at having to move. I have to tell you that the trick-lamp you have in the living room gave me a run for my money." He chuckled. "I had to distract the buyers when it did it's on-and-off routine." Tom smiled nervously, twiddling a ballpoint pen in his long fingers. "Must need a new bulb, right? Oh well, you can never tell with electricity, can you?"

The note Tom left for us after the next showing made my mother very upset. "Walk-through went great until we hit laundry room. Bad smell drove us right back out. If there are problems like that, please let me know before I show the house. Closed the door so smell wouldn't permeate everything—Tom."

"Well I never," mom said heatedly. "What does he think? We are on a well, after all. A little sulfur won't kill them."

"I changed the filter yesterday, Liz, it couldn't be that," dad said.

Our water, coming up through layers of sulfur, picked up a faint smell that we'd all learned to live with, but once the filter was changed, all traces of the smell and color were usually erased.

"I simply have no idea what he could be talking about," mom fumed. "That laundry room is cleaner than the day we moved in and we've added all those lovely white wall cupboards. I've wiped everything out very carefully. There's no odour!"

Dad and I dutifully trooped into the laundry room to give the room a giant sniff while mom stood with hands on hips, watching us from the doorway.

"Well?" she asked. "What do you smell?"

"Pine Sol," dad said. I nodded my agreement.

"Exactly," she replied, her eyes flashing with anger. "A smell indeed! This is insulting!"

The following Saturday, I'd been out for the day, riding Chuck with my other horse friends, working hard to keep him under control and grousing about the move. I was in a bad mood already when I came home to find mom and dad stewing over the most recent and puzzling note of all from our realtor.

"Hi guys: if you have trouble getting house ready for showing, call me, we'll re-schedule. Thankfully clients running late. Had enough time to cancel. Need to hear from you before re-booking—Tom."

"It maddening," mom said. "When we walked in here, the house looked exactly as it did when we left, right?"

Dad simply nodded his agreement and frowned at the hand-written note.

The faint scent of flowers, from a drug store aerosol still lingered in the air as they stood at the kitchen counter together. I knew they couldn't have been home long. The kitchen was still spotless, although a lone cupboard, tall and narrow, housing half of the large pantry on one side of the galley-style kitchen had been left open … but surely that had been Tom, trying to show off the kitchen. Everything looked fine to me.

"Well, I'm gonna go change," dad said, heading down the hall.

"Me too," mom agreed, following him. "Then I'm calling Tom."

I'd already turned to walk out of the kitchen, intent on watching some cartoons to try and salvage my day, when behind me, I heard a strange growl, followed by a sharp wooden bang!

Whirling around, the empty kitchen stared back at me. The only difference was that lone, open cupboard door was now firmly closed.

I could hear the muted sounds of my parents as they continued their conversation in their bedroom down the hall.

Someone was playing games again.

Backing out of the room in a defensive crouch, I kept backing up all the way to my room. Who was doing this? Was it coincidence that it happened as soon as my parents left the room? Had I imagined that weird growl?

That menacing sound changed things in my mind. What were we dealing with here? This was no longer just some confused spirits. My earlier fears surfaced anew. Something was actively trying to keep us from leaving, and I was willing to bet it wasn't Bobby.

In the days and weeks that followed, the people Tom brought to look at the house seemed to leave as fast as they arrived. No one wanted to buy my home. Wasn't I getting what I wanted? So how come I was so scared?

Leaving a mess of toys or making a bad smell was the kind of childish prank I might have thought of, but I knew I was innocent. If only my parents shared that belief. So often lately, they looked at me with accusing glares after they read another of Tom's now infamous notes.

Later that day, I walked in on another meeting, this time conducted in the front hallway. We were preparing to leave the house so another prospective buyer could take a walk-through. "Let's just walk through together," suggested Tom. "I have a very motivated buyer!"

"How motivated?" dad asked him, as they moved off through the house.

"Well, this fellow has apparently driven by about a dozen times, he knows some of your neighbours, and he's talked with them about the property and its history. I understand he's an avid horseman, so I'll show the barn and riding ring first."

"Hmm, a horseman," dad said, scratching at his chin. "Just a single guy?"

"No, he's married with a couple kids, and his wife is expecting again. From what I understand she couldn't come today."

"Hmm, without his wife, this guy might not be that interested in spending time looking at the house. Wouldn't you say?"

"Perhaps not," Tom replied, peering into each room cautiously as he went.

"Might be more interested in the barn, then?"

"Possibly," Tom agreed.

"That might be a plus," mom muttered. The adults didn't seem to notice that I was following them.

Dad turned to Tom. "You say he talked with our neighbours? What for?"

"Don't know," Tom replied. "Perhaps getting a feel for the neighbourhood."

"And he knows the history of the land? What do you mean?"

"Well, he asked me for the date that the house was built, and it's my understanding that he's looked into it a bit with the city records, that kind of thing. Nothing specific. Why?"

"Not important," dad said, and reached out to shake Tom's hand. "Good work Tom, let us know how it goes. We appreciate it."

"Of course," Tom said. "Ah, one more thing. You are positive there are no sewage or plumbing problems with the house? I feel ridiculous asking you again, but ..."

"None at all," dad quickly assured him. "The water has some sulfur in it, but I just changed the filter."

"Ah, well maybe that's it," Tom said.

"I don't know," dad agreed. "But the place was perfectly fine both when we left and when we got home. Nothing out of place. You sure about those games and puzzles? You didn't pick up anything?"

"Not me," Tom replied.

"Well, imagine that, another odd thing." The sarcasm in his tone seemed to leave the realtor puzzled but he said no more about it.

Tom smiled his practiced realtor smile. "Oddities are a dime-a-dozen in my profession, Will. Don't worry, I'll call you when I get back to the office," he said. "Hopefully soon we'll be celebrating."

The grass crunched underfoot as I strolled out through the back field, hands crammed into the pockets of my jeans.

I would miss this place, I knew. Even more, I would miss the little boy that I now realized had come to me asking for help. I couldn't help but feel I'd let him down.

The injustice of it made me mad. How could I possibly help him when I didn't know how? For some reason, he was trapped here, that much was obvious. Why he couldn't find his way to Heaven, I didn't know, but I had some idea that it had to do with the dark entity he called 'John'. Angrily I kicked at a clump of dried mud and watched it explode into dust off the end of my toe. "John's not your friend" he'd told me. Yeah, no kidding, I thought. How about some useful information though, like what could I actually do about it?

Continuing to stomp around the field, while shaking my head and muttering to myself, I was glad my parents were busy inside the house. They were in full swing with an idea Tom had pitched a few days ago.

Signs proclaiming that there was an 'Open House' were posted all up and down our street, and balloons decorated the corners of the house and mailbox. If our realtor was right about this, an Open House usually brought in buyers.

I was doomed to leave. And without my help, I knew Bobby was doomed to stay.

Kicking fiercely at the small rocks that peppered the landscape, I wished for the thousandth time that he could come to me again, but I already knew he wouldn't. It was like wishing for a blizzard in the middle of July.

The flowers in the garden were hardy Chrysanthemums and despite it being Fall, dad had wound back the cover and vacuumed the pool. It sparkled in the sunshine.

All in all, it was a perfect day for a party, but instead, we were having an Open House for a bunch of realtors.

"So I suppose that's it, then?" I said, my tone dripping acid.

"What's it?" mom said, placing a stack of napkins on the kitchen table beside a plate of chocolate chip cookies, still warm from the oven.

"You're just going to sell the house out from under me, no matter what I say about it?"

"Yup," she said, not looking at me. We'd been over this many times before and I knew mom wasn't interested in going there yet again.

"Well fine, then!" I shot back, my tone rising with my temper. "You go, but I'm staying!"

"What?" Mom turned to look at me in surprise. "What are you talking about? Where are you proposing to stay?"

"I don't know," I admitted. "I'll live under a bridge or in a ditch someplace."

Mom's startled look gave way to stifled laughter and she turned away from me, her shoulders shaking with mirth.

I, on the other hand, wasn't in a laughing mood. I knew what I'd said didn't make any sense, but I was past caring. This was my home and they were selling it out from under me. It wasn't fair.

Humphing into the air, I stomped out of the room and went outside.

"Don't slam the door," I heard mom say as the door slammed closed after me.

"Whoops, clumsy me," I muttered, stalking away.

Connections

39

That night, I lay in my bed and gave in to the swirling thoughts in my head. I was so tired.

I'd done my best to avoid the prospective buyers and realtors who came to our Open House, running from one location to another as they crawled all over our house and outbuildings like a bunch of ants.

Even in my sleep, I felt both physically and mentally drained. I slipped easily into a dream-state where I realized at one that someone was trying to talk to me. Strange, disjointed pictures whirled through my dreams. I shook my head at the interruption. I needed to rest.

"Go away," I muttered. But the dreams came anyway.

I dreamed of my own house, but it was different somehow. None of the furniture was right. Right place, wrong time.

A dark haired woman worked to clean the large glass doors, methodically spraying and wiping, the circular motions almost hypnotic.

Suddenly, the glass she was wiping started to move.

The woman stopped working with a frown and simply waited.

The dream played like a T.V. show. It felt familiar.

The door was part way along the track, revealing five or six inches of open air. She chaffed her arms against the cold that poured through, and peered through the glass into the yard beyond.

The view through that window was familiar. This was my yard. How could that be? I didn't know this woman.

Closing and re-locking the door securely, she went back to work.

Only a few minutes elapsed, however, before a telltale click sounded and once again, the door moved along its track.

"David," I heard her call to someone outside of the room. "Can you come in here?"

She regarded the open doorway with an expression I'd seen on my own face many times. Grasping the handle severely, she slammed it and slid the lock home with a resounding metallic clank.

"This is crazy," she muttered, walking from the room. "David, where are you?" I heard her call.

In my dream, the empty room looked enormous, but I saw something that the dream woman did not.

A tell-tale shadow hovered just outside the glass door. The shape was fuzzy and featureless but I recognized him in an instant.

I watched like a voyeur as the normally brightly lit room, with its large bright windows, grew perceptibly darker, although it was the middle of the day. The soft scraping of metal on metal indicating that the lock securing the glass door was receding.

The woman in my dream had still not returned.

Somewhere at the opposite end of the house, a puppy barked incessantly and a little boy's laugh quickly followed. Flashes of colour followed. I could see the young woman now. She smiled fondly at a little boy and his puppy as they played a fast game of tag.

She didn't see that the glass door now stood partly open.

Rag and spray bottle still in her hands, she began walking back toward me and the open door, when suddenly another sound caught her attention.

"David?" she called, turning to investigate. "Are you here?"

She smiled gently at the small boy as she passed him, where he sat on the floor with his dog. He looked different to me as he sat there, playing happily. His face was vibrant. So alive.

"Mommy will be right back. Stay here." With that she disappeared from the room.

My view shifted. The small puppy gave a short, excited bark and in one swift movement, he flashed through the now fully open doorway, followed closely by the little boy, his short legs pumping to keep up.

"Dammit! The door!" The young mother rushed into the room seconds later. Her hand gripped the edge of the glass door as she slid to a stop, confusion distorting her features.

This was my house. How was I seeing this?

"Bobby!" She called, leaping nimbly through the open doorway she stood on the concrete patio, looking around for her small son. "I told you to stay inside!"

"Bobby?" She walked briskly to the north end of the house, just as a screech of truck tires and air brakes rent the air. The look in her eyes made the tears standing in my own begin to fall. "No-o-o-o!" She screamed, breaking into a run.

She was running for the road.

I screamed with her and ran at her side, knowing it was already too late.

Out of breath, we arrived at the scene of the accident together. Energy spent, the air stolen from our lungs, we took in the horror in front of us and couldn't face it.

We were too late.

A small, lifeless body lay on the hard surface of the road. Blood discoloured the golden hair and his glorious eyes, still open, stared lifelessly at the sky.

Several feet away, the hulking form of a huge dump truck blocked out everything. The driver's door stood open and a tall man wearing a heavy sweatshirt huddled in the road, his body folded in on itself. He rocked back and forth as he clutched at his eyes and head cried piteously.

"I didn't see him, I didn't see him, he's just a child ... Lord, No!" he repeated.

Together, the young mother and I collapsed onto the road. Our world crumbled into chaos.

An anguished scream pierced the silence and I awoke, startled to realize it had been my own.

Tears had pooled in my ears and I sat up quickly, wiping at my face in confusion.

"It's only a dream," I panted, my arms wrapping around my body, as I too began rocking back and forth on my tangled quilt, the tears hot and stinging. I looked around carefully at my four walls, forcing myself to find some comfort in its familiarity.

It had have been a dream, but it was so real.

Mom appeared in my doorway a moment later, a weary look of concern on her face. "Ginny, are you okay?" she whispered urgently.

"Yeah ... I think so," I whispered back. The tears had already subsided, and I wiped away the rest of them with the back of my hand.

"Nightmare?"

"Yeah." My heart was still beating fast and I felt an uncontrollable urge to tremble, which I tried to hide beneath the bedcovers.

"Mmm," she said, stifling a yawn. "Do you need me to stay with you?"

"No, it's okay," I mumbled.

"Okay," she yawned, covered her mouth with the back of her hand and blinked sleepily. "Are you sure?"

"I can manage."

"Alright, do you think you can get back to sleep?"

"Yeah."

"Ok," she yawned again and turned back to her own room. "If you need me, I'm right here."

I listened to the sounds of my mother's sleepy footsteps, dragging back across the carpet and heard the creak of the mattress as she settled back into her bed. I lay awake for a long time, staring at my ceiling and puzzling at the clarity of the dream that was more like an experience.

The emotional pain I'd felt when kneeling on the pavement with the young mother still stabbed at my heart. I had actually *felt* the small rocks on the road digging into my knees.

How could I be experiencing this?

I was going back to see Julia in the morning. She and I had lots to discuss.

~~~~~

The next day dawned clear and surprisingly warm for October. School was a minor inconvenience to me. Something that had to be endured. As I pedalled my bike through the crisp morning air, my thoughts were riveted on what I would say to Julia. I knew I had to be coherent, concise and not what my mom would call 'flighty'.

By the time I was pedalling home again, I had a well-rehearsed script, which I wasted no time in relaying to Julia soon after she admitted me to her home.

"Well, you're a very helpful girl. I'm not surprised that you get such dreams," she said. "When I was a girl, people used to say that events 'coloured the landscape'. I'm quite sure that I interpreted it differently from most folks, but people don't say this anymore. I suppose it's fallen out of fashion. I wish they would though, because it's true. Traumatic events, like the one you describe, they leave a mark." Julia talked easily with me as we worked, removing the dried wisps of plant matter from the planters at her front porch. She was so casual; she could have been discussing the weather.

I looked sideways at her. "Dad uses that expression, but I don't think he means it in quite the same way."

"I'm sure he doesn't," she chuckled. "But to a couple of gals like us, we can still feel the change in the air, can't we?" She smiled and dusted her hands together. "Let's go inside and wash up," she said. Wide by side at the kitchen sink, the water rinsing the dark earth from our hands, she spoke again.

"Sometimes strange dreams are just that. But sometimes they are more. Perhaps this was more."

My eyes widened.

"It's just a theory," she said, smiling. She reached for a towel and handed me another.

"So what do you think it means?" I asked her.

"I don't know. It was your dream," she began, "you are the only person who can really interpret the dream, if indeed it *needs* interpreting. It could just be a case where you knew some of the facts, and your sub-conscious mind created the rest. I know how badly you feel for this boy."

I frowned, trying to piece together what I'd been told by my parents about Bobby's death. "Do you believe that?"

Julia looked away.

"Julia, you lived here then, didn't you? You know what happened." I tried to keep the accusation out of my voice and failed.

"Yes, although I often wish I didn't." She passed a weary hand across her forehead. "It was a very sad, sad day. No one could really believe it happened. His mother had to be hospitalized for awhile, you know."

"I didn't know that."

"Yes, poor dear. It was a blessing when they put the house up for sale. It was the only thing they could really do, you know?"

"Yeah," I said. "But I wonder why they didn't keep the dog?"

"The dog," she said wonderingly. "Oh, you mean Fred? Well, honey they just couldn't. Perhaps you'll understand one day."

Julia wandered away from me, a handkerchief had appeared in her hand and she dabbed at her eyes as she walked.

"I don't want to talk about that anymore," she said quietly. "How is the sale of your house coming along?"

"Alright I suppose," I said. "It feels like everyone's in such a rush, though."

"I see," she replied. "And of course, you have unfinished business, there don't you?" Julia turned to smile gently at me. "Perhaps that's where this dream has come from."

"Do you think so?"

She shrugged. "Who knows? Could be."

"I wonder ... I feel like if I could just think clearly, I could figure this out. Do you think ... maybe I could try that exercise again?" I was desperate to know more, to be able to connect my dream to something tangible. To help my friend.

"Didn't you try it on your own, as I suggested?" she asked.

"Well, no. I was scared I'd get it wrong. Are you sure it's *just* a relaxation exercise?"

"Oh," she said, and her eyes crinkled at the corners. "You've seen through my little fib."

I tilted my head at her and just waited.

"Well, let's see what we can do. Do you remember how it starts?"

"Breathing, I think. Right?"

Julia chuckled. "Yes. Breathe in and out, like the waves of the ocean. Let's sit here." She led me to sit down opposite her at the breakfast bar in her kitchen.

I breathed.

"Now, some people use this ... *exercise*, as a way of really opening up their other senses. You know about the five senses, right?"

"Yes," I responded eagerly.

"Keep breathing," she admonished, watching me until I resumed the rhythmic breaths once more. "People actually have six senses, but we don't always use that last one. In some, that last one isn't strong enough for them to even realize they have it. Do you understand?"

"Maybe," I breathed. Indian Magic, I thought happily. She's teaching me Indian Magic. Was this part of what she called my *gift*? I'd heard about what people called the *sixth sense*. Did I have a sixth sense too? Did she?

My pulse raced and I licked my lips nervously. "I want to learn though. I'm ready."

"Are you?" She smiled indulgently at me, as though I were a small child asking to drive the family car. "We'll see if that's so. Do you feel relaxed now?"

I thought about that for a minute. "Yeah, actually I do. Is that the breathing?"

"Yup," she answered. "Now, let me ask you something important."

"Alright."

"Are the things you see in your mind real, or are they imagination?" Julia cocked her head to one side and jutted out her chin. "Keep in mind, that includes dreams." She wiggled her eyebrows at me.

"I-It's not that easy," I complained. "I guess sometimes, they could be … but how can I decide when I don't know anything yet?" This was very awkward, I thought, considering I'd just related my most recent dream.

"You know more than you think," came the sage reply.

"And what if I'm wrong?" I whispered.

"What if you're right?" Julia sat forward suddenly on the upholstered stool and held out her hands to me.

I was staring. I could feel my eyes start to water as the need to blink intensified but I felt frozen.

Julia, sensing my rising panic, cleared her throat. The unexpected sound made me jump. "Are you alright, dear? Would you like a lemonade?"

"I don't think—I don't know," I said. "Yes please."

Julia didn't answer; she just smiled gently and got up to pour me a glass of the tasty drink.

I looked out the large windows while I waited. Her wooded yard seemed to exist in sharp contrast to the small, orderly garden plot, with its slowly wilting greenery. How could everything outside that window look so normal while inside, things were anything but?

"Here you are," Julia handed me a tall glass and sipped from another. "Good stuff. Homemade."

"Yeah, it's good."

"You're frightened, but there's no reason to be. Perhaps you need more time to feel comfortable." She looked genuinely concerned and I hastened to explain.

"I guess I'm just so confused. Everything seems so strange. This is coming too fast."

"In what way?"

I looked down at the space between us and saw that her hands were outstretched again, waiting for mine. There was no answer I could give that wouldn't sound childish and silly. Consciously pushing back my doubts, I carefully placed the half-empty glass on the counter and placed my warm hands in her cool ones.

So far, Julia's had been vague and non-committal when it came to my doubts and fears. Although still kind, she was vague. In spite of that, I felt understood which, looking back on it now, was just what I needed.

"You're a special person," she said to me as we sat there together. My hands rested loosely in hers. "I feel like you and I are kindred souls." She stopped speaking and just looked at me, my sweating hands still cradled in her cool ones.

"Thank you," I answered. "Julia... you want me to choose, but I can't. What if none of it is real?"

"Can't you?" she asked. "What do your senses tell you?"

I shook my head. "I can't seem to focus."

"Maybe this will help. Think of the meaning behind the word 'real'. Do you question whether your sight is real? Or déjà vu, or whether Mary really did have a vision when the Angel of the Lord came to her all those years ago to announce the coming of our Savior?" Julia's eyebrows arched. "The question you should be asking is how real does it have to be?"

We sat there for long moments after that and I thought carefully about what she'd said. There was no doubt about where her beliefs lay. I looked around the room, taking in, for the first time, how many crucifixes and religious paintings and artwork she had in her home. Julia was a devout Catholic and although she never flaunted it, her faith was always at the forefront of everything she did and said.

Finally, she let go of my hands and stood up. She walked slowly back to the kitchen. "I promised Father Pat a lasagna. Would you like to learn?"

I was getting to know Julia's ways and this was one of them. I took the hint and shifted gears right along with her. That day, with a million thoughts whirling through my head at the things she'd almost said, the only thing I could truly say I'd learned was the fine art of lasagna-making.

311

Help Me

40

I was in the oak tree again. Sitting in my favourite place, legs bracing against an adjacent limb. It was pleasant, surveying the beauty of my home in the sunshine. I looked down at my clothing and felt mildly perplexed. I was wearing shorts, my bare legs seemed tanned. Off to the left of our yard, the swimming pool, instead of being wrapped up for winter, glistened invitingly.

This was all wrong.

Was I dreaming again? I had to be.

But this time, it felt like re-living a memory.

In the long driveway that led to the barn, a small figure huddled on the ground. My heart seemed to skip a beat as a recognised him.

Bobby!

I remembered this! He seemed to be arguing with someone, but there was no one there.

This must be what other people see when they look at me, I thought drily.

Slowly, as though I could magically turn up the volume on my hearing, faint voices reached my ears and I knew that somehow, I was hearing the conversation that was taking place on the opposite side of my yard.

Impossible, but audible, nonetheless.

"... but why?" I heard a small voice ask. I was sure it sounded like Bobby's voice.

A low mumbling was the only answer.

"Where are my mommy and daddy? I'm lost."

Another sound, so low I almost missed it, seemed to answer his question.

"No," he said, and I could hear him start to cry. "Help me ..."

My clock radio read 3:45 A.M.

My body sprawled awkwardly across my bed, the bedspread and other blankets twirled about my feet. I realized I'd been dreaming again. This time, it'd been so intense; the gathered corners of the bed sheets had come off and begun to wrap me up like a cocoon.

Blinking again at the clock radio, I understood, probably for the first time, that I had a responsibility. It didn't matter if I didn't understand. Maybe one day I'd be able to, but for now, I just needed to *do* something.

In times of doubt, my best friend always helped me figure things out, but unlike most girls, my best friend was pen and paper. Creeping quietly to my desk, I hauled out my orange duo-tang and began flipping back through the numerous entries. I turned the pages fast, almost without looking.

The entries, written in rounded, childish handwriting filled the pages, their edges curled.

At last, my fingers stopped. Without questioning why, I started reading.

June 23rd, 1979 Dear Journal: We've lived here exactly a month and I can tell you this place is weird. I was trying to read in the living room today and the light in there kept going off by itself. Dad came and looked at it, but he's just as frustrated as I am. I can tell. He wiggled the cord, turned the switch a couple of times and told me it must need a new light bulb. Right. I've never seen a light bulb burn out and then come back on again. I don't think it's possible. I asked my teacher and she thought I was kidding. I know how light bulbs work. Why would dad lie to me? Doesn't he trust me to tell the truth?

June 28th 1979 Dear Journal: I don't know what to do. My friend Bobby said the weirdest thing today. "Adults don't see me" is what he said. Now why would he say that? Not can't, but don't. Something doesn't add up ... it just makes my head hurt. I wish I could talk to someone, but who can I trust with my secrets? Just you I guess, Journal.

June 28th, 1979 Dear Journal: It was the last day of school today, but somehow I don't feel as excited as I should. Here I am writing in a stupid notebook when all the other kids are doing something exciting. I'm not like them, but I could never tell that to my family. They'd get all weird about it.

I flipped some more pages, anxious to discover the answer, or even a discernible pattern.

October 20th, 1979 Dear Journal: Getting ready for Halloween. Pointless. My friends at school are talking about going to some weird party where they're going to have a 'haunted house' and fake cobwebs and stuff. Ooh. Spooky. What a laugh. Haunted house? Hah. I live in one.

November 12th, 1979 Dear Journal: Remembrance Day yesterday. Dad laid a wreath at the monument they call a cenotaph. So much preoccupation with death. I didn't want to go, but mom said I had to be respectful, so I stood out there in the rain with everyone else, trying to look somber and respectful. What a confusing day. I didn't know any of the people who died, so why did I have to be there? And why did those weird people in uniform have to stare at me like that? My parents didn't even notice! Dad said people act funny when they're sad. Maybe that's it. There were lots of men in different coloured uniforms standing amongst the old, grey haired veterans in their suits with all their medals pinned to their chests. These guys didn't have medals on them; maybe that's why the old guys wouldn't talk to them. So much for respect! The poor soldiers, I felt really bad for them, so I tried smiling, but they just stared at me. It made me feel weird. I tried to ask mom about it, but she said she couldn't see who I was talking about, which is just plain ridiculous, because they were right there in front of us. To tell the truth, it was maddening.

November 24th, 1979 Dear Journal: It's weird, but I have dreams that I've lived here before. mom thinks it's déjà vu, but it's more than that. I just wish I could explain...

December 18th, 1979 Dear Journal: I don't know how to explain this. I know what mom said about Bobby, and I know that I can't argue about it anymore, but it's difficult to trust. Trust him, trust myself ... what will happen if I don't? Am I strong enough? Can I even help him? He asked me to. I heard it, as clearly as I hear my own mother. I think maybe he's just as afraid of that scary man as I am. I just want to set him free. No one deserves this.

The book fell from my fingers before I noticed I'd let go. The splat of it hitting the ground made me jump. I was reading as though a different person had written these entries.

How could I not see?

A peculiar sense of calm settled over me. I don't remember falling asleep, but when I next opened my eyes, the clock read 7:30. Time to get up for school.

It was hard to concentrate on socials studies that day. Having made the decision to help my friend no matter what the consequences, I just wanted to get it over with. Bobby was scared, I could see that now. He didn't have anyone to help, and somehow, John was the reason. I knew it instinctively. The minutes dragged by, and the teacher's voice droned on and on about things I couldn't bring myself to care about.

After school I pedalled hard, the green five-speed bike my parent's had given me seemed impossibly slow.

I had to hurry, I had to hurry.

The sign that greeted me when I pulled into my own driveway nearly sent me into a skid.

SOLD!

The letters were done in a slash of red pasted diagonally across the real estate sign that had marked our front yard for months.

It was really happening. Apparently the 'serious buyer' my parents had been waiting for had stepped forward.

I was out of time. I had to make a choice.

"... so now I'm sure," I finished, standing in our kitchen, the telephone receiver pressed to my ear. It felt hot in my hands as I gripped it, trying hard not to tremble.

"I see. Well, if you've decided the dreams are real, that puts a new spin on it," she said. "Alright, think it through carefully. You believe this dark entity was there before? You think it ... *caused* the accident with the little boy?" Julia's voice was like a lifeline on the other end. I clung to each word desperately.

"Yes."

"Well, given what I know about you and the situation, I don't know what you can...."

"There's got to be something." I paused and looked around, making sure I was alone. "Even if Bobby is lost, I can't simply walk away knowing this will keep happening over and over ... I want it gone. It's ... here. *Inside*." I whispered the last word urgently into the phone.

"Calm down child, calm down," she said, her voice low. "Tell me, are you sensing things or ...?"

"Seeing them is more like it," I interrupted, worried that she was trying to minimize the problem or worse still, trying to convince me that nothing was happening. "Julia, if we move, will it follow us?"

"You say it's *inside* the house?"

"Yes," I whispered.

"Hmm ... your folks go to church," she stated. "Do you have any religious articles in the house? Can you get your Pastor to come?"

"Religious articles?" My mind drew a blank. "Like a bible or something?"

"Sure," her voice was hesitant. "But I was thinking more like a crucifix for the wall, or a religious picture or something that might have been blessed by the Church?"

"Um ... no. I don't think so ... wait! I have a silver cross necklace. Mom and dad just gave it to me. Do you think *that* was blessed?" The silence on the other end of the line made me think that maybe we'd gotten disconnected. "Julia? Are you still there?"

"I'm here," she said. "I was just wondering if I'm really the best person to help you with this, that's all. Can you get your Pastor to –?"

"Oh no! Please don't say that! No one else believes me. Besides, he's been here already. He blessed the house. I guess it didn't work."

"Now don't say that," she admonished. "I wouldn't say it didn't work, just sometimes things need a little more *oomph*."

"Oomph?" I repeated, truly puzzled.

"Look sweetie," she continued. "You mustn't blame your parents; in their eyes, it's dangerous to believe in this sort of thing. They're worried, no doubt, that people would label them crazy, or you, or your sister. In time, they would watch the price of their beautiful house dwindle down to nothing. They're right to be careful you know. If anyone ever discovered their secret, it could be very serious for your family. Especially for you."

I was astonished; the problem now facing me seemed insurmountable. "How do people do this?" I asked, my voice cracking with emotion.

She paused and let out a long breath into the phone.

"Most people just refuse to believe, Ginny. As I've said, it's the *smart* thing to do, and it's much safer."

I pressed the phone to my ear harder. "I've already tried that."

"I know, honey," she said, and I heard her sigh again. "Come to my house later. I think I have an idea."

"Mom and dad aren't here. They left me a long list of chores. If I don't do them all, I can kiss my freedom goodbye. They're in a 'grounding' sort of mood."

"Well then, wait until they get home. Tell your mom that I'm giving you something to help sell the house."

"What?"

"I'll talk to you soon," Julia said. "Goodbye."

"Uh-huh," I responded lifelessly. The line went dead, but I continued staring at the receiver in my hand long afterward. What was she talking about? What was she going to do? Didn't she understand that Bobby needed me? How could I move away now? I just wanted that other one, John, to be gone. Why couldn't she help me with that? I chewed nervously at my lower lip as I carefully replaced the telephone receiver in its cradle.

Did I do the right thing? I'd done exactly the opposite of what my father told me. I'd blasted this wide open and there was no going back. If my parents suspected I was loony before, now they'd be sure to take me to a shrink. Hanging up religious items in our house? But what options did I have? A loud click from the laundry room door told me someone was opening it, and I moved away from the phone quickly, anticipating my parent's arrival. As the seconds ticked by and no one appeared, however I grew suspicious. Cautiously, I approached the door and peered through the glass in the top section of the Dutch door.

Only inches from my outstretched hand, with sudden and terrifying force, the open door slammed, cracking one of its small panes of glass.

I screamed and jumped back, heart thudding.

"Cut that out!" I screamed at the empty space. "I can't take this anymore! Leave Bobby alone and leave me alone too!"

I ran from the kitchen and straight out the front door, slowing to a halt on the front lawn. The grass felt cool under my bare feet. Behind me, the house sat ominously quiet. The empty driveway was a testament to the fact that mom and dad were still out.

They'd been rounding up cardboard boxes and packing tape in preparation for moving. I wished that I could feel happier about it, but the only thing that kept circulating through my head was *moving isn't the answer*.

I knew instinctively that we couldn't escape what was happening in the traditional way, with cardboard boxes and a moving van. Even if we left, Bobby would still be lost and I couldn't deal with that.

Walking purposefully to the broad living room windows, in my socked feet, I stood looking at them from the safety of the front lawn. It certainly *looked* like a nice, comfortable home. There was no visible sign that a dark entity was waging war on the inside. Once the new people moved in, what would happen to them?

Half an hour later, I was still outside on the grass, when my parents arrived home.

"Ginny!" mom cried in surprise as she alighted from the car. "What are you doing out here? Is something wrong?"

"Everything's wrong," I whispered.

"What?" mom was too far away to hear me, but I didn't repeat myself. Wearily, I walked over to the car to help them bring in the empty boxes we would use to start packing. My body felt as though I had lead weights tied to my wrists and ankles as I carried the boxes inside.

What was I going to do?

The house I had once loved was driving me insane.

~~~~~

"Julia? Did you think any more about that problem we talked about yesterday? You said I should hang things up on the wall?"

"Indeed," she said cheerily. "But not just any thing will do. Be patient. I'm expecting a call any minute."

"A call?" Uh-oh.

"Oh, not to worry. I needed something, that's all. You said you didn't have any religious articles in your house and I'm taking care of that."

~~~~~

"Oh Julia, it's beautiful! It's perfect. How very thoughtful and so kind." The gleaming cross, draped with the prostrate form of Jesus, cast in silver, was indeed a work of art.

Mom gently cradled it in her hands as she spoke with our friend and neighbour, the telephone receiver pinched between her shoulder and ear, the long curly cord twirling and spinning as she moved.

"Sometimes I wish we were more religious," mom said. "We go to church, and we've enrolled Ginny in Catechism of course, but sometimes …." Her words trailed off and I watched as she listened intently to what Julia was saying on the other end of the line. "Well of course dear, we do what we can. Perhaps you're right though. Every house needs a little something. I'm still nervous that the whole deal could fall through." Mom nodded several times as she held the receiver to her ear. "Yes," she said at last. "Tony said we won't know for sure until after the 27th. That seems

318

like forever, so you see, we can use all the help we can get." Mom was chuckling a little, but I couldn't help feeling like her words were truer than she wanted them to be.

"What was that dear?" The tone in Mom's voice had changed and it drew my attention like a magnet. "Now why would we do that?" Mom listened intently, purposely turning her back on me when she saw me standing there. "Uh-huh ... okay ... are you sure? Well yes, but ... oh! And when should we do this? ... okay, well if you think it'll make a difference, you'd know more about that than I would." When she turned back around, I busied myself with changing the placemats on the kitchen table. "Alright dear, yes, I'll see to it myself. Oh, I know," she smiled and nodded at me and I knew Julia must be thanking her for sending me over. "Not at all, it's me who is thanking you. You're a good friend Julia. Take care. I'll talk with you soon. Bye now."

The concern in my mother's eyes as she hung up the phone was troubling. There was no doubt she'd keep her conversation a secret from me, but I couldn't help wondering what sort of instructions Julia had given her. Whatever it was had given her that line of worry on her brow.

"I know just where to put it," mom said, as though to herself.

"In the kitchen?" I asked hopefully. "There's a beautiful spot right here." I pointed to a place just above the doorway that led into the family room.

"Oh, yes exactly ... perfect." Mom followed my gaze and squinted, as though trying to envision it there.

The next day I was startled by the sight of my mother on a stepladder, the crucifix from Marie in her hands. "Ginny," she called. "Where did you put that crystal necklace?" Mom was trying to seem casual, with her elbows resting casually on the top of the ladder, but there was a hard edge to her voice that she couldn't control.

"Um, in my underwear drawer," I said. "You want it?"

"Mm-hmm, please," she said.

Some time later, I watched carefully as she wound the gleaming chain of my crystal necklace around the top edge of Julia's gift to us.

"Now it's perfect," she said cheerily.

~~~~

Whether it was the strength of the powerful object now hanging in our house, or merely good timing, it ceased to matter when our realtor stopped by a few days later with exciting news.

"It's done," he said.

Dad blinked at him and mom clapped her hands.

I stood back. Here we go, I thought.

Trust

41

"We're leaving you know." I spoke the words aloud in the semi-darkness. The overhead lights did little to dispel the gloom of the barn at night-time. "I guess you won."

Taking a deep breath to steady my nerves, thinking over my strategy for the hundredth time, I tried to figure out if I was crazy or what.

"I suppose you'll go on scaring whoever moves in here, won't you?" My voice echoed in the empty barn. "It's not fair you know. It just isn't. These people did nothing to you. I've done nothing to you. How could a little boy have threatened you so much you'd want to hurt him?!" My shouted words echoed back at me.

A prickling sensation wove its way up and down by backbone. Was this a sign that I wasn't alone, or was it just a bi-product of my own fear?

"I've been afraid of you long enough," I said defiantly. "Won't you answer me? Are you really here?"

I listened hard, was I counting on vague impressions and fear-based responses to tell me that something really did lurk in that barn? What if all of it was in my own head?

What if there were no ghosts at all? The thought struck me like a physical blow. Then what about Bobby? He was real enough, wasn't he? The events of the past year and a half weren't in my head. Were they? *And how real does it have to be*? Julia's words came back to me in a rush.

I shook my head to banish those negative thoughts. She was right. Somehow, this needed to end, whether it was only my fear, or whether something evil really did lurk in the dark spaces, waiting to invade someone else's mind, it had to stop.

But realizing this didn't make it any easier. I chewed at my lower lip and felt a deep frown developing. I didn't know if I could fix the so-called 'damage' my friends and I had caused when we used the Ouija board—Julia said things like that made a haunting ten times worse—but I knew I had to try.

Angrily I shouted into the emptiness, unable to control my emotions anymore. They lashed out. "Show yourself, you coward! I'm here! I know you're real, but you insist on hiding!"

The hard edges of the silver crucifix at my neck dug into the palm of my hand, while I leaned wearily against the plywood wall for support. Dark spots appeared in front of my eyes and I felt my knees start to buckle. I recognized the symptoms and, letting go of the necklace, I sat down heavily, the cold of the concrete floor seeping immediately through the seat of my jeans. Spots hovered in front of my eyes and I concentrated on taking deep, even breaths.

I might have written it all off as an attack of nerves if it hadn't been for the sounds. They were faint at first, like a distant police siren or an approaching storm. Gradually, almost as if it gained confidence, the sound grew louder, until I could finally make it out for what it was.

Laughing. Someone was laughing at me!

Diana?

Instantly, I got up off the floor and managed to peer outside, making sure the driveway was still empty.

It was. I was truly on my own.

The thought should have terrified me, as I stood in the wide-open doorway waiting for something else to happen, but I felt strangely calm.

Turning towards the sound, I focused on it, and visualized the dancing colours I'd seen in the center of the crystal medallion. My breathing slowed and my vision, free of those floating dark spots, sharpened, every detail jumping to significance.

Now we're getting somewhere, I thought.

Slowly building, like a gathering wave, the air around me began to change. I felt it happen. But this time it felt different. It felt like it was coming from *me*!

A simple prayer fell from my lips. A willing heart and a fierce desire calmed my shaking hands.

I looked with new confidence at the unpredictable shadows. Would it work? Could I really do this?

"Shadows, huh? Is that all you've got? Shadow isn't even possible without light, you know." Talking to myself this way helped me keep a firm grip on reality.

The words of the simplest prayer I knew swelled in my mind and I whispered it again, taking small steps forward across the hay strewn floor.

"Our Father, who art in Heaven," I began.

The words felt good on my lips and lent me the power of clarity. My mind and heart soared.

I am loved. I am cherished. God loves me. God protects me.

Not always. That thought came unbidden and I stopped in my tracks, startled at the ugliness behind those words.

Images of myself flashed through my mind. Falling from the hayloft, running, terrified down the path as something unknown chased me, cradling my suddenly bleeding hand, staring transfixed at the mirror in my own bathroom as terror spread across my face.

But I knew I'd narrowly missed the sharp edge of a wheelbarrow I hadn't noticed when I fell from the ladder, and the dark shadow that chased me and haunted my thoughts was just that: a shadow. Although I'd been terrified, I was still alright.

This time.

The whispered statement was like a wayward thought, but the malice was unmistakable. That wasn't my own subconscious. It was a threat. A dull headache had formed over my eyes as the constant pressure I'd felt earlier grew in intensity.

I knew if I had fallen only 2 inches to my right, I would have hit the metal-edge of that wheelbarrow in the barn. It would have been … I couldn't finish the thought. Thoughts like that were dangerous. This thing thrived on fear, doubt and terror. It would get inside my mind again if I let it.

But I wasn't going to.

"Hallowed be Thy Name," I whispered to the silence. Silence echoed back at me as I stood there, wondering whether I'd imagined it all, but knowing deep down that was impossible.

The small surge of triumph I'd felt earlier as the words of that familiar prayer buoyed up my courage had faded and I now felt small and alone.

Get out!

The force of those words knocked me backwards before I could react. As I caught my breath, I looked around in confusion, realizing I was standing outside. A crushing weight settled on my chest and I felt the deep sadness that I had experienced at the loss of Charlie once again. Tears formed in my eyes.

Backing up into the waiting sunshine felt like Heaven. As the sun's rays warmed the frigid skin of my hands and arms, my senses were held in a state of euphoria.

What was I doing here? I couldn't seem to remember.

Walking back down the pathway to my own back door, the negative thoughts that had swirled through my brain were gone, replaced by a deep sense of foreboding for the innocent building my grandfather had built. The sense of confusion left me as suddenly as it had come and I found myself staring back at the barn, trying to make some sense out of it.

"What's going on?" I whimpered into the stillness. "What am I supposed to do God? Tell me!" Coming to a halt on the path, I gripped the cross at my neck for emphasis, the gravel under my feet making crunching noises where my feet still nervously flexed inside the pale blue sneakers. "It was so clear before, but now? I don't know anymore."

A word popped into my brain like a burst bubble. I could almost hear the sound of it.

Trust.

"Trust?" I said aloud. "Trust ... who? Myself? God? Julia? My parents? Come on ... I need more than one word here!"

My frustration built up inside of me and I stormed back to the house. This wasn't working out at all as I'd planned.

~~~~

The more I thought about it, the angrier I became. I knew there was only one more thing I could so. One last gift I could give to Bobby.

I had to try.

Once again, I felt it engulf me as I stepped inside. The air was thick, as though it should take extra effort to breathe it in. By now, the feel of it was uncomfortably familiar. It was startling when I felt it touch my mind. At first it was tentative, like a small push, almost like a headache than began and withdrew, over and over again.

I couldn't have said how I knew this, but I realized it was testing me. *Worthless!*

The self-doubt assailed me like bullets.

This is a stupid plan.

No one believes me.

As I stood there, trembling slightly, I had no choice but to listen, only I didn't like the words.

The negative thoughts swarmed through my head, ripping at my self-esteem. I could feel it choking me, robbing me of the thickened air. Clenching my hands against the onslaught, I fought for breath, tensing my muscles until I felt something dig painfully into my palm.

It was the figure of Christ cast out of silver. It had several sharp edges. The painful intrusion served its purpose and I drew on that sensation to wake up my senses and drag more air into my lungs. Standing a little straighter, acting on instinct alone, a shield formed in my mind's eye and I focused all my attention on it.

It didn't matter that no one believed. *I* believed, and I would rely on myself if no one came to help me. Had I been thinking clearer, I would have laughed at that.

Help me? How could they do that? Besides, my journal entries proved I'd already been helping myself for months.

Trust.

It was all I had to go on, but it might just be enough.

I wondered, not for the first time, what price I would have to pay when this confrontation was over.

A price beyond compare.

Not my words. The phrase skittered through my head and was gone. Part of the darkness at the far end of the corridor seemed to detach itself and cross through the narrow beam of light let in by the doors at the far end. It happened so fast I couldn't be sure, but I tensed instinctively nonetheless.

The air grew more dense, and I could feel it pressing in all around me. Gathering my courage in both hands, I marched to the far end of the barn and hauled at the door to let in some daylight.

Instead of easily giving way, however, the heavy door repelled my efforts. There was no lock on this door, no way to stop it from sliding on its metal overhead track, so why wouldn't it budge?

All I wanted to do was run away. I could feel something in front of me. That same sensation I'd encountered the night when the lights went out was now right in front of me. The urge to step back was strong, but instinctively I knew that if I did, I would be lost. Everything looked normal, but it wasn't. That was its stock in trade. Every day it tricked people into thinking there was nothing here, and then it came at you when you least expected. Realizing how it would look to someone if they entered the barn at that moment, I almost laughed at the absurdity of the whole thing. A child, her stance wide, ready for a fight in an otherwise empty livestock barn.

I had to stop thinking like that. It could get into my mind so easily. I didn't want to give it anything for free.

I'm already there.

Choking back the whimper that sprang to my throat, I tried to swallow, but the lump wouldn't budge.

Get out! I hurled the thought at the shadows.

I was out of ideas. I literally had no clue how this stand-off was going to end. Sooner or later, I was going to have to let the horses into the barn for the night, and I was pretty sure I wasn't going to be allowed to do that.

A moment later, I felt a familiar presence by my side and a sense of motion. A whisper of sound accompanied that movement. Fabric rubbing against fabric ghosted through the darkness to my ears. Instead of panic filling my heart, however a deep sense of calm settled over me.

I didn't have to see him to know he was there. His familiar presence is one I will never forget.

I managed a small smile. We stood there together, Bobby and I, facing down our nightmare. I literally felt the pressure of his small hand in mine.

"We can do this," I whispered.

"*Don't let go*," the whisper was barely audible, and seemed to float in the air. Whether I'd imagined it or he was, somehow, really there, it no longer mattered.

One of the overhead lights suddenly exploded, sending shards of glass flying everywhere. I ducked, instinctively covering my face.

"In nomine Patris, et Filii, et Spiritu Sancti ... Amen." The image of our pastor as he'd said these words filled my mind. A moment later, I realized I was parroting those words back into the darkness.

Straightening and carefully dusting glass from my hair, I felt the air around me begin to change. It was charged, like one of those science fair exhibits that make your hair stand on end.

So attuned to my environment and my own senses, I realized with surprise that somehow, it was coming from me!

My hands were clasping the crucifix and I willed them to relax. My thundering heartbeat echoing in my ears, seemed to slow, and I was acutely aware of my own breathing. All of these things happened in mere seconds.

And then I just wasn't there anymore.

I hadn't run away or even moved. In fact, I could see that I still stood just as I had. But I simply wasn't there. I no longer participated in the scene unfolding in the shadowy barn: I simply watched it. Even now, I'm having difficulty with the description of something I was barely aware of.

Calmly, I watched the silver crucifix, with the thin metal chain of my crystal necklace dangling from it, swinging back and forth hypnotically. The crystal seemed to catch fire with a myriad of light.

My arms now held the crucifix crushed to my chest.

Remote and unable to move, I simply watched, as a thin ribbon of color seemed to appear. It looked ridiculously like some over-exposed film I'd once seen, hues of red and yellow melding together in the middle of a black void, taking various shapes as it undulated and changed. The blues and greens of the crystal that dangled from the crucifix I still clutched, seemed to spread outwards, as the crystal, now hanging away from the surface of the silver figure, spun in lazy circles. The colours danced at the edges of my vision, as though, in another moment I would pass out. It must be a dream, I thought. It felt like a dream.

My arms hung like they had weights tied to them. It was too much effort to move them. I heard a voice, or at least I thought I did. Someone was there with me. Bobby? Someone else?

If only I could open my eyes wider, I thought. *Maybe I could see. But they won't go any wider. I can't make my body respond.*

Maybe, I'm not standing here at all. Maybe I'm just asleep. I feel like I'm asleep … I feel like I'm dreaming.

Fresh hay, horse manure, sweet feed … the strange combination of smells registered on my senses with equal importance. *Where are the horses?* The random thought floated through my mind and was gone.

I saw my own hands and was surprised when I couldn't make them work. I felt as weak as a newborn kitten. I knew I wasn't sleeping, but couldn't understand what was happening.

The curtain in front of my eyes was still there, unmoving, like some sort of strange fog. Why wouldn't it move? *Let me see!*

Maybe my sister was right. Was any of this real?

Please let me wake up.

"Virginia, snap out of this, right now!" My mother's voice sounded harsh in my ears, and I felt my eyes leaking tears. The effort it took just to blink was exhausting.

"Come now Gingerbread, talk to us," the deep baritone of my father's voice, coming from outside my immediate field of vision was a comforting sound. I wanted to smile but couldn't.

A moment later, the image of their faces became clouded and wearily I gave in. My body seemed to float as I felt my eyelids sliding closed.

Full Circle

42

"It's surprising just how much can happen in 30 days," the woman said, sliding the cardboard box across the shiny surface of her new kitchen countertop.

"Yeah," her husband agreed. "Hey honey, did you see the box I brought in here earlier? It's got my measuring tape, the level and my screwdrivers in it. I put it right here on the counter, beside the dishwasher. It's labeled Mark's Tools in big, black letters. I swear I put it right here."

"Yeah," she said slowly, turning around to survey the room, taking in all the boxes, stacked on the floor, the counters and around the corners into the other rooms. "Gee, hon, I don't suppose that would be too hard to locate, now would it?"

"Okay, okay, I know there are a few boxes in here, but this one is clearly labeled."

"Tell you what?" she said. "Have at it, I've just got to grab another garbage bag, there's still a few things left in these cupboards. They must've left in a hurry!" She made a sweeping gesture with her right hand, and prepared to walk from the room.

She heard the sigh even as she crossed the threshold to the living room, but did not slow or stop. He could find it himself, she thought. He's a big boy.

"Jamie!" He called a few minutes later, just as she plucked a shiny black bag from the box in her new laundry room, aka the mudroom. "Can you come in here?"

"What is it, Mark, did you give up already?"

"Yeah, I can't find anything without you." He grinned at her. "But I did find this, what do you make of it?" As she rounded the corner, she could see her husband, still standing on a small ladder, placed by the end of her kitchen cupboards. He held something cupped in one hand. He was staring down at it intently and she approached with caution.

It was a beautiful crystal pendant, suspended on a finely wrought silver chain.

"They must have left this behind too," he said. "It's obviously worth something. They'll want it back, I'm sure."

"Well, just put it in the truck and when you make your last trip to the old house, you can drop it off at the real estate office," Jamie said. "Where did you find it, anyhow?"

"Well, that's the weird thing," he said, "it was right out in the open, right here." He indicated a small brass hook screwed into the end of the kitchen cabinetry where something heavy had obviously been hung. "I'm trying to think how a family would forget to bring something so valuable."

"They hung a chain on the wall?"

"Not just the chain. Take a look," he said. Reaching in front of him, he plucked something from the top of the ladder where it'd been resting. "This was hanging with it," he said. In his hands, he held an intricately carved wooden cross, mounted with the figure of Christ cast in silver.

"Well, any kind of decoration like that is obviously meant to go with them," she said. "You know how moving day is; they must have just overlooked it. Can you take it down to the real estate office later?"

"Sure. I think they're open until six tonight ... hey! Look at this," he said, pointing to the back of the crucifix and holding it out so she could see. "That's strange."

There, on the back of the crucifix, scratched into the wood's smooth surface, were letters. The childlike scrawl read: B-O-B-B-Y.

"Bobby?" She read aloud. "Who's Bobby? I thought the previous owners only had girls."

"Yeah, I thought so too. Maybe it's a nick-name?"

At the end of the shadowed room, the old, wooden door that led to the laundry room she'd only just left, popped open and swung wide. "What now?" Irritation marred her delicate features. "Don't tell me the doors are warped in this place? I knew we shouldn't have skipped that home inspection!"

"Oh honey, relax. Hey, the place isn't brand new, we should expect some settling. That's all it is." The young curly-haired man crouched before one of the bottom cupboards and looked up at her. "Try to remember that we did get this place for a song. Can you blame them for wanting to expedite the sale? Their oldest daughter just got married and she was the one who took care of the horses. I'd do the same thing if I were in their shoes."

"Hmm, is that all it was," she commented under her breath.

"What hon?"

"I just don't like the idea of doors popping open on their own, that's all. It's creepy." She wiped her hands on the front of her pants and crossed the room to shut the door, firmly. "Mark," she said, looking across the room at the front foyer. "Did you leave the light on in the hall? I thought we agreed to try and save money now that our mortgage is so high."

"Huh? I could've sworn I turned it off." He paused to scratch his head in bewilderment.

Her long blonde hair that he loved so much bounced as she shook her head. "Apparently not, it's still blazing over there. Well, maybe you just turned it on without thinking." She smiled at him and crossed back to the array of kitchen cupboards they were stocking. "See? We're already on autopilot and we haven't even been here a day, yet!" She smiled fondly at her husband and reached out to give him a hug, but her ponderous pregnant belly and the crucifix he still held made that awkward.

"Whoah," he said. "No unauthorized hugging! I don't want to poke 'junior' with this thingy. Besides, if we start that, we'll never get moved!" He chuckled as he said it, raising his eyebrows suggestively, while he hugged her back with one arm.

"Okay, okay. Seriously, though, let's get that thing back to the previous owners, okay?" she said, chewing at her lower lip. "It gives me a creepy feeling. That name on the back, it's odd, don't you think? I mean, in a house-full of girls ... it's not like a child made it or anything. That's a work of art."

"Yeah, but I'll bet if someone took a look at half the crap we toted from our old house, they'd say it was odd, too." He chuckled and grabbed a tea towel from the countertop. Jamie found herself chuckling too.

I'm over-reacting to everything, she thought.

"Where are the boys?"

"Playing in the back," he answered. They found a chicken coop."

"Ugh," she said. "This may take some getting used to."

Mark laughed and went out the back door, wrapping the item in the tea towel as he went. As he slid behind the wheel of their beat-up pickup truck, anxious to get that one last trip to the old house finished, he allowed himself a weary sigh. The crucifix, a red and white checkered bundle, lay on the seat beside him, the crystal pendant already forgotten deep in the pocket of his jeans.

Jamie smiled to herself as she watched her husband walk out to the end of the gravel path and out of sight.

"Now, maybe I can get something done," she said to herself, returning to the kitchen. She moved the ladder that her husband had conveniently left set up in the corner and climbed up a few steps to get a better look under the range hood. "Let's just see if I can figure out why this stopped working."

A moment later, light footsteps behind her announced the presence of one of her children.

"Graham!" She swished absently at her hip, as she felt a tug on the hem of her shirt. "I've gotta change this bulb first." She didn't turn from her work, her head twisted up awkwardly under the appliance, happy that her well-meaning husband was finally out of the house and wouldn't be second-guessing her every move. Graham would just have to wait a moment.

The hem of her maternity shirt tugged again, insistently. "Graham, just a sec! I swear you're so impatient," she said.

Stepping down from the small step-ladder, she frowned and looked around in wonder, seeing no one. "Where did you go, you rascal?" she said, a low chuckle in her voice. "Hey, this isn't hide and seek. Come on now, boys, where are you? I've got work to ...."

"Hey! No fair, quit shoving! Stop I said! Cut it out!"

"Why don't you make me?" The muted sounds of their childish argument seemed to be coming from outside. Jamie hurried to break up the fight, crossing through the recreation room and sliding open the tightly closed glass door, still wondering how her youngest son could have moved so fast.

Rounding the corner of the back patio somewhat breathlessly, she looked around. Her boys were nowhere to be found. "I move too damn slow these days," she muttered, laying a hand on her belly.

"Boys!" She called, cupping her hands around her mouth. "Boys, where are you!"

"Over here Mom," came the calm reply of her older son as he walked up the path with his brother. "Whatcha want?"

Her skin turned ice cold. They weren't even *near* the house. So whose voice had she heard? Did sound carry that well in the country?

As she tried to make sense out of the last couple of minutes, Jamie heard mark calling her from inside the house. "Honey, do you have the truck keys?"

"No," she called to him, trying to make her voice sound normal when her mind was working double-time. "They were in your pocket just a few minutes ago. Where did you put them?"

"Right here in the front hall. I swear, I'm losing everything today! Okay, if you're sure you don't have them, I'll check again," he said. "I know I left them right here …." his voice receded into the distance.

Turning to walk back inside and help her husband, she noticed the exterior door that led to the house's laundry room had been left open. "Men," she muttered. "Can't seem to close things behind them." Jamie had only taken two steps towards it, however when—BANG— the door slammed with such force that the windows rattled. Walking closer, she noted that one of the upper panes of glass was cracked.

"Mark?" she called wonderingly, peering through the individual window panes that decorated the top half of the thick, oak door. "Why are you slamming the …" standing on her tip-toes to peer inside she saw no one, "… door?"

"Mommy, what's wrong?" The younger of her two boys rushed forward for a hug, and her startled expression turned slowly into a big grin. Her hand rested on his blonde curls for a moment, as he glued himself to her hip. The young mother said nothing as she tried in vain to think of a response that didn't sound crazy.

Tousling his curls, she smiled down at her son. "You're in need of a trim, sir," she said, deciding to change the subject instead. "Go on and play, everything's fine." She walked him over to the back door, and catching sight of her second son coming across the patio, she added: "Daddy and I are gonna set up your bedrooms next, why don't you look in the garage and try and find the boxes where we packed your toys? That'll be a big help."

Without a backwards look, both boys took off in search of their belongings. "I wonder which one has my Legos!" One of them said.

Groaning inwardly, Jamie stepped back inside the house, wondering how long it would be before she was picking up those darn Lego pieces off the floors. Her back hurt already, just thinking about it. Sliding the lock on the door closed with an audible click, she spun back to the kitchen only to be faced with a blackness that seemed to engulf her. The edges of her vision swam dangerously and she panicked.

"Mark! Mark, I...."

The world tilted and she felt herself falling.

Mark entered the room at a run, his young face creased with worry.

"Jamie, no!" His young wife lay sprawled in the open doorway. A nasty bruise was already forming on her forehead, but from what? The collapse worried him, but as he thought it over, waiting for her to regain consciousness, he remembered the last doctor's visit. Hadn't he warned that she might be prone to fainting this time? That had to be it.

A moment later, Mark smoothed Jamie's blonde hair away from her face and watched as her eyelids flickered open.

"What? Oh! Hi."

"Hi back. Are you okay?"

"Oh ... yeah. I'm fine now," she said, sitting up carefully.

"Are you sure? What happened?"

"I don't really know," she said. "I was talking to the kids and I came in here to help you, then everything went black."

"You hit your head. Do you remember?"

What? I did?" Her fingers came up involuntarily to touch the spot, wincing as she did so. "I guess I did. Ow!"

"Remember what the doctor told you? Did you eat today? Are you taking your vitamins?"

"What? Yes, yes of course I am. Don't start on that, please. Help me up, would you?"

He helped her to stand, then backed away again, hands raised in mute surrender. She rubbed her arms against the sudden inexplicable chill, and moved away from the open door.

"Can you close that door? It's so cold. That's why I closed ... at least, I *think* I did."

"It was wide open," Mark replied, worrying anew at his wife's obvious confusion. "Are you okay? How do you feel?"

Jamie had retreated back into the kitchen to resume her work. "Fine, I'm fine. I have things to do."

"Oh, no you don't," he said. "The boxes can wait. Please lie down, honey. You're pale as a ghost."

"Quit mothering me, Mark!" she replied irritably. "Are you gonna keep this up when we have a full barn out there? People will be paying us good money to take care of their horses. You won't have time to fuss over me."

"Okay, okay," he said. "I'll quit bossing you around if you give in and rest, at least until I come back. I feel nervous leaving you." His clear hazel eyes held so much warmth it was impossible for her to be mad at him.

Finally, she breathed a deep sigh. She was tired, that much was certainly true. "Alright. I'll sit in the front room where I can at least hear the boys, okay? They're supposed to be finding their stuff so we can start on their rooms."

"Great. I don't want you doing any of that without me, though, right?"

Jamie nodded wearily.

"Hmm, I'm gonna check under the seat in the truck. The keys could've fallen under there when I put that ornament thing on the seat. How about I take the boys with me?" Half-way through the front door, the man paused and turned to look at his wife, concern etched across his handsome features. "Seriously, maybe I should call your mom; she said she could come over, remember? You shouldn't be alone and apparently I can't trust you not to overdo it."

"Don't be ridiculous, you've got things to do. I'll be fine." She smiled with an assurance she didn't feel. "No boxes. I promise." She made a crossing motion with her finger over her chest. "Are you going back to the old house or have we got everything here now?"

"There might be a few things, but mostly it's just junk. Once I get those keys, I'll go back and set out the stuff for the trash in the morning, and then we're clear. Hey, did you see the boy's new hideout? They've already scoped out the barn and now they've claimed that old chicken coop as theirs too. They love this place already." His quick grin faded somewhat. "Resting, yes?"

"Okay." She held up two fingers in a Girl Guide salute. "Guides Honour," she promised. "Honestly, I'm just tired, that's all. You know, this pregnancy's wiping me out." She didn't like it that he was so concerned, but who could blame him? The doctor's words came back to her as she leaned back in the padded armchair. The matter of fact way he'd talked to her had been almost insulting. It had the desired effect, she supposed. He could have said "complications" and left it at that, but he hadn't.

"This pregnancy is taking a toll on you, emotionally as well as physically," the middle-aged doctor had said to them only a short time ago. "I can't stress enough, the importance of preparation. I know you are determined to make this move, and Lord knows I can't stop you, but I beg of you, please be smart about it. You can't afford another miscarriage. We almost lost you last time. I'm serious Jamie."

She sank deeper into the chair, and looked around the room, realizing that she *was* very tired, despite her unwillingness to accept it. From her new vantage point, she could see the boys. They played happily in the flowerbeds just outside the giant picture windows, obviously forgetting all about the boxes she'd asked them to find. Closing her eyes for a moment, she could just hear the indistinct sound of their excited chatter. Moments later, however, her eyes flew open in alarm as screams reverberated through the silent house.

"Boys!" she shouted in panic, rocketing out of the chair, despite her awkward physique.

Jamie had already hauled open the front door when realization dawned and she sagged back against the wall. One of the boys ran at top speed, streaking past the window, squealing with excitement. Obviously a game of tag. She smiled to herself. Why had she thought they were in trouble? And why had it sounded like they were *inside* the house? This house had weird acoustics.

I wonder who's winning, she thought, happy to let her pulse return to normal. A glimpse of Dillon's red shirt and dirty-blonde hair was followed closely by the blue Superman shirt and lighter blonde curls of her younger son. She couldn't help but smile. So much energy!

Red, blue, red, blue ... brown.

What? The disturbance in the pattern got her attention immediately. There was another child out there.

Footfalls echoed across the wooden floor of the kitchen just then, and she heard the back door close. The partial wall between living room and kitchen made it impossible to see who it was, but she could guess. A small sigh escaped her lips. So, she thought, he can't even gather the boys without my help. The thought itself was enough to drain her energy and suddenly, the task awaiting her in the kitchen seemed overwhelmingly difficult. She knew he'd have a hard time convincing the boys to leave, now that they'd made a friend.

Rising ponderously from her chair yet again, she sighed. Her belly seemed heavier today.

"I'm looking forward to tomorrow," she said aloud.

Strains of disco music emanated from the kitchen. Jamie thought about the silver ghetto-blaster Mark had placed on the kitchen counter.

"Mark?" she wondered aloud. He must have turned it on when he came back inside a moment earlier. That man couldn't stand silence. "Can't a girl have some quiet?" she complained, rounding the corner. Scuffling sounds from the laundry room told her where her husband had disappeared to. "Good luck getting the boys to go with you; it looks like they've made a friend. Gee, that took them forever ... what's it been? An hour?" She waited for his answering laugh, but instead, the scuffling sounds stopped. As Jamie stood wondering why he didn't answer, the only sound was the radio, playing a phrase that seemed to fit, "... just trust in the good times, no matter how long it takes ...." She laughed. How ironic.

"Mark?" she called out. Crossing the room to peek into the laundry room, she frowned. It was empty.

"Where is that man? I swear he moves like a ghost!" She stood still, lost in thought, until suddenly, the lively music in her kitchen faded out to static, and a long hiss filled the room.

"Oh, now what? I didn't even touch anything!" She crossed to the kitchen counter with a purposeful stride. One pale-skinned hand reached for the radio knob, but recoiled with surprise at the temperature of the small silver knob. It was biting cold. In fact, the whole radio felt like it'd been thrown into the freezer for a couple of hours.

Is the fridge open? Knowing that was a ridiculous question, she pushed at the appliance to check. Both doors were firmly closed.

"Perhaps I'll just move it to a different outlet over here," she said aloud. Suiting the action to the word, she hit the power button, only to hear more static issuing from the speakers. "Maybe the station's off the air? Finally. Peace and quiet." Shrugging, Jamie reached for the power switch.

Before she could touch it however, the static abruptly changed.

"... *get ouuuut.*"

Jamie's eyes flew open in fear and she backed away, staring in disbelief. Had she only imagined the chilling phrase? Her breath came quickly as she stood there, trying to decide what, if anything, she'd really heard. As she stared at the radio, the hiss of static gradually faded, and music began to play again.

"Uh, okay, okay let's get a grip shall we?" she muttered. Wiping her suddenly tearing eyes and pressing the palms of her shaking hands together, she concentrated on breathing deeply to slow down her racing heart. "Hmm, CB radio, maybe?" She'd heard about those things, but didn't know how they worked. With all those signals bouncing around in the air, it made sense that some of them could get lost and re-routed through a household radio ... didn't it? She was grasping at straws, she had to admit, but the alternative didn't bear considering.

"A CB, yeah, that makes sense. It's someone on the CB. That's exactly what it is." Smiling to herself and breathing a sigh of relief at her own foolishness, she stretched her weary back and turned to go find Mark and the boys. For some reason, being alone didn't seem like such a good idea anymore.

Jamie walked with purpose to the sliding glass door that opened off the family room, careful not to bump her belly against the large pool table in her haste.

Pulling the door open, she called, "Boys! Where's your father?"

"O-kaay!" The indistinct reply came from inside the old chicken coop.

Grunting with the effort, she slid the door home in its track and stood there for a moment, trying to remember what box the food was in. Perhaps she was hungry? Yes, that was it. When was the last time she'd eaten anything? Eyes still on the handle of the door, she looked up slowly, aware of a subtle change, but not understanding why.

She saw his eyes first, the anger in them unmistakable. Red-rimmed and full of hate, he stared at her from the other side of the glass. A tall man. Dressed in black from head to toe.

Backing painfully into the edge of the pool table, she stared in disbelief. The image disappeared as quickly as it'd come. Her breath came out in sobs as she blinked rapidly, trying to dispel the face from her mind.

I thought ghosts couldn't hurt you? Her fingers came up automatically to clutch the crucifix at her neck and rest the other across her abdomen protectively. The figure on her pendant, raised against her fingertips, reminded her instantly of the wooden crucifix they'd removed from the wall. Were the removal of the cross and the timing of these strange events only coincidence?

"Oh my God," she whispered. "How could I be so blind?"

338

Her next thought was for her boys, but a moment later, as though they could hear her thoughts, her two sons were at the door in the old man's place.

"Mommy, let us in," they said.

As she pulled the door open with shaking fingers, she tried to breathe normally.

"Mom, are you okay?" Dillon, her oldest son, was obviously concerned. His hazel eyes squinted at her doubtfully.

"I'm fine. Just tired I guess," she said. Her voice trembled, and she fought to make it sound brave. She had to get in touch with Mark, fast. "Where's daddy?"

"He's fixing the truck," they answered.

"Fixing it? What's wrong with the truck?"

"Dad doesn't know. It won't start."

"That's because he can't find the keys," she explained. "I guess he's still looking for them."

"Oh," Dillon replied. "Can we have cookies, Mom?"

"Only if you help me find them."

"Okay!" They answered, diving into the open boxes on the kitchen floor.

"What happened to your new friend?" she asked.

"What friend?" Dillon said, turning around with a puzzled frown. "I didn't see anybody out there … got 'em!" He pulled forth a container from one of the boxes with delight.

"Really? I thought I saw someone outside playing tag with you in the front yard," she said, as she set the cookie box on the table for them. The return of ordinary conversation was having a positive effect. She started to feel almost herself again.

"Oh yeah!" her oldest son exclaimed. "I almost forgot! We did meet a boy. He's a year younger than Graham. His name's Bobby. He had to go home though."

"Oh!" The name startled her. That was the name on the back of the cross. Mentally shaking her head, she pushed aside those thoughts as coincidence. Restoring her smile, she turned back to her son. "Does your new friend live around here?"

"I don't know, probably. He didn't come here in a car, that much I know. Gray and I were playin' and he just sort of showed up in the second driveway, there." Dillon gestured over his shoulder at the driveway that led to the massive barn.

"That's nice, honey," she said, her thoughts suddenly veering off in another direction. "As long as you're having fun."

The barn was the whole reason they'd purchased this place, she thought wryly. I wish I'd had a better look at the house, she thought. I only have myself to blame for being so hasty.

"He knows his way around too," Dillon continued. "He's comin' over tomorrow again. Said he needs help with somethin'. Mom, I sort of feel like I've met him before. But that's crazy isn't it?" He laughed self-consciously and winced as his younger brother poked him in the ribs.

The boy's mother returned a weak smile. She was starting to have doubts of her own. Crazy? I wouldn't say that, exactly.

"Honey!" Mark called out from the front door. "I'm back! In fact, I never left. Can't find those damn keys anywhere, can you help me look?"

In his hands he carried additional boxes that he'd forgotten to unpack from the front seat of the truck. A potted plant was balanced precariously on top of it all.

"Jamie," he called again. "Boys?" Why couldn't they hear him? He could hear them. A low murmur of voices came from somewhere in the house, so why didn't they answer? Maybe they were outside.

"Strange." The acoustics in that place were screwed up. Walking through the open front door into his new house, he wondered how long it would take before it felt like home.

"Hmm, first thing to be done is replace this hideous carpeting," he mumbled, scuffing the toe of one shoe against the worn shag rug. "Better do it before the baby comes."

As he formed the thought, his carefully stacked boxes tumbled to the floor with a crash.

"No! Oh, great! Let's break everything. Good plan," the sarcasm was heavy in his voice. It had already been a long day, and it was getting longer by the second. As he bent to pick up the pieces of broken pottery from the smashed plant pot, it occurred to him that no matter what he'd tried to do that day, something had gone wrong. First it was the lights in the barn and workshop playing cat-and-mouse with him, and then, every time he turned around, something else had gone missing. It was downright irritating, putting something down only to have it be gone a moment later. It felt like someone was running around behind him picking things up, and forgetting to give them back.

Mark chuckled at the thought. People are gonna start saying I'm paranoid if I talk like that, he thought. Jamie's fainting spell had him more worried than he wanted to admit, though. The doctor's warning had been clear, but by then, they'd already purchased the place. What was he gonna do? They couldn't afford to hire professional movers.

Wearily, he abandoned the mess on the floor and straightened up, pushing his fists into the small of his back. He'd done everything humanly possible, so why did he feel so responsible for Jamie's collapse? He'd tried to dissuade her from participating in the move, doing most of the work himself and pressing family members into service whenever possible. He was doing his best to make sure she didn't lift anything, just as the doctor said, but Jamie was stubborn. Somehow, she'd managed to tire herself to the point of fainting.

Turning to the still-open doorway, he leaned against the foyer wall, staring absently into his new front yard. Jamie said she was cold, but the weather had been mild all day. Maybe it was a cold wind coming off the mountains? He wondered idly as he stood there, why he hadn't noticed any winds before. There certainly didn't seem to be any now. Anything powerful enough to topple over boxes full of dishes would certainly have caught his attention. Wouldn't it?

Mark only had a moment to wonder about that before the heavy wooden door slammed in his face.

Changes

Epilogue

"It's barely been five months," I heard my mother say on the phone. "You mean to tell me it's for sale *again*?"

She was talking with our ex-neighbour, Julia, and once again, I was listening in.

Our new house seemed to have optimal eavesdropping conditions.

"But really, Julia, I thought those people had plans for the place!" Mom's astonished tone made me draw closer, holding my breath in suspense. Our new subdivision home was comfortable, but it had next to no land, a fact my dad seemed to regret.

"What is it honey?" Dad's question, coming from behind me as he walked up the foyer stairs caused me to jump guiltily and blush crimson. Dad waved a dismissive hand in my direction. "Nice try. She already knew you were listening."

Mom had sunk wearily into a kitchen chair by the time dad and I walked into the room.

"The house is on the market again," she said.

Dad nodded thoughtfully but said nothing.

"Our house?" I asked unnecessarily.

"Yeah," she said. "I wonder what happened?"

"Do you *really*?" My father, the astonishment on his face as genuine as it was unexpected turned to face his wife. "Even after …?" He left the sentence hanging and they both looked at me.

I knew what they were thinking.

Mom crossed the room to wrap me in a sudden, fierce hug.

"Nevermind! All that's in the past."

Dad gave a non-committal grunt and turned to leave the room, but at the last moment, he stopped.

"We left it there, didn't we?" he asked.

"Absolutely," she said. "Remember? I hung it right back up on the wall. It was the last thing I did before we locked up. No, I wasn't about to bring that thing with us, after, well, after such an awful scare." She stepped away from me and rested one hand on her hip, a forced, teasing smile on her lips. "You had us worried, sweetheart. You really did."

"I know. I couldn't help it."

"You know, I still can't figure it out," mom said, stepping forward again and stroking my hair absently with one cupped hand. "You must have seen … someone, some-*thing*? I mean, to bring a *crucifix* into the barn?" Her tone, verging on nervous laughter only made things worse.

I regarded them both for several long seconds, their faces clearly showing the concern they felt. I knew they were both remembering how they'd found me, lying still, white and unresponsive on the cold concrete floor, Julia's gift still clutched in one hand.

I sighed. There was already so much they didn't, *couldn't*, understand.

I knew they were waiting for answers, but I didn't have any.

Where do I start? I wanted to shout in exasperation.

Instead, I abandoned all pretext of explanation and simply shook my head firmly.

It would have to remain a secret, at least for now. Maybe I'd tell them, in about 30 years.

~~~~

Once we moved away, the house where I saw my first ghost sold over and over in rapid succession. The local real estate agents were said to be quite perplexed. It was a gorgeous, desirable property with a modern home in good repair. Why wouldn't anyone stay in it longer than a year? Some were gone within months.

Our ex-neighbour Julia kept in touch with my parents over the years, and sometimes we visited her. Mom and dad would make a big show of always seating themselves in her formal living room, located on the opposite side of her house, facing away from our previous home.

I, however, often gravitated to the huge picture window in her kitchen area to stare across the road at the house that used to be my home. Carefully, I studied its huge oval-shaped front lawn where I'd spent many hours playing, and the long gravel driveway that led to the barn and more secrets. I knew I was looking for answers. Perhaps it was too late for that, but I couldn't help feeling like I'd failed my little friend somehow. He'd asked me for help. Had I really done all that I could? Was it enough? Was he finally at peace, able to let go of the place he'd once called home?

The End

Thank you for purchasing this book. It has taken me more than thirty years to tell this story. Through the creation of this manuscript, I can finally say I have made my peace with this part of my childhood. It is unknown whether my young friend ever found what he was looking for, or if he still roams the halls of his former home. Perhaps he left there in search of other children to play with.

Wherever he is, I hope he is happy.

About the Author

This is Virginia's first full-length novel. It is based on real-life events that took place in her childhood home beginning in 1979 in rural Langley, British Columbia. The names of the people involved in this story have been changed to protect their anonymity, and the address of the property suppressed to protect the people who now live there.

Virginia's fascination with the paranormal continues to this day. Please look for her next paranormal adventure, Ready to Haunt You, coming soon. The author lives in a quiet country home on acreage with her family and pets in Mission B.C.

Please visit Virginia's blog for sneak peeks at her newest novel, publishing updates and more!

http://www.virginiarenaud.blogspot.com

find her on https://twitter.com (ghoststoryV)

or search for the fan page for this title on Facebook

Made in the USA
Charleston, SC
28 December 2012